GERMAN LITERATURE
in
THE UNITED STATES
1945-1960

by

W. LAMARR KOPP

CHAPEL HILL
THE UNIVERSITY OF NORTH CAROLINA PRESS
1967

Printed in the Netherlands by Royal VanGorcum Ltd., Assen

UNIVERSITY OF NORTH CAROLINA
STUDIES IN COMPARATIVE LITERATURE

NUMBER 42

UNIVERSITY OF NORTH CAROLINA
STUDIES IN COMPARATIVE LITERATURE

Founded by Werner P. Friederich

Editorial Committee

William J. DeSua, Editor

| Edwin L. Brown | | John E. Keller |
| Alfred G. Engstrom | O. B. Hardison | Dan W. Patterson |

8. Nan C. Carpenter. RABELAIS AND MUSIC. 1954. Pp. xiii, 149. Paper, $ 1.75. Cloth, $ 2.25.

17. A. Levin. THE LEGACY OF PHILARÈTE CHASLES. Vol. I. 1957. Pp. xxviii, 248. Paper, $ 6.50.

31. Philip A. Shelley and Arthur O. Lewis, Jr., Editors. ANGLO-GERMAN AND AMERICAN-GERMAN CROSSCURRENTS. Vol. II. 1962. Pp. 350. Cloth, $ 7.50.

32. William J. DeSua. DANTE INTO ENGLISH. A Study of the Translation of the Divine Comedy in Britain and America. 1964. Pp. xii, 138. Paper, $ 3.50.

33. Francisco López Estrada and John Esten Keller, Collaborators. ANTONIO DE VILLEGAS' EL ABENCERRAJE. Introduction, Original Text and Translation. 1964. Pp. 86. Paper, $ 2.50.

35. Eugene F. Timpe. AMERICAN LITERATURE IN GERMANY, 1861-1872. 1964. Pp. 95. Paper, $ 3.00.

36. Frederic Will. FLUMEN HISTORICUM: VICTOR COUSIN'S AESTHETIC AND ITS SOURCES. 1965. Pp. ix, 97. Paper, $ 3.00.

37. Helmut A. Hatzfeld. A CRITICAL BIBLIOGRAPHY OF NEW STYLISTICS APPLIED TO THE ROMANCE LITERATURES, 1953-1965. 1966. Pp. 184. Paper, $ 7.00.

38. Jules Gelernt. WORLD OF MANY LOVES: THE HEPTAMERON OF MARGUERITE DE NAVARRE. 1966. Pp. x, 170. Paper, $ 5.50.

39. Lawrence Marsden Price. THE RECEPTION OF UNITED STATES LITERATURE IN GERMANY. 1966. Pp. 246. Cloth, $ 6.00.

40. Werner P. Friederich. AUSTRALIA IN WESTERN IMAGINATIVE PROSE WRITINGS, 1600-1960. Pp. xv, 280. Cloth, $ 7.50.

41. John Philip Couch. GEORGE ELIOT IN FRANCE: A FRENCH APPRAISAL OF GEORGE ELIOT'S WRITINGS, 1850-1960. Pp. vii, 197. Cloth, $ 6.50.

42. W. LaMarr Kopp. GERMAN LITERATURE IN THE UNITED STATES, 1945-1960. Vol. III of ANGLO-GERMAN AND AMERICAN-GERMAN CROSSCURRENTS, ed. Philip A. Shelley and Arthur O. Lewis, Jr. 1967. Pp. xviii, 230. Cloth, $ 7.50.

For Reprints from this Series see page 230.

Foreign Sales through Librairie E. Droz, 11 Rue Massot, Geneva, Switzerland.

ANGLO-GERMAN

and

AMERICAN-GERMAN
CROSSCURRENTS

Volume Three

ANGLO-GERMAN
and
AMERICAN-GERMAN
CROSSCURRENTS
Volume Three

Edited by

PHILIP ALLISON SHELLEY

Professor of German and Comparative Literature
The Pennsylvania State University

with

ARTHUR O. LEWIS, JR.

Professor of English
The Pennsylvania State University

CHAPEL HILL
THE UNIVERSITY OF NORTH CAROLINA PRESS
1967

For the sunn, which wee want, ripens witts as well as fruits; and as wine and oyle are imported to us from abroad, so must ripe understanding and many civil vertues bee imported into our minds from forren writings & examples of best ages: wee shall else miscarry still and com short in the attempt of any great enterprise. – John Milton, *History of Britain*, Book III.

All that is best in the great poets of all countries is not what is national in them, but what is universal. Their roots are in their native soil; but their branches wave in the unpatriotic air, that speaks the same language unto all men, and their leaves shine with the illimitable light that pervades all lands. Let us throw all the windows open; let us admit the light and air on all sides; that we may look toward the four corners of the heavens, and not always in the same direction. – Henry Wadsworth Longfellow, *Kavanagh*, Ch. xx.

La vraie grandeur d'un peuple ne consiste pas à ne rien imiter dans les autres, mais à emprunter partout ce qui est bien et à le perfectionner en se l'appropriant. – Victor Cousin, *Rapport sur l'état de l'instruction publique dans quelques pays de l'Allemagne, et particulièrement en Prusse*, Deuxième Section III, Conclusion.

Ein wahrhaft grosses Volk ist dann reich, wenn es vieles von anderen übernimmt und weiterbildet. – Jakob Burckhardt.

PREFACE

Volume Three of *Crosscurrents* represents a departure from the plan of the preceding volumes in the series in that instead of being a collection of studies by several authors it is a unified work of a single individual. Like its predecessors, however, it is a product of the Penn State Project on Anglo-German and American-German Literary and Cultural Relations. Like many of their components, moreover, it has drawn extensively from the resources of The Allison-Shelley Collection, the contents of which, incidentally, have been incorporated in large part in the listings of the *Supplement Embracing the Years 1928-1955* of the latest edition of *A Critical Bibliography of German Literature in English Translation* by Bayard Quincy Morgan. The present volume supplements the second volume of Professor Morgan's comprehensive bibliography in two ways: it extends the period surveyed by five years and it includes a number of additional items from the preceding ten years. It is the author's intention to continue his survey progressively and to publish it periodically in future miscellaneous volumes of the series.

P.A.S.
A.O.L., Jr.

GERMAN LITERATURE IN THE UNITED STATES

1945-1960

AAN MIJN VROUW

I acknowledge with gratitude the assistance of Philip Allison Shelley, Professor of German and Comparative Literature at The Pennsylvania State University, who encouraged and guided me in the research and writing of this study.

TABLE OF CONTENTS

PREFACE IX

I. INTRODUCTION 1
Background 1   Scope and Procedure 12
Survey of Previous Related Studies . 6

II. LITERATURE FROM THE MIDDLE HIGH GERMAN PERIOD TO THE BEGINNINGS OF THE CLASSICAL PERIOD 17

Walter of Acquitaine 17   Heinrich Wittenweiler 22
Ruodlieb 18   Meister Eckhart 23
Hartmann von Aue 19   Johannes Tauler 24
Wolfram von Eschenbach 19   Jakob Böhme 24
Gottfried von Strassburg 20   Angelus Silesius 25
Walter von der Vogelweide 20   Paracelsus 26
Ulrich von Zatzikhoven 20   Lichtenberg 27
The Nibelungenlied 21   Lessing 27

III. GOETHE 30
Early Reception 30   Dramas 42
Lyric Poetry 33   Faust 43
Goethe Anthologies 36   Conversations and Correspondence . 47
Narrative Prose 38

IV. SCHILLER 50
Early Reception 51   Lyric Poetry 58
Reception of Schiller and Goethe   Mary Stuart 59
  Compared 52   Other Dramas 60
Schiller Anthology 57

V. THE NINETEENTH CENTURY			64
Hölderlin	65	Stifter	85
Novalis	67	Kleist	85
Heine	67	Grabbe	88
Hebel	73	Büchner	88
Tieck	74	Raimund	90
Brentano	74	Grillparzer	91
Arnim	74	Hebbel	94
Chamisso	74	Gerstäcker	96
Eichendorff	74	May	97
Hoffmann	75	Keller	99
The Grimm Brothers	76	Meyer	101
Hauff	83	Hauptmann	102
Mörike	83	Schnitzler	105
Droste-Hülshoff	84	Wedekind	107

VI. THE TWENTIETH CENTURY			111
Anthologies	113	Hesse	134
Poets	117	Werfel	136
Rilke	117	Baum	139
Hofmannsthal	123	Fallada	139
George	124	Remarque	139
Wolfskehl	125	Selinko	140
Tucholsky	125	Dramatists	141
Benn	126	Brecht	144
Narrative Prose Writers	127	Dürrenmatt	148
Kafka	127	Frisch	149
Mann	130		

VII. SUMMARY 151

VIII. TITLE LIST OF GERMAN LITERATURE IN ENGLISH TRANSLATION PUBLISHED IN THE UNITED STATES, 1945-1960 154

IX. A SELECTIVE BIBLIOGRAPHY 221

Denn nicht so sehr die Originaltexte als die Übersetzungen sind es, die auf das Geistesleben eines anderen Landes einwirken.

Bernhard Blume:

Amerika und die deutsche Literatur

Der Bibliograph verhält sich zum Künstler wie der sammelnde Ordner des Vielzähligen zum schöpferischen Gestalter des Einmaligen. Diesem sammelnden Ordnen aber erwächst da eine unumgängliche Aufgabe, wo das geschaffene Kunstwerk die Berührung mit einem Empfangenden anstrebt, durch die auch Literatur erst ihr eigentliches und sinngebundenes Wesen erhält. Denn jedes Literaturwerk setzt den Leser nicht nur voraus, es hängt in seiner Lebensfähigkeit notwendig von ihm ab. So gilt es denn, Verbindungslinien zu ziehen vom Schriftsteller zum Angesprochenen, Bindungen anzuregen und zu knüpfen, die das Kunstwerk sichtbar werden lassen und es lebendig erhalten. Hier nun werden Lexikographie und Bibliographie als wesentliche Formen dieser unerlässlichen Vermittlung zwischen schöpferischem und nachempfindendem Geist zum dienenden Wirken für die Kunst.

Werner Schuder:

Preface to the fifty-third edition of Kürschners Deutscher Literatur-Kalender

I

INTRODUCTION

Background

'No man is an Iland, intire of it selfe; every man is a peece of the Continent, a part of the maine,' wrote John Donne in his *Devotion XVII* more than three centuries ago. The truth of his words is perhaps more dramatically evident in our day than it was at the time they were written. What Donne has said about the individual man can be aptly applied to groups of individuals or entire nations. With the increased ease of communication enjoyed today we have, in a very real sense, a community of nations inseparably interdependent and undeniably interrelated, if even, as in some instances, indirectly. Such interdependence and interrelationship implies and acknowledges an atmosphere in which at least a measure of mutual participation in the life, the cultural heritage, and the interests of neighboring nations occurs either consciously or unconsciously. When several nations or peoples have particularly close ties, such interrelationship becomes obvious to even the casual observer.

Through its origins and development the cultural heritage of the United States is related closely to the history and traditions of more than a single people. While the influence of the British has been by far the most pervasive, the German-speaking peoples have played what may justifiably be called a major role in this country. The Germans, in fact, have ranked first among 'foreign' contingents in the United States.[1]

---

[1] Albert B. Faust, for example, found that at the turn of the century '... the persons of German blood in the United States number between eighteen and nineteen millions, or about 27 1/2

Accordingly, the contribution they have made to the American cultural scene, from colonial days to the present, is now firmly established. The *Literary History of the United States* (ed. Robert E. Spiller, Willard Thorp, Thomas H. Johnson, Henry Seidel Canby, Richard M. Ludwig [3d ed., New York, 1963]) claims that 'at the present time the most fully explored "foreign" culture is that of the Germans,' and Harvey Wish, writing in *Society and Thought in Early America* (New York, 1950), confirms that 'the German-American has attracted the greatest number of historians among the foreign groups.' At times the German cultural contribution has been very active and gratefully acknowledged; at other times this contribution has been somewhat more indirect and less perceptible; and at still other times it has been violently denounced or even vigorously suppressed. Various aspects of German elements in the American cultural heritage and tradition have become the subject of numerous studies and investigations. An early two-volume encyclopedic survey, which, for years, was regarded as the standard comprehensive study of German-Americans, is *The German Element in the United*

percent of the total white population of the United States.... This German blood is diffused over a far larger portion of the population than is represented by eighteen to nineteen millions; it may be diffused over twice that number of persons; the question as to how far the German blood is carried through the entire American people is one beyond all possibilities of calculation. Twenty-seven and one half per cent represents the amount of German blood in the American people in relation to the other formative elements.' For purposes of comparison Faust attempted to estimate, in addition to the German group, the amount of English and Irish blood in this country, which together constituted the 'three elements [which] by far outclass the contributions from all other countries.' His investigation revealed that the English element in the United States numbered between twenty and twenty-one millions; the Irish and Scotch elements numbered around fourteen millions; and other national groups taken together totaled slightly more than fourteen millions (again for 1900). Such a comparison indicated that the Germans outnumbered every other national group in this country with the exception of the English element which, according to Faust's figures, exceeded that of the German by only two millions. Accordingly, Faust concluded: 'By adding its large contribution, between eighteen and nineteen millions (or about 27 per cent of the entire white population of the United States) to the twenty millions or more from England, it has made the American people a Germanic nation' (*The German Element in the United States*, 2d ed. [New York, 1927], II, 24-27). Much more recently Theodore Huebener stated unequivocally: 'The German element is the largest ethnic group in our midst. It is estimated that about one-fifth of our population has German blood in its veins' (*The Germans in America* [Philadelphia, 1962], p. v).

States by Albert B. Faust (Boston and New York, 1909, 2d ed., New York, 1927; German ed., Leipzig, 1912). Faust's work establishes 'the prominence of the Germans as a formative element of the American people... from the earliest period of their settlements in this country to the present time' by providing a history of the Germans in the United States together with a discussion of their political, moral, social, and educational influence. John A. Hawgood, in *The Tragedy of German-America: The Germans in the United States of America during the Nineteenth Century – and After* (New York, 1940), has inquired into the nationalistic aspirations persistently characteristic of many activities of Germans in America. He traces their resistance to assimilation or modification from the time of the first German settlers in North America, through their unsuccessful attempts to establish territorially isolated and culturally exclusive new Germanies, to the era of a socially and psychologically unassimilated German-America that terminated with the dilemma of the minority during the years of the First World War. Another more recent study is Theodore Huebener's *The Germans in America* (Philadelphia, 1962), which traces the role of the German element in the material and cultural development of the United States down through the time of the Second World War.

The most extensive study of German impact on American life has been produced by Henry A. Pochmann. In his 865-page volume, *German Culture in America: Philosophical and Literary Influences: 1600-1900* (Madison, 1957), Pochmann and his coadjutors have treated with painstaking detail the momentous contribution of German culture to the life of our nation, transmitted not only through the German-speaking persons who immigrated to this country and who here were assimilated into American life but also through philosophical and literary influences available through the printed page. Companion to this study is a compilation of more than twelve thousand items in *Bibliography of German Culture in America to 1940* (Madison, 1953), of which Pochmann was compiler and Arthur R. Schultz editor.

Interest in studying the reciprocal relationships between German literature and the literary activities of the British and the Americans has developed, for the most part, since the turn of the century. Studies devoted to the currency, reception, or influence of English and American literature in Germany and German literature in England and the United States were initiated by several individuals at about the same time. Marion Dexter Learned of the University of Pennsylvania, with the inception in 1897 of a series of publications entitled *Americana Germanica*, awakened both a consciousness of and an interest in the many lines of association among the cultural experiences of the United States and Germany. Begun as a quarterly, the periodical was continued from 1903 under a new title, *German American Annals*, first as a monthly and later as a bi-monthly. The original title, *Americana Germanica*, was retained for a series of larger monographs published as separate volumes. Edwin Miller Fogel, also of the University of Pennsylvania, replaced Learned as editor of the periodical in 1917 and continued in this capacity until 1919, when the *German American Annals* ceased publication. A. R. Hohlfeld, who in 1901 joined the faculty of the University of Wisconsin, established what he subsequently called 'The Wisconsin Project on Anglo-German Literary Relations.' With Hohlfeld's enthusiasm and under his scholarly guidance approximately twenty-five major investigations were concluded, including the important contributions of Scott Holland Goodnight, Martin Henry Haertel, Lillie V. Hathaway, Lawrence Marsden Price, Bayard Quincy Morgan, and, of course, Hohlfeld himself. The origin and growth of this ambitious program of studies has been recorded by Hohlfeld as the Foreword to the 'last and final' volume produced by the Project.[1]

The influence of the Wisconsin Project extended to scholars at institutions other than the University of Wisconsin with the result that a number of important investigations on the theme embraced by the Wisconsin Project were carried out under what Hohlfeld has labeled 'extraterritorial publications.' Bayard Quincy Morgan, while a member

---

[1] Designation of the volume *German Literature in British Magazines: 1750–1860*, edited by Bayard Quincy Morgan and A. R. Hohlfeld (Madison, 1949) as the 'last and final part' of an undertaking dealing 'with interrelations between German literature and the literature of the English-speaking world' is made by Hohlfeld himself (p. 3). In a very real sense, however, the Wisconsin Project may be said to have continued beyond this, to which assertion the publication in 1957 of *German Culture in America* by Professor Pochmann attests.

of the Department of German at the University of Wisconsin and in conjunction with the Wisconsin Project in 1922 prepared a 708-page *Bibliography of German Literature in English Translation* (Madison, 1922). Continuing his activity in the same field after moving to Stanford University, Morgan produced a 'completely revised and greatly augmented' second edition entitled *A Critical Bibliography of German Literature in English Translation, 1481-1927, With Supplement Embracing the Years 1928-1935* (Stanford, 1938). At the University of California Lawrence Marsden Price, after completing his doctorate at the University of Wisconsin, where his dissertation formed a part of the Project, continued investigations of another aspect of Anglo-German literary relations, concentrating more specifically on English literature in Germany. Harold S. Jantz, now of The Johns Hopkins University, with studies dealing with the influence of German literature in colonial New England has called attention to the early date at which German culture and specifically German literature played an important role on the North American continent.

At The Pennsylvania State University Philip Allison Shelley initiated and fostered another productive program devoted to the study of the relations of English and American to German literature and has assembled the valuable collection of some ten thousand books and manuscripts designated as The Allison-Shelley Collection which evidences the vital interaction of these literary relations. The publication of the first two volumes of *Anglo-German and American-German Crosscurrents* (Univ. of N. Car. Stud. in Comp. Lit., No. 19 and No. 31 [Chapel Hill, 1957 and 1962]) illustrates how rich a field of scholarly research this theme affords. In Volume One of the series Shelley describes what has come to be known as 'The Penn State Project on Anglo-German and American-German Literary and Cultural Relations,' and enumerates the dissertations and other studies inspired by, and comprising the products of, the Project. The present study owes its conception to the interest generated by the Penn State Project.

Survey of Previous Related Studies

With the emergence and gradual growth of comparative literature as a recognized academic discipline in the twentieth century, there has developed a corresponding interest in the bonds that link the literary activity of England, the United States, and Germany. Before the turn of the century a number of scholars had devoted their energies to this subject. In the past two decades or so, however, the number of such studies has increased considerably, due, at least in part, to the establishment of English as the major language of communication among Western peoples. Investigation of the contribution and debt of German literature to English-language literature, as well as the contribution and debt of English and American to German literature, increases in interest and importance as the cultural relationships of these nations grow ever closer with increasing social, economic, and political contact. (The selective bibliography to this volume lists some of the most important of these studies.) The investigations of Lawrence Marsden Price, Mary Bell Price, Irene Wiem, and Gilbert Waterhouse, for example, treat the currency of English literature in Germany. Various aspects of the currency of American literature in Germany have been examined by Harvey W. Hewett-Thayer, Eugene F. Timpe, Erich Leitel, and others. The study of German literature in England has engaged the efforts of such persons as Charles H. Herford, Violet Stockley, F. W. Stokoe, B. Q. Morgan, A. R. Hohlfeld, and Walter F. Schirmer.[1]

A triad of literary associations, the currency of German literature in both England and the United States, is the subject of still other related studies. The most comprehensive of these is the monumental work of Bayard Quincy Morgan, *A Critical Bibliography of German Literature in English Translation, 1481-1927...*, cited earlier. In the second edition – the product of years of devotion to his investigation – Morgan not only provides a complete bibliography of volumes translated from the German into English over a period that extends nearly half a millenium but also, by use of symbols and brief comments, critically evaluates the

---

[1] A detailed survey of studies devoted to the literary interrelationships of England, the United States, and Germany is tentatively scheduled for publication in Volume Four of *Anglo-German and American-German Crosscurrents*.

translations. And Morgan's definition of literature is not a narrow one: for the purposes of his bibliography it includes essays, travel literature, German history and biography, history of German literature, history of Greece and Rome, history and theory of art and music, aesthetics, philosophy, and personal letters, all of which taken together he designates 'humane letters.' Perhaps the unique quality of the bibliography is its breadth of scope, affording, as Morgan himself states, 'for the first time... an entire national literature... seen through the distorting medium of another language; and the resulting picture is... totally different from that given by the histories of literature or indeed any other critical source.' A supplement to this work, extending the bibliography from 1928 to 1955 has recently appeared as the companion volume to a reprint of the second edition (New York and London, 1965).

Supplemental to Morgan's *Bibliography* in the scope of its coverage, Richard Mönnig's *Deutschland und die Deutschen im englisch-sprachigen Schrifttum, 1948-1955* (Göttingen, 1957) provides a useful bibliography of works in English about Germany and of German books translated into English. As suggested by the title, belles-lettres comprise only a small part of the whole; of 128 total pages, approximately ten pages are devoted to German poetry and fiction and less than half a page to foreign fiction that employs Germany as its predominant theme. Documenting English-American-German literary crosscurrents in our own time, to which thus far little attention has been paid, this bibliography substantiates the continuation and indeed the intensification of mutual cultural interrelationships.

Complementary to Morgan's work of establishing the kind and quality of German literature that was translated into English, and supplementary to the investigations of reception by Haertel, Goodnight, and Morgan-Hohlfeld, Lillie V. Hathaway's *German Literature of the Mid-Nineteenth Century in England and America as Reflected in the Journals, 1840-1914* (Boston, 1935), a study originally pursued as part of the Wisconsin Project, provides, in addition to an invaluable bibliography of references to German literature, an examination of, and an insight into, the response which German literature elicited in the popular magazines and journals of England and America.

Concentrating on the earlier nineteenth century, René Wellek's *Confrontations: Studies in the Intellectual and Literary Relations between Germany, England, and the United States during the Nineteenth Century* (Princeton, 1965) presents six essays on the theme of 'German-English and German-American literary and philosophical relations during the Romantic age.' Written between 1929 and 1963, all of the studies had been published previously, with the exception of the first which had been originally prepared as a lecture delivered in 1963. Three of the essays examine the relationships of British writers (Carlyle and DeQuincy) to the German intellectual and literary movements of their era. Two more examine American intellectuals (the minor transcendentalists and Emerson) and their relationships to German philosophy. The introductory essay compares German and English Romanticism in an attempt to illuminate the distinguishing features of the movement in Germany.

The increasing number of studies dealing with German literature in the United States has been closely linked to the developing interest in the whole field of German cultural elements in this country. Indeed, studies devoted to this topic seldom fail to include some references, however cursory, to the literary aspects of America's debt to her German heritage, such as those by A. B. Faust, already referred to, or by John A. Walz, *German Influence in American Education and Culture* (Philadelphia, 1936); and the Promethean labors of Pochmann in his *Bibliography* and his *German Culture in America* are devoted in large measure to the contribution of German letters and men of letters to America's literary and cultural development. Apart from these works of a broader nature and in addition to the studies devoted to German literature and its relation to the whole of English literature (especially Hathaway, Morgan, and Mönnig), a number of fundamental investigations have been conducted by competent scholars both in this country and in Germany dealing with German literature in the United States.

Harold S. Jantz in 'German Thought and Literature in New England, 1620-1820' (*JEGP*, XLI [1942], 1-45) has systematically treated the earliest evidences of German influence in the cradle of American culture. His research has confirmed that even before 1820, when the first American pioneers to German universities – Edward Everett, George Ticknor, George Bancroft, and Joseph Cogswell – returned from Germany to New England, there was an intense interest in things German. He has shown that actually this interest was quite advanced already in the early and middle seventeenth century, but that it gradually diminished through the turn of the century; that around 1790 it culminated in a new intensity directly responsible, a quarter of a century later, for the atmosphere receptive to Madame de Staël's *De l'Allemagne*, the reading of which inspired the pilgrimage to German universities of the several young men destined to attain distinction in America's cultural development. Orie W. Long has treated this aspect of German intellectual and literary influence on early American men of letters in *Literary Pioneers: Early American Explorers of European Culture* (Cambridge, Mass., 1935). Chronologically continuing Long's study, Stanley M. Vogel's *German Literary Influences on the American Transcendentalists* (Yale Stud. in English, Vol. CXXVII [New Haven, 1955]) examines the impact made by the literary forces of Germany upon four major groups of the Transcendental circle: the men of letters, the theologians, the critics, and the translators. J. Wesley Thomas' *Amerikanische Dichter und die deutsche Literatur* (Goslar, 1950) surveys German influence upon American men of letters from the colonial period until the early twentieth century.

Supplementing these investigations are two related studies – parallel to one edited by Morgan-Hohlfeld treating German literature in British magazines – which deal with the currency of German literature in American periodical publications: *German Literature in American Magazines Prior to 1846* by Scott Holland Goodnight (Madison, 1907) and *German Literature in American Magazines, 1846-1880* by Martin Henry Haertel (Madison, 1908). These provide a picture of the introduction and expansion of German literature in America from colonial days through most of the nineteenth century. They illustrate, through their exhaustive lists of references to German literature that appeared in literary journals, the extensiveness of American interest and attitude. The years extending from the last decades of the nineteenth century to the First World War remain to be investigated through analysis of magazine references.

A treatment of the immediately following era, *Das deutsche Buch in Amerika: Übersetzungen der Jahre 1918-1935* (Zeulenroda [Thür.], 1937) by Hans Frese, is a work of questionable merit. Although the amount of German literature translated into English and circulating in the United States is impressive, he concludes, these books do not represent the true German spirit. Each book translated from the German, he asserts, can be classified within one of three categories according to the purpose it seeks to promote: pacifistic ideals, Germany and democracy, liberalism and the individual. These, according to Frese, are not really characteristic of the whole body of German literature, and hence Americans remain ignorant of what is truly representative in contemporary German literature. Using Frese's conclusions as a starting point, Günther Dietel, in 'Studien zur Aufnahme und Beurteilung der deutschen Literatur in Amerika, 1919-1939' (unpubl. diss., Jena, 1952), explains the indifference in the United States to certain German writers and books by concluding that subject matter alone is the determinant of American reaction to German literature and to any other literature. Thus the *Heimatdichter* and the *Arbeiterdichter* have virtually no chance for popular success in this country. In arriving at his conclusions Dietel examined quite extensively the reviews of German translations in several popular American magazines; in this way his work relates, at least in method, to that of Goodnight and Haertel.

While as yet there have been no published studies devoted to German literature in the United States during the Second World War, Henry C. Hatfield and Joan Merrick, in an account in the *Modern Language Review* (XLIII [1948], 353-392) entitled 'Studies of German Literature in the United States, 1939-1946,' have sketched the production of American scholarship dealing with German literature during and immediately after the war. Their conclusion, that American Germanists, while very active, have failed to establish significant contact with the cultivated public and by so doing contribute toward German literature's isolation, includes a directive that 'the base of American interest in German literature should and could be broadened, without any sacrifice of scholarly precision.'

Ulrich Weisstein, at the Second Congress of the International Comparative Literature Association which was held at the University of

North Carolina in September, 1958, delivered an important address, later printed in the Proceedings of that congress, on 'The Reception of Twentieth Century German Literature in the United States' (*Comparative Literature*, Univ. of N. Car. Stud. in Comp. Lit., No. 24 [Chapel Hill, 1959], 548-557). In his address, which he called 'an aesthetically oriented paper in literary sociology,' he examines not the influence exerted by, but rather the reception accorded to, German literature of this century. Calling attention to the importance of the various strata in which reception is effected, he enumerates four distinct classes of readers, each of which, he points out, requires special interpretation before any complete picture of a particular writer's reception can be accurately and comprehensively ascertained. These classes are the *Germanisten*, the textual anthologies, book series such as The Modern Library, and best sellers, which he unqualifyingly places on the lowest rung of the sociological ladder. Weisstein, in classifying the twentieth-century German authors who have achieved an audience in the United States, summarizes his conclusions as follows:

> Using the aesthetic criterion of literary excellence as a yardstick with which to measure the sociological phenomena pertaining to the reception of contemporary German literature in America, I venture to offer the following categories: 1) Authors whose present American reputation matches, or nearly matches, their actual literary achievement (Thomas Mann, Kafka, Rilke, Brecht and Hesse); 2) Authors, who, having been popular at one time, are now justly forgotten (Toller, Feuchtwanger, Wassermann and Emil Ludwig); 3) Authors whose popularity in America was much too shortlived (Georg Kaiser, Arnold Zweig, perhaps also Werfel); 4) Authors whose work is, and always has been, unduly neglected (Heinrich Mann, Ernst Jünger, Gottfried Benn and Carl Zuckmayer); and 5) Authors whose fame has barely begun to spread beyond the German-speaking countries (Max Frisch, Ingeborg Bachmann). Far from complete, this list could be augmented by a catalogue of individual works still awaiting translation.

Another brief treatment of essentially the same theme is Bernhard Blume's 'Amerika und die deutsche Literatur' (*Deutsche Akademie für Sprache und Dichtung, Darmstadt, Jahrbuch 1959* [Heidelberg and Darmstadt, 1960] pp. 137-148). He is unconvincing in his attempts to provide reasons for his observation that practically no living German authors are known in this country and that for the twentieth-century German writers as a whole, only the names Thomas Mann, Rilke, and Kafka – and possibly a fourth, Brecht – can be said to be read in America. For his treatment of this subject Blume was vehemently criticized by an East-German critic, Hermann Kant ('Darmstädter Dilemma,' *NDL*, VIII [August, 1960], 161-163) in a non-objective criticism that seems not so much to question the accuracy of Blume's observations as to attack American ignorance of German literature. Another article elicited by Blume's address, 'Amerika und die österreichische Literatur' by Robert Rie (*Wort in der Zeit*, VII [April, 1961], 42-45), while generally praising Blume's treatment, emphasizes that any critical evaluation of German literature currently read in the United States must differentiate carefully between literature as required reading in school texts and reading matter found 'auf dem "Markte."' Rie laments the failure of the majority of Americans to distinguish between Germany and Austria, and expresses regret that great Austrian writers have become victims of 'eines intellektuellen "Anschlusses."'

Still another brief but penetrating treatment of the subject is 'Die moderne deutsche Literatur in Amerika' (*Die Sammlung*, IX [1945], 247-253), in which the author, Stanley R. Townsend, distinguishes among three groups of American readers in whom foreign literature, including German literature, finds its audience: 'die Akademiker, die Intellektuellen und das gebildete Publikum.' Townsend, in examining, for example, the contrast that marks the American reception of Herman Hesse with that of Franz Werfel concludes: 'Im allgemeinen können wir sagen, dass die am meisten gelesene deutsche Literatur in Amerika immer aus den Werken bestanden hat, deren Stärke nicht im Stil, sondern im Erzählerischen liegt.'

The above sketch of previous related studies is suggestive of the degree to which English-American-German crosscurrents have captured the attention of scholars in the last sixty years. It also shows that the currency of German literature in translation in the United States during the years following the Second World War remains unexplored. This exploration is the intent of the present study.

As a survey of studies devoted to English-American-German literary interrelations shows, relatively little detailed attention has been given to date to the phenomenon of German literature in the United States during the years following the Second World War. More than two decades have passed since American troops crossed the Rhine to defeat Naziism. Germany, the arch enemy, at the time judged by many as totally synonymous with Naziism, was conquered. News reports were filled with details of Nazi atrocities. Germany's disastrously evil role in mid-twentieth century defied comparison with the darkest episodes of brutal injustice. Today in retrospect the evils of Naziism seem no less serious. But the intervening years have revealed that the common picture of Germany in 1945 was not quite complete, that Naziism even in Hitler's totalitarian state could not be equated entirely with the whole of Germany. It is more clear today than twenty years ago that, while the forces of evil in Germany were masterminding the conquest of Europe, still another segment – small but potent – of that same people was keeping a fearful but incessant vigil over the rich German cultural heritage that no negative force, no matter how pervasive, could erase either from the records of history or from the hearts and minds of its twentieth-century guardians. Some of that segment chose exile: Thomas Mann, Brecht, Werfel, to name only three, came to the United States; others went to Switzerland or France or elsewhere; some, such as Ernst Wiechert, Manfred Hausmann, and Erich Kästner, chose an 'innere Emigration.' While the Nazi Germans executed the plans which eventually led to their own annihilation, representatives of that other Germany continued to nourish a cultural heritage of which a tradition of literary excellence constitutes no small part. Today this fact is somewhat more intelligible than it was a quarter of a century ago.

This study traces the publication of German literature in translation in the United States from 1945, when things German represented primarily either the products of an enemy or an emigrant, to 1960, by which time the political relations between Germany and this country had developed into a partnership within the Atlantic community. One purpose of the present study is to record, by means of an extensive title list, the translations from German literature published as independent volumes in the United States during this sixteen-year period; a second purpose is to evaluate and interpret the significance of that bibliographical record. The title list establishes both the extent and the nature of the contribution of German literature to literary interests in the United States; it also constitutes, at least in part, a record of its currency. That record reflects the one side of what certainly is a reciprocal relationship, forceful and stimulating in our own day as it has been frequently throughout the past. It is also a record of the reception accorded to German literature, measured, not by aesthetic standards of excellence, but by statistical evidence and subjected to critical evaluation. Such a study aims not to conclude whether the translated German works represent uncompromising standards of literary excellence or conciliatory submission to uncultivated taste. It cannot acclaim the meritorious nor disdain the meretricious. It does not suggest that perhaps certain literary products ought to have been imported, while others should have been denied an American reception. It does not even attempt to answer fully the question of why certain books have appeared. The present study proposes rather to establish a record of the vast panorama of German literature which has undeniably become a part of America's recent literary experience.

The term 'German literature,' when undefined, is ambiguous, for both 'German' and 'literature' can be variously interpreted. In this study the term 'literature' means, broadly speaking, *schöne Literatur*; it excludes works that deal primarily with philosophy, theology, art, or science, except in the case of early writers who are generally included in studies of literature. Thus, included are writers such as Ekkehardus I, Meister Eckhart, Johannes Tauler, and Jakob Böhme, e.g., mystics whose imaginative literary quality constitutes an important segment of the body of German literature. On the other hand, systematic philosophers, such as Kant and Schopenhauer, are omitted. Children's literature constitutes an essential portion of the bibliography, but, for purposes of limiting the scope of the subject, is not treated in the discussion. 'German' here means works written originally in the German language, i.e., works written in German irrespective of the author's birth, nationality, or residence. Hence, as is often customary, Swiss and Austrian writers are automatically included, as are such figures as Chamisso and

Kafka. Also included are those persons who emigrated either temporarily or permanently and who continued to constitute a legitimate part of the heritage of German literature. Authors who began writing almost exclusively in English some time after their immigration to the United States (for example, Vicki Baum) are not represented in the title list.

This study is limited to those translations in separate volumes actually published in the United States during the years 1945 through 1960. On occasion a translation may have been published simultaneously in the United States and in England and, at times, also in Canada, Australia, or New Zealand. But English translations not published in the United States are excluded from consideration, even though they may have circulated, even widely, in the United States. Works written in German and published in the original language in the United States are not considered here, since their appearance could not possibly have made any appreciable impact upon the American reading public as a whole but necessarily remained confined to a restricted segment of readers in this country. Anthologies which are devoted exclusively to translations from German are included. No attempt has been made to itemize or treat translations of works from the German which are included in general anthologies.

Currency of German literature in the United States, within the definitions given above, is measured by an extensive title list of German literature translated into English and published in this country from 1945 through 1960 and given *in extenso* as the second part of this study. Compilation of the title list was accomplished by reading through many pages of book lists, such as the *Index Translationum*, the *National Union Catalog*, *A Catalog of Books Represented by Library of Congress Printed Cards*, the *Cumulative Book Index*, Mönnig's bibliographies, *Books in Print*, *Paperbound Books in Print*, and publishers' catalogs.

The title list of translations had been completed prior to the appearance of Morgan's *Supplement*; however, the present list has been checked against his. Works published between 1945 and 1955 (the concluding year of Morgan's recent volume) and not contained in the *Supplement* are marked by an asterisk.

In the ensuing analysis the discussion follows a chronological arrangement of authors according to the era or movement with which they have generally been associated, down to the twentieth century, where, due to the multifarious literary nature of these years, the authors are treated according to genre. Because of the large number of twentieth-century writers represented in the period under consideration, it was necessary to exercise some selectivity generally in favor of those authors best known in the United States and ignoring those whose reception here was considerably limited during the sixteen years surveyed.

2

LITERATURE FROM
THE MIDDLE HIGH GERMAN PERIOD
TO THE BEGINNINGS OF THE CLASSICAL PERIOD

In the United States during the years surveyed in the present study, a total of fourteen authors, with volumes devoted exclusively to selections in English translation, represent the literary development of Germany throughout the centuries that precede Goethe and the classical period of German literature. Of these fifteen authors only a few have had more than one or two volumes of their works published in this country in translation. Most of these translations are related in origin and production to the interests of individual scholars at American universities and thus manifest more largely an academic interest. Hence the works represented may be said to reflect little popular appeal to the general American reading public, and the translation and publication of these works may rightly be considered an activity closely associated with the interests of Germanists and other academic persons.

Earliest of all specimens of Germanic literature appearing at this time in English translation in the United States are two compositions that, in one sense of the word, are not German literature at all, for they were written in Latin and as such illustrate the persistence of intellectual activity pursued and preserved in the monasteries during a time of general disinterest in written literature and in an era certainly not propitious to literature in the native tongue. One such poem, *Waltharius manu fortis*, is itself a translation and presumably an elaboration of an Old High German text no longer extant. An English translation of this heroic epic in Leonine hexameters made by F. O. Magoun, Jr., and H. M. Smyser was published in 1950 as Connecticut College Monograph No. 4, which contains, besides *Walter of Aquitaine*, the stanzas dealing with Walther contained in the *Nibelungenlied* and also the Graz and Vienna fragments of the Middle High German romance of Walther of Aquitaine and Hildegund of Burgundy. A decade earlier this English version of the *Waltherii Poesis*, as it is referred to at the end of the poem, had been included in a volume containing selections translated for the first time from Old Norwegian and from Medieval Latin into English by the same two scholars. The volume containing it, entitled *Survivals in Old Norwegian of Medieval English, French, and German Literature, Together with the Latin Versions of the Heroic Legend of Walter of Aquitaine*, was published as the first of the Connecticut College Monographs (Baltimore, 1941). Avowing that, inasmuch as interest in many older texts is related to historical documentation rather than to great literature, prose translations are quite adequate, Smyser and Magoun expressed the hope that 'in the case of the Poem of Walter, a work of genuine literary merit, ... we may some day be given a "literary" translation, perhaps one of such successful hexameters as those of Hermann Althof's German rendering' (p. ix). This hope, as yet, has remained unrealized.

A translation of a second specimen of Latin literature written during the era of the Saxon emperors, the Latin epic *Ruodlieb*, makes available for the first time to readers of English the fragmentary novel 'second to none in importance as a document of the eleventh century in the field of imaginative literature,' as the work is characterized in the Preface to the volume entitled *Ruodlieb, The Earliest Courtly Novel (after 1050)*, (Univ. of N. Car. Stud. in Germ. Langs. and Lits., No. 23 [Chapel Hill, 1959]). The scholarly interests of Edwin H. Zeydel, translator of this work, are reflected in a number of other translations of older German literature published for the most part as volumes in the series designated as the University of North Carolina Studies in the Germanic Languages and Literatures. Initiated in 1949, this series is performing an important service to American letters by presenting not only older and classical works but also modern works of German literature in English translation. Like a related series of monographs – the University of North Carolina

Studies in Comparative Literature – this one also includes studies of literature prepared by American scholars.

Zeydel has translated two additional important works from the Middle High German *Blütezeit* that have been published in the former series. In collaboration with Bayard Quincy Morgan, he has translated into rhyming couplets Hartmann von Aue's version of the medieval Oedipus legend, *Gregorius* (Univ. of N. Car. Stud. in Germ. Langs. and Lits., No. 14 [Chapel Hill, 1955]). Another translation of the same work, but which goes beyond Zeydel's translation by providing a textual analysis, was made by Sheema Z. Buehne and presented as a doctoral dissertation in 1960 at The Pennsylvania State University ('A Metrical Translation of *Gregorius, the Good Sinner*, by Hartmann von Aue, with Critical and Interpretive Notes'), which further substantiates the observation that older German literature has generated interest chiefly in academic circles.[1] The other Middle High German work translated by Zeydel, again with the collaboration of Morgan, is Wolfram von Eschenbach's *Parzival* (Univ. of N. Car. Stud. in Germ. Langs. and Lits., No. 5 [Chapel Hill, 1951]). Here the translators have not attempted to present the lengthy epic in its entirety; rather, they have translated into English verse all of the most important parts and joined them with connecting summaries that enable the reader to follow the events without interruption. A complete prose translation of Wolfram's epic poem, with the division into sixteen books, together with an introduction and textual notes, made by Helen M. Mustard and Charles E. Passage – the latter known for his important recent translations of a number of Schiller's dramas – was published just one year beyond the concluding date of the present study by Vintage Books as a paperbound volume (New York, 1961). Zeydel has made available in English still another important piece of very early German writing with his translation of *The Lay of Hildebrand* in Volume 1 (pp. 463-464) of a two-volume anthology entitled *The Heritage of European Literature* (ed. Edward H. Weatherly, A. Pelzer Wagener, Edwin H. Zeydel, and Avrahm Yarmolinsky [New York, 1948]).

[1] Mrs. Buehne's translation, with an introduction by Helen Adolf, was recently published by Friedrich Ungar (*Gregorius, the Good Sinner* [New York, 1966]).

Similar to Zeydel's *Parzival*, with summaries connecting the translated portions, is his version of *Tristan and Isolde* by Gottfried von Strassburg, which was published by the Princeton University Press for the University of Cincinnati in 1948, prior to the initiation of the series of studies at the University of North Carolina mentioned above. Supplementing Zeydel's abridged translation is one by A. T. Hatto of Gottfried's epic in its entirety, bound together with the surviving fragments of the *Tristan* of Thomas of Bretagne and published in 1960 in Gloucester, Massachusetts, and simultaneously in England as one of the Penguin Classics – an edition which through its vehicle suggests an attempt to reach a wider reading audience. Professors Zeydel and Morgan again worked together on the translation of thirty poems by Walther von der Vogelweide, thus providing English readers with one of the very few separately published collections of recent translations of Middle High German lyric poetry by means of a selection, published as a paperbound volume by the Thrift Press, of some characteristic examples of this genre from its most celebrated exponent, with emphasis 'placed upon poems of perennial significance' (*Walther von der Vogelweide: Poems; Thirty New English Renderings in the Original Forms, with the Middle High German Texts* [Ithaca, New York, 1952]). Translations by various translators of twenty lyric poems from twelve Middle High German poets constitute a part of the volume entitled *Lyrics of the Middle Ages* (New York, 1959), alleged by the editor, Hubert Creekmore, to be 'the first anthology to present only medieval poetry in translation in a broader than national scope.' In the collection are assembled translations of lyric poetry from the years 500 to 1500 in fourteen major European languages. One other specimen from the brief span of years in which Middle High German poetry reached its zenith, Ulrich von Zatzikhoven's *Lanzelet* (New York, 1951), was translated by two other university professors, Kenneth G. T. Webster of Harvard and, after his death, Roger Sherman Loomis of Columbia. This translation was published as Number XLVII of the series entitled Record of Civilization, Sources and Studies.

From the preceding it can be noted that, while nothing of Old High German literature and only two pieces of writing from the early Middle

High German period are represented through translations, the most important epic poets and the most important lyric poet of the Middle High German *Blütezeit* have been represented in English through translations published in the United States between the years 1945 and 1960, in the case of Wolfram and Gottfried of their *magna opera*, and in the case of Hartmann of one of his major poems. It should be noted that in 1944 an English version by Charles Maxwell Lancaster of what many scholars consider Hartmann's *magnum opus* had appeared. Published by the Vanderbilt University Press, Lancaster's version of *Der arme Heinrich*, as well as his version of a portion of Gottfried's *Tristan* in the same volume, was based upon literal prose translations, by John G. Frank and Carl Hammer, of the original Middle High German text (*Two Moods of Minnesong: An Adaptation into English Verse of Gottfried von Strassburg's First Part of Tristan and Isolde and of Hartmann von Aue's Complete Poem of Hapless Henry*). In the nineteenth century the story of Hartmann's court epic had been introduced into English for both British and American readers by two gifted poets. In America Longfellow made use of it in *The Golden Legend* (1851).[1] In England in the year 1846 or 1847 Dante Gabriel Rossetti wrote a paraphrase of Hartmann's poem, *Henry the Leper*, bringing his version to completion about 1871 (published in two volumes in a limited edition in Boston, 1905, Volume One containing the text and Volume Two containing a facsimile of the manuscript). Rossetti had also begun to translate the *Nibelungenlied*, but unfortunately no trace of this effort remains. Although beyond the span of years surveyed in the present study, it is significant that in 1962 there appeared *The Song of the Nibelungs: A Verse Translation from the Middle High German Nibelungenlied* (Detroit), by Frank G. Ryder, the first new translation into English of this important epic since 1911, published by the Wayne State University Press. An older translation of *The Nibelungenlied*, by Margaret Armour, first published in London

---

[1] For an evaluation of Longfellow's role as a cultural mediator between Germany and the United States as demonstrated in his accomplishments as a translator of German lyrics and ballads, see the article by Carl J. Hammer, Jr., 'Longfellow's Lyrics "From the German," ' (*Studies in Comparative Literature*, ed. Waldo F. McNeir, Louisiana State Univ. Stud., Humanities Series, No. 11 [Baton Rouge, 1962], pp. 155-172).

in 1897 and chosen for inclusion in Dutton's Everyman's Library as early as 1908, was reprinted, together with an introduction by Franz Schoenberner, by the Limited Editions Club in 1960. The following year the same translation, with an introduction by Edy Legrand, was republished by the Heritage Press.

Thus, while many significant pieces of Middle High German literature continue to be available only in Middle High German or modern German versions, the undisputed masterpieces are now available to American readers in recent English translations. The translation of Ulrich von Zatzikhoven's *Lanzelet*, an epic poem of comparatively less merit, may be related to a broader academic interest in the period of development and decline of the Arthurian romance and the relationship of German literary production in this field to French sources. The deterioration of the Middle High German court epic into the comic, usually satiric poems descriptive of peasant life is represented in a translation of Heinrich Wittenweiler's *Ring* by George Fenwick Jones, another volume published in the University of North Carolina studies (*Wittenweiler's Ring and the Anonymous Scots Poem, 'Colkelbie Sow'; Two Comic-Didactic Works from the Fifteenth Century*, Univ. of N. Car. Stud. in Germ. Langs. and Lits., No. 18 [Chapel Hill, 1956]). More than two decades earlier the scholarly efforts of Clair Hayden Bell of the University of California had made available an English version of *Meier Helmbrecht*, another work illustrating the same deterioration, together with a contrasting work, *Der arme Heinrich*, showing the epic at its height, in a volume published by Columbia University Press (*Peasant Life in Old German Epics: Meier Helmbrecht and Der arme Heinrich, Translated from the Middle High German of the Thirteenth Century* [New York, 1931]).

Representative poetry of the seventeenth century in Germany appeared in modern English translation in a very recent volume by George C. Schoolfield entitled *The German Lyric of the Baroque in English Translation* (Univ. of N. Car. Stud. in Germ. Langs. and Lits., No. 29 [Chapel Hill, 1961]), containing, in addition to an introduction and a biographical index, the German texts and translations of nearly two hundred poems from some ninety authors. The relation of the publication of this volume to scholarly interests and academic pursuits is evidenced not only by the person of the author but also by his own statement of purpose expressed in the Preface:

> The present book has been written to serve three ends. First, it is meant to introduce the German lyric of the seventeenth century to people who, while perhaps interested in European literary matters, cannot read German well enough to make out Baroque texts, and who, most likely, are not aware that Germany possessed a literature in the seventeenth century. The German Baroque, so well known to cultured Americans in its musical and architectural manifestations, deserves to be made accessible from its literary side as well.
>
> In the second place, the book is intended to aid those undergraduates who have decided to concentrate in German. It may help them to understand Baroque German a little better; it may make them realize that, despite the evidence of Gryphius's tragedies and Opitz's *Buch von der deutschen Poeterei*, the seventeenth century can offer genuine reading pleasure.
>
> Finally, the book has been written because the author enjoyed writing it, a confession, to be sure, which may cause his dishonorable discharge from even the disciplinary battalions of scholarship.

In contrast to the above works, nearly all of which were published by university presses or were otherwise associated with scholarly pursuits, the works of four writers from among the German mystics seem to reflect a persistence, in the United States of the twentieth century, of an early interest in German mysticism and its later development, pietism, illustrated by certain long persisting religious groups such as the Moravians, the Schwenkfelders, and the Amish.

The recent publication in the United States of several volumes devoted to the works of Meister Eckhart supports the observation that an increasing interest in German mysticism is in evidence, particularly since, according to Morgan's *Bibliography*, only one of Eckhart's works in English translation had been published in the United States in the first four decades of this century. In 1941 a collection of twenty-eight sermons, together with some fragments from sermons, and including a translation of Eckhart's 'Defense' – the latter allegedly translated into a modern language for the first time – was published under the title *Meister Eckhart, A Modern Translation* (New York and London), by Raymond Bernard Blakney; this volume was then reprinted in 1957 as a paperbound Harper Torchbook. Blakney also translated Eckhart's

Sermon on Beati Pauperes Spiritu (Pawlet, [Vt.?], 1960), of which 210 copies were printed. Harper also published, in a series entitled Classics of the Contemplative Life, *Treatises and Sermons of Meister Eckhart* (New York, 1958), a collection of translations from both the German and the Latin works, together with an introduction, by James M. Clark and John V. Skinner. The same volume was simultaneously published in London by another publisher. James M. Clark's *Meister Eckhart, An Introduction to the Study of His Works, With an Anthology of his Sermons*, published one year earlier by Thomas Nelson and Sons (London, New York, etc.) was prepared, as stated in the Preface, to correct the lamentable fact that Eckhart had been so ignored in English, while a 'vast amount of learned work [has been] published during the last seventy years or so on the Continent,... A recent bibliography of Eckhart contains two hundred works written in French, German, Italian and Dutch, but not one in English,...' Clark's book is intended to fulfil 'the purpose of assembling the results of Continental scholarship in a lucid and intelligible form.' In 1957 the Philosophical Library published *Meister Eckehart* [sic] *Speaks; A Collection of the Teachings of the Famous German Mystic* (New York), a booklet of a devotional character containing a collection of nineteen short essays, introduced by Otto Karrer. The slender volume, also published in England, of seventy-two pages is a translation by Elizabeth Strakosch from the German, *Meister Eckehart spricht*.

The religious literature of mysticism is further represented by a volume, also edited and translated by Elizabeth Strakosch, containing twenty-one sermons of Tauler entitled *Signposts to Perfection; A Selection from the Sermons of Johann Tauler* (St. Louis, 1958), and by a spurious work attributed to Tauler (*The Book of the Poor in Spirit, by a Friend of God* [New York, 1954]).[1] The later development of the literature of mysticism is represented by several volumes from the writings of Jakob Böhme. In 1946 *Way to Christ* appeared in Los Angeles and in 1947 in

---

[1] Evidence of early interest in the sermons of Tauler among English-speaking persons is provided, in addition to the published items cited by Morgan, by the existence of a manuscript collection of his sermons translated into English, contained in The Allison-Shelley Collection and attested by the Assistant Keeper of the British Museum to be from the seventeenth century.

New York. In 1954 his *Confessions* appeared in New York. *Personal Christianity* was published in 1958 and brought out in a paperback edition in 1960. A translation of *Vom übersinnlichen Leben* was published in 1958 (*Dialogues on the Supersensual Life* [New York]). Of the several volumes only one, *Six Theosophic Points, and Other Writing* (Ann Arbor, 1958), was published by a university press. Interest in the non-theological literature of the German mystics is reflected by the publication of *Death and the Plowman* by Johannes von Saaz, a translation from the modern German version of Alois Bernt by Ernest N. Kirrmann and appearing as another of the University of North Carolina studies (Chapel Hill, 1958). Together with this volume the publication of *The Cherubinic Wanderer* of Angelus Silesius (New York, 1953), in a translation by Willard R. Trask, and with an introduction by Curt von Faber du Faur, makes available in English specimens of the religious poetry of mysticism from around the year 1400 and again from two and a half centuries later.

Another instance of current interest in mysticism is the recent publication of two quite unusual volumes which first appeared in German around the middle of the nineteenth century. *The Life of Our Lord and Savior Jesus Christ, Combined with The Bitter Passion and The Life of Mary; From the Revelations of Anna Catharina Emmerick, as Recorded in the Journals of Clemens Brentano* (Fresno, Calif., 1954), edited by Carl E. Schmöger, alleged to be 'a photographic reproduction of the first and only English version... published in 1914... as *The Lowly Life and Bitter Passion of Our Lord and Savior Jesus Christ and His Blessed Mother, together with The Mysteries of the Old Testament*' (see *The National Union Catalog; A Cumulative Author List Representing Library of Congress Printed Cards and Titles Reported by Other American Libraries: 1953-1957*). In Morgan's Bibliography (no. 1454), however, is recorded *The Dolorous Passion of Our Lord Jesus Christ; From the Meditations of Anne Catharina Emmerich*, published in London in 1862. Schmöger's biography of Emmerich was translated by Helen Ram and published in London in 1874 and again, in two volumes, in 1885. *Life of the Blessed Virgin Mary; From the Visions of Anne Catherine Emmerich* (Springfield, Ill., 1954), also recorded in the journals of Brentano from which they were translated by Sir Michael

Palairet, with notes by Sebastian Bullough, was published in the same year.

Interests other than those strictly literary are responsible for the publication of translations of several volumes from the writings of Paracelsus. His *Volumen medicinae paramirum*, translated by Kurt F. Leidecker and published by The Johns Hopkins Press (Baltimore, 1949), had been preceded by the publication of other specimens of his medical expositions by the Institute of the History of Medicine in 1941, the year marking the four-hundredth anniversary of the death of Paracelsus. Undoubtedly the Second World War was at least partially responsible for the fact that this anniversary passed virtually unnoticed in the United States. A more popular interest in this controversial sixteenth-century figure and his relation to twentieth-century preoccupation with scientific pursuits was delayed until after the close of the war. In 1951 appeared Henry M. Pachter's biography *Magic Into Science: The Story of Paracelsus* (New York, 1951); in the same year was published *Paracelsus: Selected Writings* (New York, 1951), which achieved a second edition in 1958, further evidencing a more general if belated interest in this Renaissance man of magic and science.

From the age of the mystics and the days of Paracelsus it is a long stride, chronologically and ideologically, to the age of classicism in Germany. The promise of flowering furnished by the Renaissance had remained largely unfulfilled in Germany. While in Italy, France, and England literature flourished, in Germany the energy released and developed by the Reformation produced, in the Thirty Years War, violence so intense that Germany's cultural life was fundamentally disrupted for nearly a century. It is not too surprising, therefore, that, since Germany exhibited so little literature of enduring merit during the war-torn seventeenth century, few translations into English of that epoch have appeared.

The eighteenth century and the beginnings of the German classical period are represented, in translations published in the United States during the period under study, by two figures, one of whom had never before been represented by the publication in the United States of any of his works in English translation.

Like Paracelsus, Georg Christoph Lichtenberg is not strictly a literary figure. His writings had appeared in English translation but once before, when *The Reflections of Lichtenberg*, selected and translated by Norman Alliston, was published in London in 1908. Quite recently Lichtenberg has become the subject of attention in the United States with the publication, within a period of two years, of several volumes devoted to his life and works. *The Lichtenberg Reader: Selected Writings* (Boston), translated, edited, and introduced by Franz H. Mautner and Henry Hatfield, published in 1959, contains a miscellaneous selection of several hundred of his aphorisms, twenty-seven of his letters, and four of the essays Lichtenberg wrote for the *Göttingischer Taschenkalender* of which he served as editor from 1778 until his death in 1799. Also in 1959 there appeared a volume entitled *Lichtenberg: A Doctrine of Scattered Occasions; Reconstructed from His Aphorisms and Reflections* (Bloomington, Ind.). One year later there was published *A Reasonable Rebel, Georg Christoph Lichtenberg* (New York and London, 1960), a translation by Bernard Smith of a biography written by Carl Brinitzer and originally published in German as *G. C. Lichtenberg; die Geschichte eines gescheiten Mannes* (Tübingen, 1956).

The second figure of the early eighteenth century represented in translations of his works published in the United States between 1945 and 1960 is Lessing. During the years covered by the present study, eight separate volumes devoted entirely to Lessing's works appeared in this country. Two of these, *Emilia Galotti*, translated by Anna Johanna Gode-von Aesch (Great Neck, N.Y., 1959), and *Nathan the Wise*, translated by Guenther Reinhardt (Brooklyn, 1950), which appeared in Barron's Educational Series – originally largely interlinear but more recently of greater literary value – reflect the role of Lessing's dramas in the classroom where courses in general or comparative literature of the eighteenth century often include a study of these two works. But recent interest in Lessing has not been confined to the classroom. For instance, *Nathan the Wise, A Dramatic Poem in Five Acts* (New York, 1955) has also appeared in an English verse translation by Morgan, long noted for his interest in translations and in translating as an art. This same drama is currently available also in Everyman's Library, a reprint of a volume first published in London in 1930, containing, in addition, *Minna von Barnhelm* and *Laocoön* (New York, 1959). Interest in Lessing's treatise on the limits of painting and poetry, when judged from the number of translations published, has not merely persisted but has remained quite active, for in addition to its inclusion in the above mentioned volume, a reprint of an early translation that had been made by Ellen Frothingham and first published in the year 1874 was published at New York in 1957 as a separate, paperbound volume. A recent translation of *Laocoön* by Edward Allen McCormick, originally announced for publication in December, 1959, appeared in 1962 as a volume of the Library of the Liberal Arts, which series is now issued by Bobbs-Merrill. In contrast to the majority of translations from the earlier periods of German literature, all translations of Lessing's works have been published by firms other than university presses, except for some selections from his theological writings, translated by Henry Chadwick and entitled *Theological Writings: Selections in Translation* (Stanford, 1957).

It is not without significance that during the years of the Second World War Lessing's *Nathan* was produced on the stage in New York City on two different occasions, providing convincing evidence that interest in Lessing extended well beyond purely academic preoccupation with the historical development of German dramatic literature and, perhaps even more significantly, that Lessing's *Nathan* was accepted as important dramatic art which extended above and beyond any general antagonism to things German. Adapted for the American stage by Ferdinand Bruckner, *Nathan the Wise*, with Herbert Berghof portraying the titular hero, opened on March 11, 1942, as a presentation by the Studio Theatre at the New School for Social Research on West Twelfth Street. This production by Erwin Piscator was such a success that a few weeks later, on April 3, the 'celebrated play,' as Brooks Atkinson in one of two reviews referred to it, was brought uptown to the Belasco Theatre. Hailing it as 'the sort of drama you rarely see on Broadway' (New York *Times*, March 12, 1942, p. 25) and as 'the first work of real intelligence to appear in our neighborhood for a long time' (New York *Times*, April 4, 1942, p. 18), these and other reviews could not avoid pointing out that Hitler had burned this play of religious and social tolerance in 1933 on Unter den Linden. Piscator revived the production for a brief run in February, 1944, at the Studio Theatre once more. While much less enthusiastic than two years earlier, one reviewer credited Lessing's drama with 'moments of compassion and dignity' (New York *Times*, February 22, 1944, p. 26).

This important stage production doubtless aided the survival in the United States of a more popular awareness and appreciation of German literature and undoubtedly contributed toward the much fuller reception of German letters in this country which the years following the cessation of hostilities between Germany and the United States were destined to bring.

German literature of the Middle High German and Early New High German periods published in the United States between 1945 and 1960 is related only remotely to the general American reading public. For the most part these works are related, firstly, to the interests of Germanists, as a part of their own scholarly studies, reaching a wider circle of readers through the classes in literature in which they are read, and, secondly, to a surviving interest in mysticism and pietism. Few, if any, of these works can be said to reveal any large popular interest or to have made any appreciable impact upon the general reading public. With the beginnings of the classical period this situation changes: to a limited degree with Lichtenberg and more clearly with Lessing the currency of German literature in the United States extends beyond strictly academic circles to a wider literary audience.

3

GOETHE

The reception of Goethe in the United States has, by and large, been generous and enthusiastic, though not, at times, without controversy, criticism, and even condemnation. Initially, in America as in Germany and other countries, his reputation was based primarily upon *Werther* so that in these countries and to his own displeasure he was known chiefly as 'the author of *Werther*.' This reputation subsequently developed into a fuller, more mature recognition of the universal nature of his genius. Today, to the majority of the American reading public, he is best known as 'the author of *Faust*.'

Three forces, in the main, were responsible for determining the nature and extent of Goethe's initial and early reception in the United States.[1] Firstly, Goethe's works in the original, as published in Germany, were to be found, in very modest numbers at first, in important public and private libraries of New England, which from colonial times had contained numerous German books.[2] The presence of Goethe's works in the late eighteenth and early nineteenth centuries, therefore, was by no means unusual. The Boston Athenaeum, for example, included German

---

[1] See Eugene Oswald, *Goethe in England and America*, 2d ed., rev. and enl. by L. and E. Oswald, Pubs. of the Engl. Goethe Soc., No. XI (London, 1909); also a review of the foregoing with numerous additions: Frederick W. C. Lieder's 'Goethe in England and America,' *JEGP*, x (1911), 535-556; and Henry A. Pochmann, et al., *German Culture in America: Philosophical and Literary Influences, 1600-1900* (Madison, 1957), pp. 327-346.

[2] See Harold S. Jantz, 'German Thought and Literature in New England, 1620-1820,' *JEGP*, XLI (1942), 1-45, especially 4-20.

books among its holdings and acquisitions. In 1827 its only work by Goethe was a copy of the translation of *The Sorrows of Werter* (Chiswick, 1822), although several additional works, most of them in the original German, were on order; by 1840 the library had acquired Hayward's translation of *Faust* (London, 1834), Carlyle's translation of *Wilhelm Meister's Apprenticeship* (Boston, 1828), Sarah Austin's *Characteristics of Goethe* (London, 1833), and one volume in the original German, *Kunst und Alterthum* (Stuttgart, 1827).[1] At an even earlier date there was a substantial number of German works temporarily in the Boston Athenaeum, although they were not intended for circulation, for it was here that John Quincy Adams deposited his personal library, containing works in German, during his absence (1809-1817) from the United States in Russia following his appointment by President James Madison as Minister Plenipotentiary to the Court of Saint Petersburg.[2] From this collection, during its owner's absence, George Ticknor borrowed a German copy of *Werther*, from which he made, in 1814, what for about a century and a quarter was the only American translation of the story.

Secondly, Goethe was known personally by a number of the young men who were destined to became leading literary intermediaries. The English translation of Madame de Staël's *De l'Allemagne* was printed in the United States in 1814, having been published in England just one year before. Its vogue was truly phenomenal, affording countless Americans their initial acquaintance with Germany, its cultural accomplishments, its literary development, and its leading literary figures,

[1] See the *Catalogue of Books in the Boston Atheneum* [sic]; *to Which are Added the By-Laws of the Institution and a List of Its Proprietors and Subscribers* (Boston, 1827); and the *Catalogue of Books Added to the Boston Athenaeum since the Publication of the Catalogue in January, 1827* (Boston, 1840).

[2] For a discussion of the German books in the Adams library see *A Catalogue of the Books of John Quincy Adams Deposited in the Boston Athenaeum, With Notes on Books, Adams Seals and Book Plates*, by Henry Adams, with an Introduction by Worthington Chauncey Ford (Boston, 1938). See also Walter John Morris' 'John Quincy Adams: Germanophile' (unpubl. diss., Pa. State Univ., 1963), esp. the Appendix, pp. 238-241, for a part of a list of books shipped by Adams from The Hague, 1797, and from Berlin, 1801, compiled from Adams' 'Catalogue of Books,' and which, comprising about nine percent of Adams' total catalogue, includes 'works in German, works about Germany and/or Germans in German or other languages, works by German authors in other languages, and works related to Adams' research and writing on German Literature.'

including Goethe. It was responsible for the intensification of interest, already stimulated and lively, among several young Americans in travel through Europe, especially Germany, and in study at a German university, particularly Göttingen. George Ticknor and Edward Everett were the first two of the first generation of Americans that subsequently included Joseph Cogswell and George Bancroft, who made the journey to Germany, usually took 'The Road to Weimar,'[1] and personally met 'the author of *Werther*.' As a matter of fact, it was as an exercise for learning the German language, in anticipation of his journey, that Ticknor had translated Goethe's *Werther* into English. Upon their return, their intellectual development stimulated, partially molded, and significantly influenced, by their direct contact with Germany, these literary pioneers fostered in their fellow Americans a heightened interest in things German, in German literature especially, and in Goethe in particular.

Thirdly, a wide range of Goethe's works, beginning with the appearance of *The Sorrows and Sympathetic Attachments of Werter* in Philadelphia in 1784, gradually became available in English translations, some of which, to be sure, did no honor to Goethe, while others more memorable were creatively done by translators who themselves, in a number of cases, were poets and literary scholars of the first order. Most translations of his works that were published in England also circulated in the United States, and reviews of others, not yet available in English translations, circulated through American journals and newspapers, extending the acquaintance of Americans with Goethe beyond his *Werther*, to his *Elective Affinities*, his *Memoirs, Wilhelm Meister, Iphigenia*, and to some of his poetry. Not all reaction, by any means, was favorable, just as in his own country Goethe was not without his opponents and outright enemies. His moral standards and his naturalistic philosophy were frequently examined by the Puritan conscience and found wanting. The appearance of the translation by C. C. Felton of Wolfgang Menzel's history of German literature, in which Goethe comes under severe

---

[1] See Bliss Perry's 'The Road to Weimar,' *Amer. Scholar*, I (1932), 272-291, and, especially, O. W. Long's *Literary Pioneers: Early American Explorers of European Culture* (Cambridge, Mass., 1935).

attack, published in 1840 as the seventh, eighth, and ninth volumes in George Ripley's series entitled Specimens of Foreign Standard Literature, contributed toward further condemnation. But he also had his American champions; foremost among them was Margaret Fuller who, with her translation and interpretive preface to *Conversations with Goethe in the Last Years of His Life, Translated from the German of Eckermann* also included as the fourth volume in Ripley's Specimens (1839), and with her essays in his defense in the *Dial*, did much to temper American judgment of Goethe and to encourage a more mature interpretation of his works, the major ones of which were available in English translation by about the middle of the century.

Today Goethe's works continue to experience a generous reception in the United States unmatched by that accorded to few, if any, other German authors. Of no small significance to Goethe's recent popularity in this country were the activities planned and carried out in connection with the bicentennial celebration of his birth in 1949, reinforcing, as it did, the renewed devotion to his memory elicited by the centennial commemoration of his death only seventeen years earlier, in 1932. It was particularly these celebrations which served to intensify the consciousness of, and arouse special interest in, Goethe's unexampled contribution to a common literary heritage, just a few years after the conclusion of hostilities between Germany and the United States.

Lyric poetry has generally proved the most intransigent of all literary genres to transference into a foreign language. Perhaps this fact explains why, in spite of Goethe's general popularity in the United States gauged by the number of translations of his works, relatively few translations of his poems have taken root and become familiar to English-speaking readers.[1] A few of his poems have become familiar, of course, by having been set to music by Schubert, Wolf, and other composers; yet in most performances these are sung in the original German, often with program

---

[1] See Lucretia Van Tuyl Simmons' *Goethe's Lyric Poems in English Translation Prior to 1860*, Univ. of Wisconsin Stud. in Lang. and Lit., No. 6 (Madison, 1919), and Stella M. Hinz's *Goethe's Lyric Poems in English Translation after 1860*, Univ. of Wisconsin Stud. in Lang. and Lit., No. 26 (Madison, 1928), for an analysis and interpretation of an exhaustive list of poems by Goethe in English translation down to that time.

notes supplying a translation, not infrequently in prose. 'Those who believe that poetry, especially lyric poetry, defies translation,' writes that tireless translator, Edwin H. Zeydel – one of the most recent to attempt the task – in the Preface to his *Goethe, The Lyrist* (Chapel Hill, 1955),

> will derive enough reason [for so few memorable translations in English of poems having been produced] from that belief. The studies of Miss Simmons and Miss Hinz give the answers to others. Many of the translators were too foreign to the world and thought of Goethe. Some had an imperfect command of his language. Most of them, missing the simplicity and directness of the German poet, strove to compose poems that were pretty, but lost the meaning, or spirit, or both, of one of the world's greatest lyrists. Many, even of the best, used a stilted idiom which the reader of today, familiar with Frost, Robinson, and Sandburg, can no longer relish. (p. xi)

Prior to the appearance of Zeydel's translations, B. Q. Morgan acknowledged the same problem in his bicentennial essay, 'Goethe in English':

> ...there is today no satisfactory English collection of his shorter poems. This is entirely understandable, for Goethe was perhaps the most accomplished lyricist the world has yet seen, and it is a law that the difficulty of translating a lyric is in direct proportion to its merit. On the other hand, since in this very field Goethe speaks most immediately and delightfully to those who understand the language, the loss in this case is particularly deplorable. One can only say that a part of the best of the poet must remain a sealed book to those who approach him through the medium of any language but his own. (*Southwest Goethe Festival: A Collection of Nine Papers* [Dallas, 1949], p. 110)

Also discussing this problem at about the same time, Ludwig Lewisohn, at the Goethe Bicentennial Convocation and Music Festival held June 27 to July 17, 1949, in Aspen, Colorado, delivered an address entitled 'New Versions of Goethe's Poetry,' in which he discussed the relation of Goethe's poetry to readers of English, where 'Goethe has fared ill both in the past and in the present.' In contradiction to the often repeated claim that 'poetry cannot be translated,' Lewisohn, a man of letters who has likewise translated extensively from the German, concludes 'that the great poets can be translated and that Goethe is among their number,' and he proceeds to offer in evidence of his conclusion numerous samplings from 'the writing of my own 100-and-some-odd versions of Goethean poetry.'[1]

While it is true that a number of Goethe's poems, even from their earliest appearance in English translation, have quite frequently been included in anthologies, only a few separate volumes devoted solely to his poetry have ever been published in the United States. In light of the infrequent appearance of such volumes devoted exclusively to Goethe's poetry in English translation it is quite remarkable that during the years surveyed in the present study several volumes of Goethe's poems saw publication, but it is curious that none of these appeared before, and only one in, the bicentennial year, 1949. The single group of translations to appear in that important year was a slender collection in mimeographed form, entitled *Most Famous Songs of Goethe*, translated in the original meters by Udo Rall and published by the translator in a limited edition of fifty copies (Arlington, Va., 1949).[2] Lamenting this lack of new translations, Edwin H. Zeydel, in the Preface to the volume, mentioned previously, of his own translations of some of Goethe's poems, comments: '...since two world-wide Goethe celebrations have taken place during the interim, the centennial of his death in 1932 and the bicentennial of his birth in 1949, we would have a right to expect numerous modern translations. But this expectation has not been fulfilled.' Zeydel's own translations of one hundred poems, printed facing the originals and with an appendix containing a list of musical settings, appeared under the title *Goethe, the Lyrist*,[3] published in 1955 as Number 16 of the University of North Carolina Studies in the Germanic Languages and Literatures (Chapel Hill) and achieved a second edition, revised, in 1959. In 1957 a second collection by the same translator entitled *Poems of Goethe*,

---

[1] This address, along with the other lectures presented at the Convocation, was published in a volume entitled *Goethe and the Modern Age: The International Convocation at Aspen, Colorado, 1949*, edited by Arnold Bergstraesser (Chicago, 1950), under the title 'Goethe's Poetry in the Lands of English Speech' (pp. 192-212).

[2] Also in the bicentennial year the Souvenir Program of the Bicentennial Convocation and Music Festival at Aspen, containing program notes to the sixteen concerts of the Festival, included English translations of the poems of Goethe set to music and performed at the concerts.

[3] For a very brief discussion of a few translations of Goethe's poems since 1924 – the concluding year of the study by Miss Hinz – consult the Preface to this volume.

containing some sixty poems and epigrams with particular emphasis on Goethe's later lyrical production, also presented with the originals and a list of musical settings, was published as Number 20 in the same series.

The advent of the bicentennial celebration of Goethe's birth inspired several separate anthologies containing miscellaneous selections from his writings. These were prepared, in the main, for the general reader in popular editions, offering a cross-section of his poetry, prose, drama, and criticism. Thomas Mann edited, selected, and wrote the introduction for *The Permanent Goethe* (New York, 1948), a volume in the Permanent Library Series – a series presenting, under this title, authors, both classical and modern, of international repute from various national literatures. Anticipating the important anniversary year, this anthology provided the American reader with a broad introduction or re-introduction to Goethe's works by presenting selections, many in new translations, from his lyric poems and ballads, from his longer prose fiction, three dramas, travel sketches, literary essays, letters, and proverbs. For the student, a special college edition of this volume was issued. During the anniversary year there was published a two-volume work, comprising primarily personal correspondence from, to, and about Goethe, and including selections from his literary writings that contribute to the biographical nature of the work, by Ludwig Lewisohn: *Goethe, The Story of a Man, Being the Life of Johann Wolfgang Goethe as Told in His Own Words and the Words of His Contemporaries* (New York, 1949). Also in the anniversary year was published *Wisdom and Experience*, a volume containing selections from Goethe's prose chosen by Ludwig Curtius and translated and edited by Hermann J. Weigand (New York, 1949). These two anthologies, appearing as they did in the bicentennial year, recall an earlier compilation, *Practical Wisdom of Goethe, An Anthology*, which, edited by Emil Ludwig, translated by F. Melian Stawell and Nora Purtscher-Wydenbruck, and published in England in 1933, also doubtless reflected a renewed interest stimulated by the centennial celebration of Goethe's death.

Popular interest in Goethe did not cease with the conclusion of the bicentennial celebrations; rather, they seem to have inspired an interest that, once reawakened, continued to develop, as manifested in particular by the publication in 1958 of a paperbound book by the New American Library, *Great Writings of Goethe* (New York), edited by the British poet and critic Stephen Spender, himself a prolific translator and interpreter of German literature to the English-speaking world.[1] These general anthologies, perhaps more than anything else, attest to a wide circle of interest within the United States in Goethe as a literary giant; and particularly the appearance of a pocket-size paperbound edition points to the recognition of that interest among the American reading public.

Throughout the period under survey translations of single works of Goethe have appeared at an impressive rate and in significant numbers. Some of them have appeared as editions mainly for use by students, others have been directed toward the general reader, still others have been published as volumes in series presenting great literature of the Western world. A translation of Goethe's autobiography, *Dichtung und Wahrheit*, was published by the Public Affairs Press in a bicentennial anniversary edition as *Goethe's Autobiography: Poetry and Truth from My Own Life* (Washington, D. C., 1949) in a British translation by R. O. Moon that had first appeared in the earlier anniversary year, 1932. An additional translation of the same work, by Eithne Wilkins and Ernst Kaiser, *Truth and Fantasy From My Own Life*, published in London in 1949, was republished in New York. The republication in the United States of these two British translations recalls the earliest English version of *Dichtung und Wahrheit* published here. Goethe's autobiography (those portions that had already been published in Germany) had first reached American readers already during the poet's lifetime: in 1824 *Memoirs of Goëthe [sic]: Written by Himself* – an anonymous British translation, which, castigated by Carlyle and termed by others 'a most audacious and impudent quackery,' 'a pseudo version,' and 'a miserably mutilated

---

[1] Spender has translated works by Schiller, Büchner, Rilke, Wedekind, and Toller, and has edited, or prepared introductive essays for, other translations. He was one of the scholars to address the Goethe Bicentennial Convocation in Aspen, Colorado, on 'Goethe and the English Mind,' which appears in *Goethe and the Modern Age* (Chicago, 1950), pp. 113-134. Some seven weeks earlier, on May 12, 1949, he delivered an address entitled 'The Goethean Spirit in Our Time' at The Pennsylvania State University under the auspices of the Simmons Series sponsored by the Department of German.

edition,'[1] was actually made from the French version of Aubert de Vitry of one year earlier – was published in two volumes in London and republished the same year in a one-volume abridgment in New York.

The first of Goethe's works ever to have appeared in English – his immensely popular *Werther* – was, in both England and the United States, long the most widely read of all of his works. The immediate appeal which the story had is demonstrated by the fact that, before the close of the century in which Goethe wrote it, four English translations had appeared in print, two of which, together with a fifth that was printed after the turn of the century, made repeated appearances in the United States throughout the nineteenth and even in the twentieth century.[2] The influence of the almost phenomenal vogue of *Werther*,

---

[1] See Robert Alan Charles' 'French Mediation and Intermediaries, 1750-1815,' in Volume One of *Anglo-German and American-German Crosscurrents*, ed. Philip Allison Shelley, Arthur O. Lewis, Jr., and William W. Betts, Jr. (Chapel Hill, 1957), esp. p. 24; for a somewhat fuller treatment of the subject, see Charles' 'French Intermediaries in the Transmission of German Literature and Culture to England, 1750-1815' (unpubl. diss., Pa. State Univ., 1952), esp. pp. 68-69.

[2] See O. W. Long's 'English Translations of Goethe's Werther,' *JEGP*, XIV (1915), 169-203; also *Goethe's Works with the Exception of Faust: A Catalogue Compiled by the Members of the Yale University Library Staff*, ed. Carl F. Schreiber (New Haven, 1940); and also Long's 'Werther in America,' *Studies in Honor of John Albrecht Walz*, ed. Fred O. Nolte, Harry W. Pfund, and George J. Metcalf (Lancaster, Pa., 1941), pp. 86-116.

The first of the translations of *Werther* into English achieved seven reprints in the United States by 1808. *The Sorrows of Werter: A German Story*, the title of its first English translation, by an anonymous translator, earlier believed to be Richard Graves but more recently held to be Daniel Malthus, was published in London in the year 1779 and was made, not from the German original, but from the French version by George Deyverdun, published three years earlier in Maastricht – one of three French versions that had already appeared by that time. Five years later, in 1784, this translation from the French, published in Philadelphia, became the first American edition of *Werther*, as *The Sorrows and Sympathetic Attachments of Werter; A German Story, by Mr. Goethe, Doctor of Civil Law*. An anonymous translation of 1786, *Werter and Charlotte, A German Story*, was the second to appear; it was made directly from Goethe's original German version but achieved only one edition and hence was never published in America. Likewise, the third English version, by John Gifford, in 1789, translated from the French of Phillippe Charles Aubry, had only one edition. William Render's translation, first published in London in 1801, was based upon Goethe's second version that had appeared in Germany in 1787. The appeal of this translation was doubtless to be assured by the translator's claim, asserted in his preface, of personal acquaintance with the author and the protagonists of the story, 'documented' by the inclusion of an 'Appendix: Containing an Account of a Conversation which the Translator Had with Werter, a few days preceding his death.' When Render's

sometimes referred to as the 'Werther-fever,' was not limited to transtions of Goethe's story but extended to numerous imitations and adaptations, its theme recurring in drawings and paintings, poetry, and drama.¹

The first translation of *Werther* made by an American was never accorded publication until 1952, some hundred thirty years after it was completed. As a young American student, George Ticknor, destined to become 'America's first great scholar in belles-lettres,'² translated the story in the year 1814, having borrowed John Quincy Adams' German copy from the Boston Athenaeum, as noted earlier. In the century and a half since that time *Werther* has continued to attract American readers, and indeed, next to *Faust*, is probably the most widely known of Goethe's works in the United States. In our own day *Werther* remains the representative prose work of Goethe. In the bicentennial year Victor Lange edited a volume containing *Sorrows of Young Werther* based upon Goethe's second version of the work and R. D. Boylan's translation of 1854; in the same volume were also included *The New Melusina*, translated by Jean Starr Untermeyer, and *Novelle*, translated by Lange himself (New York, 1949). Lange subsequently edited *Great German Short Novels and Stories* (New York, 1952), which contains Goethe's epistolary novel in a translation by the Englishman William Rose, first published in London in 1929, and which constitutes a volume of the Modern Library, a series reflecting the reading

---

version was reprinted in the United States in 1807 it included, in addition to the Appendix and a ten-page discourse 'On Suicide. By William Paley, M.A.,' also 'The Letters of Charlotte To A Female Friend, During Her Connection With Werter,' an independent work by William James published anonymously both in London in the year 1786 (with a dedication 'To Her Most Excellent Majesty, The Queen'), in Dublin the same year, and in 'Newyork' in the year 1797. The most popular English translation in the United States was that by Dr. Pratt, which after its first American printing in 1807, received ten reprints.

¹ See Stuart Pratt Atkins' *The Testament of Werther in Poetry and Drama* (Cambridge, Mass., 1949) for an account of the influence which Goethe's *Werther* has exerted upon European poets and dramatists, demonstrated by the products it has elicited during the years since its appearance. See also Herbert Ross Brown's, *The Sentimental Novel in America, 1789-1860* (Durham, N. C., 1940), 'Werther-Fever and Suicide,' pp. 155-165, for an account of the relation between Goethe's *Werther* and the suicide motif in early American fiction.

² See Frank G. Ryder, ed., *George Ticknor's The Sorrows of Young Werter* (Chapel Hill, 1952), p. ix.

interests of a large number of American readers. Lange's edition replaces an earlier volume (1933) of the Modern Library with the same title, edited by Bennett Cerf, in which *Werther* was also included, not in the translation by Rose, but one attributed to Orson Falk – a translation that, as far as can be determined, has never been reprinted elsewhere. George Ticknor's translation of *Werther*, after extensive efforts to locate the manuscript had failed and it was subsequently presumed lost, was rediscovered by Frank G. Ryder who edited it and published it, with a full introduction, under the title of *George Ticknor's The Sorrows of Young Werter;*[1] it appeared in 1952 as Number Four in the University of North Carolina Studies in Comparative Literature.[2] The most recent translation of this work was made by B. Q. Morgan and published in 1957 in the College Translations Series with a title that more accurately conveys the German original than any of the previous ones: *The Sufferings of Young Werther* (New York).

Of two other works of Goethe that appeared in the United States during the period under study, both were early British translations that in the intervening years have become classics. Thomas James Arnold's translation into heroic couplets of the hexameters of *Reineke Fuchs*, which first appeared in the year 1853, was republished a century later, in 1954, with an introduction by Edward Lazare, as *The Story of Reynard the Fox* by both the Heritage Press and the Limited Editions Club. The latter organization also republished in 1959 for its members Thomas Carlyle's translation of *Wilhelm Meister's Apprenticeship* with an introduction written by Franz Schoenberner. Carlyle's translation

---

[1] Less than a decade before the rediscovery of this translation, O. W. Long, on the basis of information supplied to him by members of the Ticknor family, had reported that 'unfortunately, most of Ticknor's manuscripts have been destroyed, among them this translation' ('Werther in America,' p. 91). Ryder's own brief account of his important discovery is recorded in the Preface to his edition; see also Ryder's 'George Ticknor's *Sorrows of Young Werter*,' *Comp. Lit.*, I (1949), 360-372.

[2] The publication of this early translation nearly a century and a half after its completion recalls the fate of an even earlier significant translation. John Quincy Adams' translation of Wieland's *Oberon*, made while Adams was resident in Berlin, from 1797 to 1801, as United States Minister Plenipotentiary to Prussia, was published only in 1940: *Oberon: A Poetical Romance in Twelve Books, translated from the German of Wieland by John Quincy Adams*, ed., with introduction and notes, by A. B. Faust (New York, 1940).

of the *Lehrjahre* had first been published in London in 1824 in three volumes; in the United States his translation of the *Lehrjahre* was first published, likewise in three volumes, in Boston, in 1828.[1] While other translations of Goethe's *Wilhelm Meister* have been made, Carlyle's has been by far the most frequently published. According to Morgan's *Bibliography* the Carlyle translation had been most recently republished in 1931. The interest, thus, of the Limited Editions Club and of the Heritage Press in making available literary classics in classic translations is responsible for the still more recent appearances of both Goethe's *Wilhelm Meister* and his *Reynard the Fox*.

The scientific interests and achievements of Goethe are also represented by recent English translations published in the United States. *Goethe's Botany: The Metamorphosis of Plants (1790) and Tobler's Ode to Nature (1782)*, (Waltham, Massachusetts), translated, and with a detailed introduction, by Agnes Arber, was published as a volume of Chronica Botanica, a series comprising an international collection of studies in the methods and history of biology and agriculture. Another translation of this same scientific essay is included, along with other scientific treatises of Goethe's, in *Goethe's Botanical Writings* (Honolulu, 1952), translated by a Germanist of the University of Honolulu, Bertha Mueller, for which volume Charles J. Engard, botanist at the same institution, supplied the introduction in which, examining Goethe's prominent role 'in the rise of a great scientific era,' he enumerates the important achievements illustrative of Goethe's relationship to the field of science:

---

[1] See Philip Allison Shelley's 'A German Art of Life in America: The American Reception of the Goethean Doctrine of Self-Culture' in Volume One of *Crosscurrents*, 241-292, for a study of the relationship of *Wilhelm Meister* to the development of the humanistic ideal of self-culture in the United States. Martin L. Kornbluth traces the record of reception achieved by Goethe's apprenticeship novel in the United States down to the close of the nineteenth century in an article entitled 'The Reception of *Wilhelm Meister* in America,' *Symposium*, XIII (1959), 128-134, where he finds that 'although Goethe's novel has not played, perhaps, a major role in shaping American literature, its career is a barometer of American taste, and its over-all role one that should not be overlooked if we are to understand and appreciate fully both the backgrounds of our fiction and the current of American literary criticism' (p. 128).

> ...this was the man who ...was to have a genus of plants (*Goethea*) and a mineral (goethite) named for him; who was to coin and be the first to use the word morphology; who was to contribute to our understanding of the physiology of color; who was to rediscover and describe the intermaxillary bone in man, propound the vertebral theory of the skull, formulate a concept in botanical morphology that persists to this day, discover the volcanic origin of a mountain, establish the first system of weather stations; who was to be among the first to use the comparative method in biology, to make the first systematic classification of minerals; and, finally, was to come unwittingly close to achieving the fundamental concept of organic evolution. (p. 3)

In the United States today Goethe is perhaps best known as a dramatist, and, more specifically, as the author of *Faust*. But apart from the number of new translations and new editions of older translations of Goethe's *magnum opus*, relatively few new translations, or even reprints of older translations, of his dramas have recently been made available to the American reading public. This fact may well be related to a general disinterest on the part of a large segment of American readers in drama as literature.[1] It is noteworthy that even the bicentennial year did not inspire the publication of any of Goethe's dramas other than *Faust*. For the most part, interest in Goethe's dramas is confined in general to Germanists and other literary scholars. Before 1955 the English translation of *Egmont* published last in the United States was the one by Anna Swanwick, originally made in 1850 and most recently published in an anthology of world drama in 1933 (see Morgan's *Bibliography*, no. S2614).[2] A new translation, by Willard R. Trask, appeared in 1960 in Barron's Educational Series.[3] The publisher of the same series is responsible for the availability

---

[1] See 'Armchair Broadway,' *New York Times Book Review*, August 16, 1964, p. 8, where the author, Lewis Nichols, addressing himself to the question of published Broadway plays, states categorically: 'The publishing of Broadway plays is a small item in the overall ledgers of publishing, ...' and again: 'Broadway plays usually don't make the bestselling book lists, ...' Recognizing Random House as the leading publisher in this field, he relates this fact to the personal interest of the president of the firm, Bennett Cerf, whose quoted statement reveals an ulterior motive in play publishing: 'You make a bit on some of them, lose a bit on others, but from publishing his play you sometimes get an author, just as we got Moss Hart's "Act One." '

[2] Morgan does list the appearance, in 1941, of a literal translation (translator unidentified) reproduced from typed copy (*Bibliography*, no. S2604-1).

[3] Morgan dates this volume (*Bibliography*, no. S2615-1) 'ca. 1955,' giving the publisher's catalog as his source of information. Apparently, however, the work had been listed prematurely and was not published until 1960.

of a translation by Sidney E. Kaplan of *Iphigenia in Tauris* (Brooklyn, 1953). Another translation of the latter work, by B. Q. Morgan, was published by Academic Reprints (Stanford, 1954), a fact further substantiating the claim that a scholarly rather than a popular interest has been focused on Goethe's dramas.[1]

The existence of a microfilm of a typewritten copy, made at Columbia University, of an unpublished version of 'Iphigenia in Tauris: A Play' (1958) by the English scholar Roy Pascal, who has otherwise distinguished himself by his studies of the *Sturm und Drang* period and the German novel, is recorded by the *National Union Catalog*, which also records a microfilm of a typewritten copy, likewise made at Columbia University, of 'Stella: A Drama for Lovers,' a translation from the original version of 1775 by B. Q. Morgan (1958).[2] Publication of a new translation of *Torquato Tasso* by Ben Kimpel and T. C. Duncan Eaves (Fayetteville, Arkansas, 1956) initiated a new series to be known as The University of Arkansas Editions, which, as far as it has been possible to determine, has not been continued, at least with the publication of other translations from German authors.

If attention paid to Goethe's dramas other than *Faust* is disappointingly small and limited to specialized interests, the appeal of *Faust*, judged from the number of translations and editions published in the United

---

[1] Since so few of Goethe's dramas have been performed on the American stage, it is worth noting the production of *Iphigenia* in Sanders Theatre, Cambridge, Massachusetts, March 22, 1900, by the Irving Place Theatre Company of New York City, the performance of which, carried out under academic auspices (the Department of Germanic Languages and Literatures of Harvard University), occasioned the publication of Anna Swanwick's translation (1843) of *Goethe's Iphigenia in Tauris*, accompanied, on facing pages, by the Weimar text (Cambridge, Mass., 1900).

[2] Concerning these unpublished translation of German dramas and how they became available on microfilm at Columbia University, B. Q. Morgan, in a letter of November 29, 1964, to Philip Allison Shelley, writes: 'Some years ago I got acquainted with Eric Bentley, and we corresponded about translating and translations. On learning that I had a number of unpublished translations of German dramas on my shelves, he asked to see them. I shipped them to him, and as he was then teaching at Columbia (maybe he is now), he had them microfilmed and deposited in the Columbia Library. From there they got into the LC list. Bentley sent the MSS back to me, and they are here now.

'Practically speaking, the microfilming amounted to a sort of publication, since (I suppose) anybody can borrow those films and use them at will.'

States, continues to be extensive.[1] Some of the editions published between 1945 and 1960 represent a continuation or revival of interest in earlier translations that have since become classics; others are new translations reflecting a positive acknowledgment in our own day of the universal and timeless character of the work.

The oldest English translation that reappeared after 1945, and one of the earliest complete translations of Part One ever made, is that by John Anster, whose version of Part One was first published in London in 1835,[2] of Part Two in 1864, and the vogue of which, owing to distortion of the original, Morgan calls 'discouraging' (*Bibliography*, no. 2659). Frantz, in his study *Half a Hundred Thralls to Faust* (Chapel Hill, 1949), enumerates a total of thirty-two editions and reprints of Anster's translation. This version, including both Part One and Part Two, together with Marlowe's *Doctor Faustus*, was published as two volumes in one in both England and the United States (1946) by the Oxford University Press in the series Oxford World Classics, replacing, in the series, the translation by the American Bayard Taylor. The same publishers in 1952 and 1954 issued an abridged version of Parts One and Two in a new British translation, made in 1951 for a broadcast performance, by Louis MacNeice, who, adding those scenes he had not previously translated, completed his version of Part One for inclusion in Spender's *Great Writings of Goethe*. The popularity of this translation is attested to by the fact that it attained a fifth printing already by 1959. The British translation by Sir Theodore Martin, Part One of which had

---

[1] For a critical judgment on earlier translations of Goethe's *Faust*, including fragments, see Lina Baumann's *Die englische Übersetzungen von Goethes Faust* (Halle, 1907); for a study of all English translations of *Faust* up to the bicentennial year (Part One, complete, Part Two, complete, or both parts, but no fragments) see Adolf Ingram Frantz's *Half a Hundred Thralls to Faust: A Study Based on the British and the American Translators of Goethe's Faust, 1823-1949* (Chapel Hill, 1949). For an investigation of the influences of the Faust legend, and particularly Goethe's *Faust*, on American literature, see 'The Fortunes of Faust in American Literature,' by William W. Betts, Jr. (unpubl. diss., Pa. State Univ., 1954).

[2] Frantz records the names of five persons, all Englishmen, whose translations of *Faust*, Part One, preceded Anster's: Lord Leveson-Gower, 1823; Abraham Hayward, 1833; John Stuart Blackie, 1834; David Syme, 1834; Warburton Davies, 1834. In 1835, the year of Anster's translation, The Honorable Robert Talbot also published his translation of Part One.

first appeared in 1865 and Part Two in 1886, was published, with revisions and annotations by W. H. Bruford, by Dutton in both England and the United States as a volume in Everyman's Library – replacing the translation by Albert G. Latham that had served at least from 1908 to 1928. Bayard Taylor's translation was first published in two volumes in Boston in 1870 and 1871[1] and since that time, along with the translation by Anna Swanwick, has been one of the most widely circulated and most frequently reprinted versions. Frantz records no less than forty-nine editions and reprints of Taylor's translation, forty for Anna Swanwick's. Morgan refers to Taylor's version as 'still the best English version, though not uniformly ideal. Admirable both in form and spirit. Close fidelity to rhyme, meter, and sense' (*Bibliography*, no. 2802). Morgan himself edited the Bayard Taylor translation of Part One for publication in New York in 1946 in Crofts Classics. The Taylor version was issued by another New York publisher in 1947. Taylor's translation of Part One was published again in 1950, with an introduction by Victor Lange, as one of the volumes in the Modern Library.

Other more recent translations made before the opening year of the present study and republished again after 1945 include one by Alice Raphael of Part One made in 1930, which was republished with an introduction by Jacques Barzun in 1955; the same translation, with an introduction by Carl F. Schreiber and a note by Mark van Doren, republished by the Heritage Press, in 1959; a translation by George Madison Priest for the centenary edition in 1932, republished in 1955 by the Encyclopedia Britannica as Volume 47 of Great Books of the Western World; and that, by the British translator John Shawcross, of 1934[2] – the last British translation to be made prior to 1945 – with a

---

[1] Although the date of imprint of both volumes is 1871, the first volume was actually published on December 14, 1870, as witnessed by the fact that the copyright notice is dated 1870, that a celebration in honor of publication was held in Boston on December 14, 1870 (see *Life and Letters of Bayard Taylor*, ed. Marie Hansen-Taylor and Horace E. Scudder [Boston, 1884], II, 542), and that a copy was presented by Taylor to his intimate friend, Richard Henry Stoddard, on the same date (see Frantz, p. 293).

[2] This translation had been limited to a single edition and had received very limited circulation since the firm responsible for its publication (the Scholastic Press, London) was liquidated before the publication was complete (see Frantz, p. 290).

foreword by G. P. Gooch, republished in 1959 in New York. In 1947 appeared, as a reprint of a translation that first came off the press in 1941, 'an American translation' by Carlyle F. MacIntyre, printed together with the German text and published by New Directions. The same company, in 1949, in both a regular edition and in a paperbound college text edition, and again in 1957, issued Part One in 'a new American version based on the translation by Carlyle F. MacIntyre.' MacIntyre, 'the most unconventional American translator of Goethe's *Faust*,' according to Frantz, 'tried, according to his own statements, to make a version of *Faust* in the living, contemporary, English idiom, unhampered by the poetic inhibitions of the past' (p. 90).

In addition to the translation by Louis MacNeice, other entirely new translations made since 1945 and supplementing those which had appeared earlier provide additional evidence of the persistent interest in Goethe's *Faust*. A translation by John Frederick Louis Raschen of Part One and selected sections of Part Two, published in 1949,[1] was one of several new American translations of Goethe's *Faust* to appear after the Second World War. In his evaluation Frantz places this translation 'among the best English versions of *Faust*' (p. 96). Also in 1949 appeared a two-volume edition containing Parts One and Two of the original German text facing a new prose translation made by Max Diez (Bryn Mawr, Pa.). B. Q. Morgan, too, prepared a prose translation of Part One, published in 1954 in the Library of Liberal Arts by the Liberal Arts Press (more recently acquired by Bobbs-Merrill); this was followed in 1957 by a volume adding Act Five of Part Two, also in prose translation by Morgan. Most recently Morgan's translation of the whole of Part Two has been published (1964). A translation by Philip Wayne of Part One, first published in England by Penguin Books in 1949 and 'reprinted 1951, 1953, 1954, 1956 (twice), 1958, 1960, 1961,' appeared in Baltimore from the same publisher in 1958 as Volume I, which was followed by Wayne's translation of Part Two as Volume II in 1959. The Philosophical Library in 1958 published Part One in a new translation by Bertram Jessup. Evidence of a continuing appeal of *Faust* to

[1] 'Although the translation bears the imprint of the Goethe bicentennial, it actually came off the press in December, 1948' (Frantz, p. 95).

the translator and the reader beyond the concluding year of the present study is provided by the publication of *Faust, Part One, and Selections from Part Two* (Garden City, New York, 1961), containing 'the original German and a new translation and introduction by Walter Kaufmann.' The degree of recent interest in this masterpiece is further demonstrated by what apparently is the first translation into English of the earliest surviving form of Goethe's *Faust*. The translation, by Douglas M. Scott, of *The Urfaust* (Great Neck, New York, 1959) is unique in that it represents the only work of Goethe's that appeared in English for the first time during the years following the Second World War.

From the above it is evident that during the sixteen years embraced by this study the number of publications in the United States of English translations of Goethe's *Faust* reflects an intense interest in this work among American readers, not only in specialized circles but also quite generally. Certainly no other single work of German literature has been translated so frequently by so many persons, nor have so many earlier translations of any other single work been reintroduced. While for many Americans most of Goethe's literary achievements remain unknown and while to the majority of American readers Goethe is solely the author of *Faust*, yet to very few of them are Faust, Mephistopheles, and Gretchen unfamiliar characters – their familiarity doubtless supported also by Gounod's opera (1859), based, as it is, on Goethe's drama.

In the bicentennial year appeared *Words of Goethe, Being the Conversations of Johann Wolfgang von Goethe, Recorded by His Friend, Johann Peter Eckermann* (New York, 1949). Prior to the publication of this volume the last English version of Goethe's *Gespräche*, so far as Morgan's *Bibliography* shows, had appeared in the United States in the year 1935; this was a translation by John Oxenford which had first been published in 1850 and which itself had been based upon the earlier American translation by Margaret Fuller in Volume Four (Boston, 1839) of George Ripley's Specimens of Foreign Standard Literature. Although the 1949 edition fails to identify the translator, a comparison of texts confirms it to be identical with the Oxenford version, contrary to Morgan's notation (*Bibliography*, no. S3051-5). Havelock Ellis wrote the introduction for the 1935 edition, Wallace Wood for the one printed in 1949.

In connection with the bicentennial celebration New Directions published a volume, edited by Berthold Biermann, entitled *Goethe's World as Seen in His Letters and Memoirs* (New York, 1949), for which Walter Sorell contributed the new translations included and also revised the major part of the older translations. This volume presents selections depicting the world of Goethe gathered from miscellaneous writings and correspondence of Goethe to others, from others to Goethe, and by others about Goethe. A British compilation, entitled *Letters from Goethe*, published in London in 1957 and republished in the United States the same year, contains 595 letters, which, translated by M. von Herzfeld and C. Melvil Sym and selected from the approximately thirteen thousand preserved pieces of Goethe's correspondence, portray both a picture of Goethe's personality and of the age in which he lived. Publication of these two volumes, together with the two-volume compilation by Ludwig Lewisohn referred to earlier, evidences the broad interest in Goethe as a universal genius generated by the bicentennial celebration and continued throughout the subsequent years. Not since the year 1915 had a single volume of letters of Goethe been published in English translation, and not since the year 1885 had a separate volume of Goethe's correspondence been published in the United States.

Goethe, as a universally acknowledged representative of wordly wisdom and literary genius, has nearly always enjoyed a welcome reception in the United States. Translations of his writings, both poetry and prose, have long formed a significant part of the literary experience of American readers. Propitious to that literary experience is the fact that, little more than a decade after cessation of hostilities between Germany and the United States during the years of the First World War, the one-hundredth anniversary of Goethe's death in 1932, and less than a decade after the Second World War the two-hundredth anniversary of his birth in 1949, served to remind Americans – and the world – of Goethe's stature as an illustrious representative of human genius. Both the centennial and bicentennial celebrations inspired new critical evaluations of his enormous contribution to the history, philosophy, and literature of the Western world. They served to focus the attention of American readers on the enduring values of his masterpieces, presented, as they were, through new editions of earlier translations, through new translations, and, in some instances, through the introduction of writings previously unavailable in English translation.

4

SCHILLER

If it is true, as one scholar asserts, that 'the centennial anniversary of Schiller's birth in 1859 witnessed a more spontaneous and widespread demonstration of devotion to the German poet of youth and democracy than had been manifested for Goethe's memory in the centenary of his natal year,'[1] the same comment is wholly inapplicable to the bicentennial celebration of the birth of Schiller when compared with the bicentennial commemoration of the birth of Goethe. This is at least true when measured by the number of English translations of Schiller's works published in the United States, either specifically in the bicentennial anniversary year, 1959, or even throughout the period of sixteen years under study – a number which contrasts unfavorably with the number of translations of Goethe's works. In 1959 in this country only four individual volumes consisting entirely of translations of Schiller's works were published as an anniversary tribute to his memory. To be sure, numerous papers, criticisms, and articles about the poet were presented to various literary assemblies and in newspapers, periodicals, and journals as part of the activities commemorative of his birth two centuries earlier. But more important for an accurate indication of the reception accorded to any writer, foreign or native, is not so much the panegyrics

[1] John T. Krumpelmann, tr., *The Maiden of Orleans: A Romantic Tragedy, by Johann Christoph Friedrich Schiller, Translated into English in the Verse Forms of the Original German*, Univ. of N. Car. Stud. in Germ. Langs. and Lits., No. 24 (Chapel Hill, 1959), 2d ed. rev., No. 37 (Chapel Hill, 1962), Preface.

of critics and scholars, but rather the dictum of the reading public as it pronounces judgment by acceptance or rejection as recorded by its reading preference.

The difficult question concerning the factors that determine sucess or failure of certain authors or specific works in their appeal to the general reader not only has been a topic of investigation for literary scholars but has been treated as well by historians, psychologists, and social scientists.[1] Answers to the question can seldom be established with unequivocal conclusiveness and must generally remain quite subjective.

The historical record of Schiller's reception in both England[2] and the United States stands as an almost diametrical opposite, a kind of antithesis, to that of Goethe's. Introduced to American readers in 1793 by the American printing of A. F. Tytler's translation of *The Robbers*, first published in London the preceding year, Schiller – like Goethe, whose *Werther* had introduced him thirteen years before – was, until after the

[1] See Frank Luther Mott's *Golden Multitudes: The Story of Best Sellers in the United States* (New York, 1947 and 1960), especially Chapter I, 'Vox Pop' (pp. 1-5), and two chapters on causation, Chapter XLIII, 'Is There a Best Seller Formula' (pp. 285-291), and Chapter XLIV, 'What Makes a Best Seller Sell' (pp. 291-297) for a discussion of the elements of popular appeal in books. For a record of best sellers in this country see *Sixty Years of Best Sellers, 1895-1955* by Alice Payne Hackett (New York, 1956). For a study of popular books in America to 1950 see James D. Hart's *The Popular Book* (New York, 1950). Briefer but valuable analyses and discussions of popular books and books of genuine and enduring literary merit are John Harvey's 'The Content Characteristics of Best-Selling Novels,' *Public Opinion Quarterly*, XVII (Spring, 1963), 91-114 and Malcolm Cowley's 'Classics and Best Sellers,' *New Republic*, December 22, 1947, pp. 25-27. Granville Hicks, succinctly formulating the elements of popular success, suggests '...a lively story, largely romantic in theme and setting, with conventional characters and plot and some pretention to a message or thesis, apparently profound but really commonplace' ('The Mystery of the Best Seller,' *English Journal*, XXIII [1934], 621-629). Edward Weeks, analysing the success of just one work, *Gone With the Wind*, trenchantly concludes that '...the novelist captures the ideas in the air at the time and puts them into words' ('What Makes a Book a Best Seller?' *New York Times Book Review* [December 20, 1936], p. 15).

[2] See Frederic Ewen's *The Prestige of Schiller in England, 1788-1859* (New York, 1932) in which the reception of Schiller is traced through three phases fittingly described by the titles to the first three parts of the book: ' "Blood and Thunder": 1788-1813'; 'Nature's Noblemen: 1813-1844'; 'The Sainthood of Schiller: 1844-1855.' See also *Schiller in England, 1787-1960: A Bibliography*, Pubs. of Engl. Goethe Soc., N.S., XXX (1961), compiled by R. Pick. For an earlier study of the reception and influence of the dramas and poems of Schiller in England during the first half of the nineteenth century, see Thomas Rea's *Schiller's Dramas and Poems in England* (London, 1906).

turn of the century, known predominantly by his earlier works. It was, again as in the case of Goethe, Madame de Staël's *De l'Allemagne* that reintroduced Schiller, the embodiment of idealism in both his poetry and his personal temperament. The censoring Puritan conscience, offended by Goethe's alleged moral laxness, rejoiced in Schiller's impeccable character and the expression of that character in his writings equally exempt from censure.[1] Carlyle's confirmation and reaffirmation of Schiller's 'morality' in his *Life of Friedrich Schiller, Comprehending an Examination of His Works*, published anonymously in London, 1825, and reprinted in Boston, 1833,[2] contributed significantly to an increasing

[1] An indirect but pointed indication of the high regard with which Schiller, as compared with Goethe, was held during the first half of the nineteenth century is found in Margaret Fuller's preface to her translation of *Conversations with Goethe in the Last Years of His Life, Translated from the German of Eckermann*, published in Boston in 1839 as the fourth volume of George Ripley's Specimens of Foreign Standard Literature. In response to bitter attacks against Goethe, such as those mounted by Andrews Norton in 1833 in his 'Recent Publications Concerning Goethe' (in the *Select Journal of Periodical Literature*, I [1833], 250-293) and George Bancroft (in the *Christian Examiner*, XXVI [July, 1839], 360-378), and supported by Wolfgang Menzel's history of German literature, available in C. C. Felton's English translation, Margaret Fuller formulated a witty summary of 'the objections, so far as I know them': 'He is not a Christian; He is not an Idealist; He is not a Democrat; He is not Schiller' (p. xii). She then proceeds to answer these objections one by one. From the reference to Schiller she constructs a defense of Goethe without doing harm to Schiller: 'In reply to those who object to him that he is not Schiller, it may be remarked that Shakespeare was not Milton, nor Ariosto Tasso. It was, indeed, unnecessary that there should be two Schillers, one being sufficient to represent a certain class of thoughts and opinions. It would be well if admirers of Schiller would learn from him to admire and profit by his friend and coadjutor, as he himself did.

'Schiller was wise enough to judge each nature by its own law, great enough to understand greatness of an order different from his own. He was too well aware of the value of the more beautiful existences to quarrel with the rose for not being a lily, the eagle for not being a swan' (pp. xvii-xviii).

Margaret Fuller's translation of Eckermann's *Conversations with Goethe*, aside from appearing in Ripley's series, was also issued with a variant binding lacking the label identifying it as a volume in Ripley's series, although interior indications were retained; two copies of the original issue and one of the variant are in The Allison-Shelley Collection.

[2] The American edition, likewise anonymous, was edited by Charles Follen, first instructor of German at Harvard, who designated Schiller's poetry as 'distinguished by its *moral* character.' In a fourteen-page preface Follen noted errors and infelicities in the translated excerpts from Schiller's works which he found it necessary to correct as editor of Carlyle's volume. Follen's edition appeared again, still without identifying Carlyle, four years later in New York in 1837.

veneration of the idealistic magnificence witnessed in his life and coordinately expressed in his poetry. In 1859 the observation of the centennial year of his birth,[1] celebrated with elaborate commemorative activities including ceremonies, programs, addresses, biographies, bibliographies, articles in periodicals, and translations of his works, manifested what in the following century was to be verified as the culmination of Schiller's popularity in the United States; after this high point a gradual but steady decline, interrupted but temporarily by the centennial anniversary of his death,[2] has persistently contrasted with the re-evaluation of, and growing esteem for, Goethe.

The decline of American popular interest in Schiller was already perceptible by the time of the centenary of his death in 1905 and the sesquicentennial anniversary of his birth in 1909, but recognition of the decline was restricted by the degree to which he had 'become enshrined as a "classic" in the American high school and college textbook' (Pochmann, p. 338). For example, one of Schiller's defenders, addressing the *Schillerfeier* held at the University of Wisconsin, May 9, 1905, after an enumeration of the translations of his works, concluded that 'perhaps the most significant evidence of American love for Schiller is to be found in the extent to which his works are used and are edited for use in our schools and colleges, (William Herbert Carruth, 'Schiller and America,' *German American Annals*, N.S. IV [May, 1906] 142). Yet just a few decades later, even the security of his 'enshrinement' in texts seems to have weakened, for, when his *Jungfrau von Orleans* was re-edited as a text edition in 1927, one reviewer declared:

---

[1] See Ellwood Comly Parry's *Friedrich Schiller in America: A Contribution to the Literature of the Poet's Centenary, 1905* (Philadelphia, 1905 [Reprinted from *German American Annals*, Vol. III]) for a survey of Schiller's reception in the United States to the year 1859, with a bibliography of 165 items 'of such literary material bearing on the life and work of Friedrich Schiller as was published, in book or pamphlet form, in the United States, to the end of the year 1859,' and for an account of some of the centennial celebrations held across the country.
[2] For a nearly complete listing and summary of the programs commemorative of Schiller's centenary held up to the date of the article's appearance, consult 'The Centenary of Schiller's Death,' *German American Annals*, N.S., III (June, 1905), 163-176, which is followed by a number of the addresses delivered at the various programs.

Right here I should like to make a strong plea for a complete and radical reform of our reading lists. And one of the texts that ought to go into the limbo of the past is the *Jungfrau von Orleans*. I am thoroughly conversant with the course of reasoning followed by both admirers and critics of the poet in their attempt to vindicate their respective positions. But my own experience in the classroom has long since convinced me that the drama is a most unfortunate selection. It is no longer viable. Is it because our students of today are too modern, sophisticated, sceptical, even cynical, to take the romantic claptrap of the drama seriously? Not altogether. Or is it because Schiller has become *unmodern*? Can Schiller ever become *unmodern*? Excepting *Wallenstein*, I venture to answer in the affirmative, even at the risk of being called *pietätlos* (G. A. Betz, rev. of *Jungfrau von Orleans*, ed. R.-M. S. Heffner [New York, 1927], GQ, I [1928], 45).

The sentiment expressed here must have been representative enough to account for a decline in the number of textbooks devoted to Schiller's works, for another critic of a contrary opinion, questioning why Schiller is not re-edited, laments: 'The fear to take up Schiller and his works seemingly was shared by the editors of textbooks for students and pupils, or else we should not be obliged to order dusty "Ladenhüter," most of which still preserve the old German spelling in use before 1900' (Hermann Barnstorff, 'German and American Interest in Schiller during the Inter-Bellum Period 1918-1939,' GQ, XIII [1940], 94).

The fact, confirming nearly universal judgment, that today – and quite consistently throughout the twentieth century[1] – Goethe enjoys a

---

[1] See Barnstorff, who concludes: 'Before and especially during the world war our interest in Schiller waned and it took a number of years after the great armed conflict before the study of German and German literature began to flourish again. But Schiller remained neglected and ...has been neglected up [to] the present day' (p. 97). See also 'American Schiller Literature: A Bibliography,' *Schiller 1759/1959: Commemorative American Studies*, Illinois Stud. in Lang. and Lit., No. 46 (Urbana, 1959), pp. 203-213, by John R. Frey who states: 'American popular interest in Friedrich Schiller, with its impressive culmination in the great centenary celebrations of the poet, in 1859, has been adequately investigated and presented. As for the century since, the Schiller interest of more than fleeting consequence has been almost exclusively confined to the scholarly sphere.' In another article entitled 'Schiller in Amerika, insbesonders in der amerikanischen Forschung,' *Jahrbuch der deutschen Schillergesellschaft*, ed. Herbert Stubenrauch and Bernhard Zeller, III (1959), 338-367, Frey undertakes 'die Frage nach Ausmass und Art des Schillerbildes während der letzten hundert Jahre zu untersuchen.' As this study, too, shows, 'setzt sich dieses Bild fortschreitend aus einem Weniger an allgemeinem Interesse und einem Mehr an wissenschaftlichen Bemühungen zusammen' (p. 339). Searching for factors that have determined the nature of Schiller's reception in the United States, he concludes: 'Der allgemeine Zeitgeist Amerikas nach dem Bürgerkrieg war Schillerscher Art nicht sonderlich günstig, und

position in this country not attained by Schiller can be concluded with reasonable accuracy from a comparison of the number of English translations of the works of each author published during the years 1945 to 1960. Such a comparison is particularly valid since within the sixteen-year period falls the bicentenary of the birth of each (and, in the case of Schiller, the sesquicentennial anniversary of his death), occasions which may justifiably be expected to have focused the attention of translators, publishers, and readers upon them, and would seem to have produced an exhibition of devotion to their memory. Yet if the publishing activities in 1949, which evidenced part of the tribute paid to Goethe, implied a similar demonstration of acclaim for Schiller in 1959, these promises remained unfulfilled. Possible factors responsible for this disparity are explored briefly by one of Schiller's twentieth-century champions, who sees Goethe esteemed by Americans as the 'Olympian aristocrat,' while regarding Schiller as the exponent of ideals that have since been attained or have changed:

> The first centennial of Goethe's birth arrived only some seventeen years after his death. Since that year marked the flood tide of revolution in Europe, the public had not yet come to appreciate the placidity of the Olympian aristocrat Goethe who had never been a popular personality in his lifetime or in posterity. However, when the centenary of Schiller's natal year arrived, the spirit of the revolution, although politically suppressed, was still alive, and youth was still idealistic in its enthusiasm for democracy.

es blieben somit als einzige, das Schillerbild weiterhin bestimmende Pflegestätten das Deutschamerikanertum und die Schule bzw. der akademische Bereich' (p. 367). For additional factors contributing to this phenomenon he summarizes certain comments which appeared in an unidentified newspaper article and which, although admittedly somewhat exaggerated, nevertheless provide a basically accurate analysis: 'Er sagt, dass ohngeachtet all der im ganzen Lande begangenen Schillerfeiern eingestanden werden müsse, dass Schillersche Art dem amerikanischen Temperament fremd sei. Seine Sprache müsse man als notwendiges Übel hinnehmen; seine Ideen und poetischen Bilder lägen ausserhalb des Erfahrungsbereichs des gewöhnlichen amerikanischen Sterblichen. Das derzeitige Schillerinteresse müsse "akademischem" Einfluss zugeschrieben werden und hätte ohne das deutschamerikanische Element niemals solche Ausmasse annehmen können. Zwei Eigenheiten Schillerscher Poesie finde der Amerikaner ungeniessbar: das Didaktische und das Sentimentale. Sicherlich seien Schillers ethische Themen demokratisch, aber sie blieben ausserhalb der Realität. So auch seine Dramen, deren poetische Diktion auf "unsere" Nerven gehe, und deren Charaktere zu "spekulativ" seien. Entsagung sei kein Bedürfnis des modernen Amerikaners, der wohl Idealismus wolle, aber Idealismus innerhalb der Realität der Dinge' (p. 367).

In 1949 the world celebrated the world-figure, the protagonist of World Literature, the Jovian Goethe. In the century which intervened between 1849 and 1949 Goethe's masterpiece, *Faust*, at first regarded as immoral, had become immortal. Now, ten years later, it seems impossible to expect the world to enthuse for the author of 'Das Ideal und das Leben,' for the poet who lent fame to such democratic revolutionists as Wilhelm Tell, Don Carlos and Jeanne D'Arc, and who, dramatically at least, championed the cause of Mary Stuart against Queen Elizabeth of England. The ideal of democracy has, as must all ideals, ceased with the attainment of its goal. The youth are no longer young idealists, but actualists, who live rather in the facts of today than in the fictions of tomorrow. For them democracy is no longer arrayed in a roseate nimbus of fantasy. Since at least two generations have lived and died for the 'ideal' of making the world safe for democracy, it is not to be expected that the youth of today can be too enthusiastic about Schiller, who always created his characters out of idealistic concepts. (Krumpelmann, *The Maiden of Orleans*, Preface)

Whether Schiller's more limited reception in the United States is due to changed ideals that are 'no longer arrayed in a roseate nimbus of fantasy' is difficult to establish. It might be argued, for example, that Goethe's 'placidity' cannot be appreciated nor even understood by 'the youth of today,' that, to young Americans, Werther is little more than a dull, lovesick adolescent, colorless and without recourse other than suicide; or that Faust's contract with Mephistopheles, ultimately declared null and void, can have no appeal to modern Americans – 'actualists, who live rather in the facts of today than in the fictions of tomorrow.' Statistical evidence, however, substantiates the perennial appeal of Goethe's *Faust*. It could also be argued that characters such as William Tell, Don Carlos, and Jeanne D'Arc should have strong appeal today, for they represent to contemporary readers the contemporary struggle of an individual to attain distinction, or simply recognition, as an individual in a mass society. Yet statistical evidence substantiates the apparently limited appeal of Schiller in the United States today. Whatever explanation is postulated, the fact remains that in recent years Schiller has been accorded a more limited reception in this country than his compatriot Goethe. Writes one critic: 'His writings are inspired with a noble idealism and a lofty aspiration, but they have less message for the modern world than the impartial realism of Goethe; he was the denizen of a simpler world than ours, and it is with difficulty that we of the twentieth century find our way back to that world. The hand of time has lain more heavily on Schiller's poetry than on Goethe's; but he remains Germany's greatest dramatist, and, after Goethe, the poet whose work has had the firmest hold upon the affections of his people' (J. G. Robertson, *A History of German Literature*, 5th ed., rev. and enl. by Edna Purdie, W. I. Lucas, and M. O'C. Walshe [New York, 1966], p. 335).

Perhaps the best indication of current popular reception of Schiller in the United States is expressed almost inadvertently yet succinctly in several reviews of Thomas Mann's *Last Essays* (New York, 1959), the longest of which is 'On Schiller,' written in 1955 just before Mann's death and inscribed: 'For the 150th anniversary of the poet's death. Affectionately dedicated to his memory,' Reviews of the volume were generally favorable, some enthusiastic; Mann's had obviously become a voice demanding attention and commanding respect, and even when he spoke of Schiller, his voice was heard. Yet one critic found this longest of the essays 'the least rewarding,' explaining that 'no doubt this is due to the fact that we no longer read Schiller much, having filed him away under the warning label "florid, romantic, of historical interest only,"' and he adds almost apologetically, 'so [we] cannot easily follow Mann in his enthusiasm,...' (Richard Gilman, 'Revelations of the Mind of Mann,' *Commonweal*, March 6, 1959, p. 603). Another reviewer identified Schiller as 'the classical playwright, the poet and chronicler, whose name is but a shadow in today's Anglo-Saxon world,' a shadow that recalls, however vaguely, 'the author of proud ballads reprinted in high school readers,...' (Richard Plant, *New York Times Book Review*, March 8, 1959, p. 4). A not too dissimilar attitude is apparent in England where a critic, also reviewing Mann's essays, remarked: 'The English have never, I think, been very much interested in Schiller, and it is not very likely that Mann's dutiful and affectionate essay will induce them to pay him more attention. We know that he *must* be a great writer, but we find it hard to respond to his fervent sublimities' (Philip Toynbee, *Observer*, April 26, 1959, quoted in W. Witte's 'Schiller: Reflections on a Bicentenary,' *Schiller Bicentenary Lectures*, ed. F. Norman [London, 1960], p. 147).

Commemorative of the bicentenary of his birth, a volume containing translations in English of specimens from the whole range of Schiller's writing was published in an apparent attempt to acquaint a wide American reading audience with the relevancy and appropriateness of his literary genius and production for the mid-twentieth century. *Friedrich Schiller: An Anthology for Our Time in New English Translations* (New York, 1959) provided, in addition to translations by Jane Bannard Green, Charles E. Passage, and Alexander Gode-von Aesch, the corresponding passages in the original German, on facing pages, together with a biographical account by the editor, compiler, and publisher of the volume, Friedrich Ungar. The same publisher is responsible for the initiation of a series of Schiller's dramas in new translations by Charles E. Passage, including, in addition to *Don Carlos* and *Wallenstein*, which appeared during the period under study and mentioned below, two additional volumes, the one, published in 1961, containing *Mary Stuart* and *The Maid of Orleans*, the other published in 1962, containing *The Bride of Messina, William Tell*, and *Demetrius*. It is significant that the selections from Schiller's prose writings that are included in Ungar's *Anthology* are the only specimens of his prose to appear in the bicentennial year. The same observation can be made concerning Schiller's lyric poetry; in fact, except for dramatic poetry, the only poetry of Schiller to appear in English translation in this country from 1945 to 1960, other than that contained in the above mentioned *Anthology*, is the *Song of the Bell*, which is recorded as having been 'tr. from Amilie Knoke's book,' copyrighted in 1947, with no publisher known (see *The Library of Congress Author Catalog: A Cumulative List of Works Represented by Library of Congress Printed Cards, 1948-1952*). A little known translation of *Das Lied von der Glocke* was made by Adolph W. Callisen, founder of the Belles Lettres Society of the Staten Island Institute of Arts and Sciences which published the translation dated Christmas, 1939. Callisen, in the very brief Translator's Preface, refers to the poem – 'pervaded by an earnest, moral tone' – as 'the most firmly fixed in the affections of the German people' (copy in The Allison-Shelley Collection). Before this, Schiller's *Glocke* had not been published in this country since the year 1919, at which time a translation by H. Pelman Bromwell was included in a volume of translations of German poems of which only twenty-five copies were printed privately in Denver, Colorado. Moreover, Morgan, who lists this translation (*Bibliography*, no. 7871), designates the translation with a dagger, a symbol 'comparable to the inverted thumb in the ancient Coliseum....' Three years earlier a translation of this poem, rated quite mediocre by Morgan, was included in *A Harvest of German Verse* (New York, 1916) selected and translated by Margaret Muensterberg. In view of the foregoing, American readers who know Schiller, but solely through translation, can hardly be expected to know him as a poet, historian, essayist, or critic – a fact that provides a silent comment on the kind of reception in this country afforded to that German author who, as has been seen, was alleged to be, 'after Goethe, the poet whose work has had the firmest hold upon the affections of his people.' It is true, as critics often point out, that as a historian he has been superseded, and as a lyricist he cannot be compared with Goethe. Yet for a poet who has won so enduringly the sentiment of his own people he remains unappreciated in this country. Ungar, regretfully acknowledging that Schiller 'has remained almost unknown to a wider public in English-speaking countries,' succinctly analyzes one of the reasons for this unfortunate situation:

> The language barrier is a formidable one for any poet; for Schiller, the classical poet of freedom and brotherhood, it has proved almost insurmountable. ...If Schiller has not reached a wider audience in English it is mainly because of the difficulties of translating him adequately. Although his German is limpid and in a sense quite simple, it is borne along by something outside the realm of grammar or lexicography, and this 'something,' so essential to a full understanding of Schiller, easily gets lost in an English rendering.[1] (*Anthology*, pp. 9-10)

The current acquaintance of Americans with 'Germany's greatest dramatist' is due in large measure to the success of the Broadway production of his *Mary Stuart* in 1957, in a free adaptation by Jean Stock Goldstone and John Reich that was published in 1958 by the Dramatists

---

[1] Ungar's contention contrasts sharply with that of a Schiller advocate one century earlier. Frederic Henry Hedge, in an oration delivered in Boston's Music Hall at the Schiller Festivity, November 10, 1859, called Schiller 'the most national and the most cosmopolitan' of German poets, 'the poet of Protestantism as Luther was its prophet,' 'the least idiomatically and exclusively German, the most translatable into other tongues, the most intelligent to other nations, the easiest naturalized in foreign lands' of all German poets (quoted in O. W. Long's *Frederic Henry Hedge: A Cosmopolitan Scholar* [Portland, Maine, 1940], p. 47).

Play Service.[1] Three different translations of this drama were published during the sixteen years under study, but only one of these appeared in the anniversary year. This was a new, unabridged translation by Sophie Wilkins and published by Barron's Educational Series. The same publisher provided a literal translation by Guenther Reinhardt of the same drama in 1950, republished in 1958. Aroused by the production on Broadway, interest in this drama apparently continued in spite of its dealing with an historical conflict quite unrelated to contemporary events, for in 1961 still another translation. by Charles E. Passage, was published together with his version of *The Maid of Orleans* in a single volume in the Ungar series.[2]

The latter drama achieved a second English translation by John A. Krumpelmann of Louisiana State University who in the Preface noted that his own native New Orleans '... might offer no more fitting homage to Schiller in 1959 than to present an American translation of his *Jungfrau von Orleans*....' How long these two dramas of Schiller have been neglected is reflected by the fact that *Mary Stuart* last appeared in English in Boston in the year 1904, one year before the centenary of Schiller's death, in an edition from the prompt book of Mme. Helene Modjeska

---

[1] For a detailed study of this drama in the British and American theater see Henry W. Knepler's 'Schiller's *Maria Stuart* on the Stage in England and America' in Volume Two of *Anglo-German and American-German Crosscurrents*, ed. Philip Allison Shelley and Arthur O. Lewis, Jr. (Chapel Hill, 1962), pp. 5-31; and 'Maria Stuart in America,' *The Theatre Annual*, XVI (1959), 30-50; also John R. Frey's 'Maria Stuart "Off Broadway," 1957,' *American-German Review*, XXIV, vi (August-September, 1958), 6-8, 27. For an historical survey of the production of Schiller's plays in general on the American stage from 1795 to 1959, see Karl S. Guthke's 'Schiller auf der Bühne der Vereinigten Staaten,' *Maske und Kothurn*, V (1960), 227-242. In 'Schiller in English,' *MDU*, XXXV (1943), 334-337, E. Heyse Dummer treats 'Schiller's success in English on the stage of at least one of our principal theatre centers, namely Chicago' (p. 334). Dummer refers to 'Schiller's success' in spite of the fact that it was not until 1849 that Schiller made his debut on the Chicago stage and that the 1905 production of Don Carlos (for seven performances) was the last Schiller play in English on the Chicago stage that he was able to report.

[2] For an analysis of another English translation of *Maria Stuart*, completed more than a century ago, never published, and only recently called to attention, see 'Charles Timothy Brook's *Mary Stuart*,' by Arthur Burkhard, in *Studies in German Literature* ['Festschrift' for John T. Krumpelmann], ed. Carl Hammer, Jr., Louisiana State Univ. Stud., Humanities Series, No. 13 (Baton Rouge, 1963).

(the stage version of Modjeska was also published in Indianapolis in 1883), and by the fact that in the case of *Die Jungfrau von Orleans* Krumpelmann refers to the version by Anna Swanwick as the 'standard' English translation – one made more than a century before. Until 1959, no genuine translation in English of this drama had been published in the twentieth century.[1] Still another of Schiller's dramas was published in translation during the bicentennial anniversary year. *Don Carlos*, which had not appeared in English since the first decade of the present century, and then in an adaptation rather than a translation, was published in 1959, another of the translations by Charles E. Passage, who, as already noted, has been responsible almost single-handedly, for making most of Schiller's dramas available to readers of English in a modern translation. For example, he has also translated the three parts of Schiller's *Wallenstein*, published in 1958 and again in a revised edition in 1960. More recently, Ungar, who has published all of Passage's translations of Schiller, has also published a volume containing his versions of three other dramas: *The Bride of Messina, or The Enemy Brothers: A Tragedy with Choruses; William Tell; Demetrius, or The Blood Wedding in Moscow: A Fragment* (New York, 1962).

Two other Schiller dramas appeared since the Second World War and both well before the anniversary year. Guenther Reinhardt's literal translation of *Kabale und Liebe* (New York, 1953), published by Barron's Educational Series, seems intended primarily for student use and hence unrelated in any direct way to an appraisal of wider interest

---

[1] Curiously, the Swanwick translation of Schiller's *Maid of Orleans*, in an edition which had been published in Philadelphia in 1899, was reissued ten years later with the 1899 date but in paper wrappers, which announced the contents as '*Joan of Arc*, an English translation of the play which is to be given by Miss Maud Adams at the Harvard Stadium, June 22, 1909' (copy in The Allison-Shelley Collection). The actual version presented by Miss Adams was an adaptation by Viereck which was not published until 1925 by the Haldeman-Julius Company as one of its Big Blue Books. In addition to two copies, one of them bearing the signature of the adapter and his bookplate, The Allison-Shelley Collection contains the typescript of this adaptation, with the following title page: 'FRIEDRICH VON SCHILLER'S / Romantic Tragedy / THE MAID OF ORLEANS / Adapted from the German for Maude Adams / By / GEORGE SYLVESTER VIERECK. / STAGE VERSION. / Copyright 1909 by / George Sylvester Viereck.'

in Schiller.¹ It is somewhat mystifying, however, that Schiller's *Wilhelm Tell*, the story of which is so well known to many Americans, did not appear during the period under survey in any new translation other than a literal one by Sydney E. Kaplan and published in 1954 by Barron's Educational Series. In 1952 the Heritage Press republished what Morgan has called an 'excellent translation, the only really good version available in English' (*Bibliography*, p. 427), by Sir Theodore Martin and first published in 1847. This Heritage Press edition also contains an introductory essay by Thomas Carlyle assembled from his discussion of the drama in his *Life of Friedrich Schiller, Comprehending an Examination of His Works*, first published in London in the year 1825.

Schiller's *Novelle, The Sport of Destiny*, has become available since 1945 in English translation. In two anthologies of German short stories (*The Blue Flower*, ed. Hermann Kesten [New York, 1946] and *Great German Short Novels and Stories*, ed. Victor Lange [New York, 1952]) there appear two different translations of the story, the one by Thomas Roscoe, first published in London in 1826 as one of the stories in a four-volume work entitled *The German Novelists*, and the other in a new translation by Marian Klopfer.

Of the number of significant philosophical and aesthetic treatises of Schiller, only one has appeared in English in recent years. *On the Aesthetic Education of Man in a Series of Letters* (New Haven, 1954) was translated by Reginald Snell and published simultaneously in England and the United States.

Recent reception of Schiller in the United States, determined by the currency of translations of his works published here, has not been exceptionally enthusiastic. To modern Americans the Broadway production of one of his dramas has made him solely a dramatist and, more specifically, the author of an historical tragedy, *Mary Stuart*. Discounting the translations published primarily for use by students, few of the dramas by Germany's greatest dramatist have become part of the literary experience of the current American reading public. The

---

¹ See L. A. Willoughby's 'Schiller's "Kabale und Liebe" in English Translation,' *Pubs. of Engl. Goethe Soc.*, N.S., 1 (1924), 44-66, for a survey of this play in England and the United States.

bicentennial celebration was commemorated primarily in academic circles. One scholar has pointed out: 'Unfortunately, one usually takes Schiller's measure from the hands of popularizers and schoolmasters. One should rather read interpretations by fellow artists such as Thomas Mann, who in his last lecture convincingly demonstrated Schiller's greatness in face of all his minor flaws' (Ernst Rose, *A History of German Literature* [New York, 1960], p. 191). The fact that Schiller has had so limited a popular reception in this country may be related to a general disinterest on the part of the American reading public, noted before, in drama as literature; surely a novelist can except greater popularity and currency among a reading audience than a dramatist. Schiller's poetry, essays, and historical writings also remain virtually unknown in this country. Perhaps ours has become too fully an age of realists to whom the voice of an idealist sounds awkwardly foreign, almost naive, slightly suspect. The reproof of Goethe to his daughter-in-law must doubtless be shared by persons of our own day. Mann, in his essay 'On Schiller,' mentions that late in Goethe's life Ottilie remarked that she found Schiller often boring. Turning his face away, Goethe replied: 'You are all far too wretchedly earthbound for him' (Mann, *Last Essays*, p. 90).

5

THE NINETEENTH CENTURY

Writers of the Earlier Years

English literature and American literature, both participants for differing lengths of time in an active interchange of literary ideas and works with the literatures of other national cultures, are indebted to nineteenth-century German literature for a rich legacy upon which their representatives have drawn extensively for inspiration and direction. Not infrequently German writers were introduced into England and the United States through translations and essays by the most respected English and American men of letters of their day, such as Coleridge and Carlyle, Emerson and Longfellow. Acquaintance with specimens of German writing became a significant influence in the literary development of writers like Scott and Meredith, Hawthorne and Poe. Yet relatively few new translations of nineteenth-century German literature appeared in this country throughout the first half of the present century. An examination of the translations into English published in this country from 1945 to 1960 reveals that while a relatively small number of English translations of nineteenth-century German literature was available during the years immediately following the Second World War, a modest revival of interest in German literature of the past century appears to have developed subsequently, judged from the increased number of published translations toward the end of the period under study – a trend that even a cursory survey indicates continues with possibly increasing momentum down to the present.

Although the nineteenth century in Germany witnessed the appearance of lyric poetry, both in great quantity and high quality, this genre, as noted previously, has had a very restricted introduction to American readers through translations. For the most part, the availability of English translations of German poetry is confined to volumes containing selections from poets of various countries and language areas. An important exception is a volume of more than 400 pages devoted exclusively to German poems with English translations entitled *An Anthology of German Poetry from Hölderlin to Rilke in English Translation* (Garden City, N.Y., 1960), edited by Angel Flores. Of the fourteen German poets represented in the volume, nine are from the nineteenth century and include Hölderlin, Novalis, Brentano, Eichendorff, Platen, Droste-Hülshoff, Heine, Lenau, and Mörike. Together their poems make up well over half of the anthology and as a group represent one of the largest single publications of nineteenth-century poetry in English translation during the period under survey.

In contrast to poetry a relatively larger number of German nineteenth-century dramas was published independently in English translations. But major interest in German literature of the past century centered on the short story, or *Novelle*, and tale, or *Märchen*. Certainly to present-day audiences the nineteenth century in German literature is a century of the short story and the tale, particularly the fairy tale, so familiar in the field of children's literature. The Grimms' fairy tales, for instance, could be no more a part of the imaginary yet very real story world of American children than if they had first been gathered and retold by persons, say, from Boston or Philadelphia. It is curious that the novel, as a literary genre, is represented in English translation from German literature of the nineteenth century by very few examples, other than the extremely popular Swiss *Robinsonade* by Rudolf Wyss, notably *The Swiss Family Robinson* – today considered, primarily, juvenile literature – and the Swiss stories for children by Johanna Spyri, especially *Heidi*, two works that have had an uninterrupted appeal ever since their first appearance in English translation which, in the case of the former, occurred in the year 1814 and, in the case of the latter, in the year 1884.

The belated recognition of Hölderlin as a great poet in his own country undoubtedly accounts for the fact that it was not until 1925 that an independent volume of his poetry in English translation first appeared in print. This was an American publication, a slender volume of sixty-four pages, *Short Poems by Friedrich Hölderlin* (Girard, Kansas), translated by Pierre Loving and published as one of the Little Blue Books containing what Morgan characterizes as 're-creations in modern and very free verse, but loosely connected with the original' (*Bibliography*, no. 4370). By contrast it is significant that during the years covered by this study three volumes of Hölderlin's poetry made their appearance in this country, in every case, reprints of British translations. In 1945 Transatlantic Arts published *Friedrich Hölderlin: Selected Poems* (New York), a reprint of a volume published in London the previous year, containing German originals facing translations by J. B. Leishman, the British translator of many of Rilke's poems. Revised and enlarged, this volume achieved a second edition in England in 1954 and was published in the United States by Grove Press in 1956. The second edition differed from the first by the addition of 'The Archipelago,' which had first been published independently in London in the preceding decade. In 1952 was published in both this country and in England *Hölderlin: His Poems Translated by Michael Hamburger with a Critical Study* (New York), which was the second edition of a work entitled *Poems of Hölderlin*, 'published on June 7th, 1943, the first centenary of Hölderlin's death,' the first translation of Hölderlin to appear in book form in England.[1] One additional volume, *Some Poems of Hölderlin* (Norfolk, Conn., 1943), with German originals and translations by Frederic Prokosch of fifteen poems from the earlier period of the poet's creativity, appeared in The Poets of the Year Series two years before the opening year of this study and was reprinted in 1946. The above-mentioned volumes, as far as the present writer can determine, constitute the entire body of English translations of Hölderlin that have been published as separate volumes in the United States down to and including the year 1960.

[1] In the year 1938 a volume entitled *Hölderlin's Madness* by David Gascoyne was published in London, containing poems which 'are not a translation of selected poems of Hölderlin, but a free adaptation, introduced and linked together by entirely original poems. The whole constitutes what may perhaps be regarded as a *persona*' (p. 14).

Poetry of the German Romantic School in independent volumes is represented in the period under study solely by Novalis' *Hymnen an die Nacht*. These *Hymns to the Night*, with the German original and an English translation by Mabel Cotterell, appeared in this country in 1949 (New York), having been published one year earlier in London. *Hymns to the Night and Other Selected Writings* of Novalis, translated by Charles E. Passage, was published as a volume of the Library of Liberal Arts (New York, 1960). Novalis' fragmentary novel *The Novices of Sais*, in a translation by Ralph Manheim and with an introduction by Stephen Spender, had been published in a striking edition containing sixty drawings by Paul Klee (New York, 1949). These three volumes devoted to Novalis represent the first editions of his works to appear in English, either in England or the United States, for nearly half a century.[1]

While the majority of German lyric poets have been afforded, at best, a very restricted introduction to English-speaking audiences, one of these has long enjoyed an unreservedly warm reception in this country. Few, if any, German poets have exceeded Heinrich Heine's record of currency in English translation, and during the years embraced by the present study he is by far the most translated German poet of the past century. It is no exaggeration to say that among both English and American readers his poems are the best known and best loved German

---

[1] See Morgan, nos. 6960-6971, and also Frederick Hiebel's *Novalis: German Poet, European Thinker, Christian Mystic* (Chapel Hill, 1954), p. 119, for editions of Novalis' works in the English language.

One volume illustrative of the influence of Novalis upon an American author is *The Blue Flower* (New York, 1902), a collection of nine stories, the first of which is a translation from Novalis' fragmentary novel, by Henry van Dyke, a writer whose works were best sellers at the turn of the century. The nine stories – the one from Novalis and the eight of his own – 'seemed to me,' van Dyke states at the beginning of the volume, 'like parts of the same story, ...the story of the search for happiness, which is life.... A hundred years ago, in Germany, *Novalis*, a wise man and a poet, began to write the story again (and thought to tell the whole of it), in his romance of *Heinrich of Ofterdingen*. The first book he called "Expectancy." And the second book he called "Fulfilment." But in the middle of the second book he broke off to take a long journey, from which he has not yet come back. If you would like to know something about the meaning of the search for happiness, as fully and clearly as it can be told in words, you will read the bit of *Novalis* which is translated here (somewhat freely, I must confess), and perhaps you will see why, for want of a better title, this book is named after *The Blue Flower*.'

poetry of his century.[1] The translation of his lyric poetry has engaged the creative efforts of a whole gamut of translators, a significant number of whom are first-rate poets of eras and coteries as widely divergent as those represented by Elizabeth Barrett Browning and Ezra Pound. Evidence of the enduring favorable reputation Heine has enjoyed in this country – a country which he never knew directly – is supported by the fact that the earliest public monument erected in his honor stands

[1] For a brief review of Heine's reception in this country, see 'Heine in America' in *The Sword and the Flame: Selections from Heinrich Heine's Prose*, edited by Alfred Werner (New York, 1960), pp. 91-97. For a detailed account of Heine's reception in 'the English-speaking world which has assimilated him into its cultural pattern' (p. 5), see Sol Liptzin's *The English Legend of Heinrich Heine* (New York, 1954). Examining the degree to which Heine has become a part of the literary scene in England, Liptzin remarks: 'In Germany his reputation ever ebbed and flowed. In England his position remained secure. In Germany the "Heine-controversy" raged for over a century and the excommunication of 1835 was repeated in 1933. In England there was no Heine controversy ever since his fame reached its crest in the mid-Victorian era but only various friendly interpretations of the quality of his genius. His hold upon the English imagination was never really shaken and he was at no time without sincere admirers.... If the Germans have at times laid claim to Shakespeare on the ground that they have better appreciated this genius of Britain than did his own compatriots, then the English may well claim Heine as their own, since they have felt for more than a century the force and spell of his personality and have made many of his ideas and songs a part of their own tradition' (pp. 162-163). Two older studies are H. B. Sach's *Heine in America*, Americana Germanica, No. 23 (Philadelphia, 1916) and S. G. Wormley's *Heine in England* (Chapel Hill, 1943). Clarence Gohdes, in 'Heine in America: A Cursory Survey,' *Georgia Review*, XI (1959), 44-49, concludes his essay with the following comparison: 'In general, the criticism of Heine written by Americans appears to have been less valuable than that produced in England. One finds among the nineteenth-century offerings no essays as meritorious as those written by Matthew Arnold or George Eliot. But the situation is probably reversed in respect of more recent scholarship on Heine. At the broadest level the most significant feature of his vogue with us, however, has been the astonishing dispersal of interest at various intellectual levels. In the United States Heine has never been a poet for the highbrows alone' (p. 49). Another useful study is Armin Arnold's *Heine in England and America: A Bibliographical Check-List* (London, 1959), which provides a bibliography of the English translations of Heine as well as of English and American criticism of Heine to the year 1957. Arnold's chronological list of the number of English Heine publications shows that from 1945 to 1949 the critical essays in books and periodicals (excluding reviews) numbered no fewer than twenty; for the years 1950 to 1954 they numbered eleven; and from 1955 to 1957 there were twenty-four. This most recent three-year period was likely never equaled since only one earlier five-year period exceeded this number: for the years 1940 to 1944 there was a total of twenty-seven. These statistics, when combined with the number of translations of Heine to appear, illustrate the extent of Heine's almost phenomenal reception in the English-speaking world.

in the United States.[1] Undoubtedly the early Nazi denunciation of Heine aroused in this country new feelings of appreciation for his seemingly prophetic pronouncements on Germany, and the centennial celebration of his death in 1956 served to maintain a high interest in his poetic achievements. From 1945 to 1960 more separate volumes of his poems appeared in English translation than of any other German poet.

The first volume devoted solely to Heine's poetry to appear after 1945 was *Poems and Ballads* (New York, 1948), a reprint of a volume of translations by Emma Lazarus, herself a poet remembered mainly for her lines, inscribed at the base of the Statue of Liberty, bidding the word's oppressed a welcome. Her volume of translations of his poetry had been first published under the same title in 1881 (New York), but as early as 1866, at the age of sixteen, she had already published *Poems and Translations* (New York), containing some of her translations of Heine's poetry. Her fuller volume of Heine translations was reissued a second

---

[1] Alfred Werner (*The Sword and the Flame*, pp. 91-92) supplies the following information about this fact: 'The story goes back to 1893 when, learning of the rejection by Duesseldorf and Mayence of the Heine monument, Americans of German origin organized a committee that commissioned its sculptor, Ernst Herter, to make a monument for America, but one not identical with the one that, in all three versions, had been rejected by the Rhineland cities. This fourth version was, indeed, accepted by the committee. But now the trouble began. It took the donations of thousands to pay for the execution of the monument in white Tyrolean marble. The Lorelei Fountain was en route when the committee began to find it more difficult than it had expected to obtain the proper site in New York. They had hoped to place it in Central Park, but the city fathers, turning to the New York Sculpture Society for advice, were told that, since the three Rhine maidens were nude and the Lorelei herself not "decent" either, this plan could not be recommended. Opposition arose on another front: some German-Americans, echoing the anti-Heine sentiments of the Vaterland, began a protest against the very idea of a monument to Heine. Several locations offered by New York were rejected by the committee as totally unacceptable.

'After twenty months in a New York warehouse, Lorelei and the Rhine maidens were finally permitted to make the second, much shorter stage of their journey. This one was to the Bronx where, in July, 1899, in the presence of the sculptor, who had come from Europe, the fountain was solemnly unveiled. The fountain carries no inscription other than the words "Heinrich Heine" beneath the portrait on the base. Only the initiated will understand the subtle irony in one of the two other reliefs: the youth (Heine!) about to kill a dragon, holds a pen instead of a spear, and the monster wears a wig to symbolize the German bureaucrat.' The Lorelei Fountain is located in the Joyce Kilmer Park at Grand Concourse and 164th Street.

time two years later (1950) by a different publisher. The following year two books of Heine's poems made their appearance, one a slender volume of sixty-two pages entitled *Selections from the Poetry of Heinrich Heine* (Providence, 1951), translated by K. S. Weimar, and the other, *The North Sea* (New York, 1951), containing the original German with translations by Vernon Watkins. In the centennial year of Heine's death, the Peter Pauper Press published a small, attractive edition of selections of his poetry in translations by Joseph Auslander under the title *Bittersweet Poems* (Mount Vernon, N.Y., 1956). Both the Limited Editions Club and the Heritage Press published *Heinrich Heine: Poems* (New York, 1957), containing poems selected and translated by Louis Untermeyer, perhaps the most prolific American Heine translator and himself a poet who has sometimes been referred to as 'the American Heine.' This edition of Untermeyer's Heine translations had originally been published by Holt in 1917 and contained 325 poems, for the most part short lyrics; a revised edition was published in 1923 both by Harcourt, Brace in New York and by Routledge in London (Broadway Translations); an edition expanded to some 500 translations subsequently appeared in 1937 in New York by Harcourt, Brace and in 1938 in London by Jonathan Cape. Together with the expanded 1937 edition of Untermeyer's translations his well received biography of Heine was published as 'the first biography of Heine which has been prepared by a poet,' as the dust jacket proclaims.

Although the above seven volumes are devoted exclusively to poems, two publications appeared which contained English translations of selections from both his poetry and his prose. The first of these, entitled *The Sea and the Hills: The Harz Journey and the North Sea* (Boston, 1946), was translated by Frederic T. Wood. The second, *The Poetry and Prose of Heinrich Heine* (New York, 1948), edited by Frederic Ewen, previously mentioned as the author of a distinguished study of Schiller in England, is a work of nearly 900 pages for which 110 of the poems were newly translated by Aaron Kramer and for which all of the prose selections were specially translated by the editor. This work was reissued as a paperbound book in 1960. For *The Sword and the Flame: Selections from Heinrich Heine's Prose* (New York, 1960), Alfred Werner, prompted by 'the enormous revival of interest in Heine's work in the past decade,' as is asserted on the dust jacket of the volume, edited what claims to be 'the first book in English to contain full texts of the major prose works'; these derived from translations made by Charles Godfrey Leland[1] in the first eight volumes of the twelve-volume edition of Heine's works in English published in England at the turn of the century (1891-1905). An even older translation of selections from Heine's philosophical writings, published by John Snodgrass in 1882 and entitled *Religion and Philosophy in Germany: A Fragment*, reappeared (Boston, 1959) with a new introduction by Ludwig Marcuse, whose biography of Heine, published in Germany just at the beginning of the Nazi era (*Heinrich Heine: Ein Leben zwischen gestern und morgen* [Berlin, 1932]), made its appearance in English one year later (*Heine: A Life between Love and Hate* [New York, 1933]). Heine's story-telling art was illustrated for readers of English, in addition to the selections included in the above volumes of his prose, by the publication of *The Rabbi of Bacherach: A Fragment* (New York, 1947) containing Heine's letters on the story, in a translation by E. B. Ashton, the pseudonym of Ernst Basch, who will be seen to have translated a number of works from the German. A translation by Basil Ashmore of Heine's ballet scenario, *Doctor Faust: A Dance Poem; Together with Some Rare Accounts of Witches, Devils, and the*

---

[1] Gohdes offers the following resumé of Leland and his role as a Heine intermediary: 'The most widely-read translator of Heine into English was a Philadelphian, Charles Godfrey Leland, journalist, vastly popular author of the humorous Hans Breitmann verses, and man of letters so catholic in his taste as to have established a Rabelais Club and discovered a previously unknown Gypsy dialect called Shelta. He occupies in the history of Heine in England and America a position comparable with that of Bayard Taylor in the annals of *Faust* in translation. After graduating from Princeton, Leland continued his education at several German universities, but while he was in Paris in 1848, he apparently never attempted to visit Heine. The violinist Ole Bull encouraged Leland's study of Heine during conversations in Philadelphia, but there is no record of the inception of his activities as translator. Leland's version of *Die Reisebilder* was first published in 1855; by 1863 it had gone into a fourth revised edition; three years later it was reissued in both New York and London, and by 1882 appeared in a ninth edition. In 1864 Leland also brought out a collection of Heine's poems, for the most part translated in the original meters, which was reprinted at least three times by 1881. Ten years later he began publishing, in London, the most extensive edition of Heine's works projected in our language in the nineteenth century. Before his death, he completed in all eight volumes in a series of twelve, as well as a version of the *Familienleben*' (p. 46).

Ancient Art of Sorcery (New York), originally published in England, also made its appearance in this country in 1952. Heine's popularity as a story-teller is further attested to by the inclusion of his stories in anthologies of writers of various nationalities, such as Marjorie Fischer's *Strange to Tell* (New York, 1946) and Hermann Kesten's *The Blue Flower* (New York, 1946). The Jewish Publication Society of America was responsible for the appearance, in the centennial year of Heine's death, 1956, of *Heinrich Heine: A Biographical Anthology*, edited by Hugo Bieber with translations by Moses Hadas.

The abundance of volumes of Heine's works, both poetry and prose, published in English translation in this country affords an indubitable manifestation of the interest generated by, and the reception accorded to, Heine in the United States. It is paradoxical, however, especially in view of the renewed interest accorded Goethe and Schiller in connection with their several anniversaries, that the centennial year of Heine's death, 1956, was marked by only two American volumes, one a small gift edition of poems, and the other a biographical anthology. Perhaps this fact provides some foundation for the contention that to American readers today Heine remains a living poet of contemporary significance and magnitude. It is primarily upon Heine as a representative that readers of English are forced to depend for an acquaintance with the rich world of an entire century of German lyric poetry.

In contrast to the limited representation of German nineteenth-century lyric poetry in English translation, nineteenth-century German literature, generally speaking, must certainly appear to American readers, as already noted, to be the era of the short story and the tale because of their comparative prevalence in English translation. The *Novelle*, consciously introduced into his country's literature by Goethe, was developed into a leading literary form by the German Romanticists, but was redefined and modified by representatives of each of the succeeding literary schools. Even today the *Novelle* – generally translated as 'short story' – remains a distinct literary genre in German literature, distinguishable, at least by specialists, from the short story and tale.[1] The

---

[1] For a discussion of the qualities that distinctively characterize the *Novelle*, the short story, and the tale, and distinguish between each of them, see Johannes Klein's *Geschichte der*

short story and the tale account for, by far, the largest number of English translations from German literature of the nineteenth century published in the United States from 1945 to 1960. Representative specimens are available from all the major literary movements in German literature since Goethe, appearing either in multinational anthologies, in anthologies limited to German authors, or in separately published volumes.

Although many volumes containing translations from nineteenth-century German literature have been published in this country, the works of Johann Peter Hebel, whom, with reference to his poetry, Bayard Taylor denominated 'The German Burns,'[1] were included in only a very few of them; Morgan lists only nine such collections, nearly all of them containing fewer than a half dozen of his poems and none of them containing any of his stories. It is of special importance, therefore, that Hebel, who in English translation is virtually unknown as a poet, and as a teller of tales has been totally excluded, is represented, if even in a limited way, by the publication of an independent volume, *Francisca, and Other Stories* (Lexington, Kentucky, 1957), translated by Clavia Goodman and B. Q. Morgan, in an edition limited to 175 copies. Hebel is, thus, the only literary figure of this period to be introduced to American readers during the period under consideration, and his *Francisca*, together with the other tales included in the volume, are the only pieces of literature, first published in the nineteenth century, to make their appearance in English in a separate volume for the first time.[2]

The tales of the German Romanticists have long abounded in English translation, and their appearance in recent American publications has continued with seemingly unabated frequency. Specimens of German Romantic tales are included in nearly all anthologies of German short

---

deutschen Novelle (4th ed. [Wiesbaden, 1960], pp. 15-25), and his articles 'Kurzgeschichte' and 'Novelle' in *Reallexikon der deutschen Literaturgeschichte* (2d ed., ed. Werner Kohlschmidt and Wolfgang Mohr, I [Berlin, 1963], 685-701). See also Benno von Wiese's *Die deutsche Novelle von Goethe bis Kafka: Interpretationen*, I (Düsseldorf, 1956), 11-32, and Hellmuth Himmel's *Geschichte der deutschen Novelle* (Bern, 1963).

[1] See Bayard Taylor, *Critical Essays and Literary Notes* (New York, 1880): 'The German Burns,' pp. 55-91 (dated April, 1862).

[2] Hebel's *The Hussar, Kannitverstan*, and *Unexpected Reunion*, all translated by Paul Pratt, are included in Robert Pick's *German Short Stories and Tales*, published by Knopf in 1954 and, as a paperbound Pocket Library edition, in 1955 and 1959.

stories published in the United States from 1945 to 1960, such as *Great German Short Novels and Stories* (New York, 1952), edited by Victor Lange and published as a volume of the Modern Library, *German Stories and Tales* (New York, 1954; Pocket Library ed., 1955; 3d ptg., 1959), edited by Robert Pick, *Nineteenth-Century German Tales* (Garden City, N.Y., 1959), edited by Angel Flores, and *Great German Short Stories* (New York, 1960; 3d ptg., 1963), edited by Stephen Spender. But the German Romantic tale is also found frequently in other anthologies of international scope. Ludwig Tieck's[1] *Auburn Egbert*, in a translation by Thomas Roscoe that was first published in London in 1826, Brentano's *Loreley and Marmot*, translated by E. B. Ashton (pseudonym of Ernst Basch), and Arnim's *The Mad Veteran of the Fort Ratonneau*, translated by William Metcalfe, along with stories by Kleist, the Grimm brothers, Hoffmann, Keller, Grillparzer, and others, appeared in *The Blue Flower* (New York, 1946), an anthology of Romantic stories from thirteen countries, edited by Hermann Kesten. Two other German Romanticists were represented during the period under study by the reappearance of two familiar stories, the one in an early British translation and the other in a new American version. Adelbert von Chamisso's *The Wonderful History of Peter Schlemihl*, as translated by William Howitt and first published in 1843, was republished more than a century later in 1954 by Story Classics, a division of Rodale Press (Emmaus, Pennsylvania). Joseph von Eichendorff's *Memoirs of a Good-for-*

---

[1] Although, during the period under study, Tieck is scarcely represented in English translation, a detailed study of the nature and extent of his reception in the United States down to 1900 by Percy Matenko (*Ludwig Tieck and America* [Chapel Hill, 1954], Univ. of N. Car. Stud. in Ger. Langs. and Lits., No. 12) shows that while the influence of America on Tieck was virtually negligible, the influence of Tieck in America was 'various and extensive' (p. 93). Matenko, in the Preface to his volume, postulates that since 1900 Tieck's reception in the United States has been 'confined to academic, chiefly Germanistic circles.' He then raises a question concerning the future: 'Will this regard for Tieck spread to the American cultivated public in general as it did between the second and fifth decades of the nineteenth century?' Maintaining that the reception of Tieck in America is determined by the reception in the United States of German romanticism as a whole, he ventures to say: '...it is by no means inconceivable that we might again have a general revival of interest in German romanticism in America which would carry with it a general revival of interest in Tieck as well' (p. 96). It would appear, however, from the present vantage point that the answer to Matenko's question remains a negative one.

Nothing appeared in a new translation made by B. Q. Morgan and published by Ungar in 1955 in the College Translations series, and in a paperback edition in 1960.

Tales of Hoffmann (New York, 1946 and 1959) – whose author, the editor of this collection, Christopher Lazare, claims, is, 'with the possible exception of Heine,... the best known of German Romanticists' – was presented as 'the first publication in modern translations of Hoffmann's famous tales' (p. 9). Capturing the imagination of a number of British and American writers, including Robert Louis Stevenson, Hawthorne, Longfellow,[1] and especially Poe,[2] Hoffmann's tales, seri-

---

[1] An interesting comment on Hoffmann, affording an insight into his general appeal both in Germany and the United States at the beginning of the twentieth century and a view of his specific interest to Longfellow, was elicited by the production of Offenbach's 'Conte d'Hoffmann' (presented by Oscar Hammerstein at the Manhattan Opera House beginning November 15, 1907) in two letters to the editor of the *Nation*. Robert H. Fife, Jr., referring to the erroneous legend of Hoffmann's life that had developed, writes 'not to assist in the thankless destruction of the picturesque Hoffmann saga, but merely to call attention to the unfading attraction of those weird, unrealistic tales of his. Every one of his contemporaries, except the eccentric Heinrich von Kleist, has ceased to be more than a name to the German reading public, but each year brings a new edition of one of Hoffmann's fantastic tales' ('The Real E. A. Hoffmann,' *Nation*, LXXXV [November 28, 1907], 491). This letter evoked a response from J. M. Hart who, calling attention to 'Longfellow's introduction of the Hoffmann legend in the "Hyperion,"' made an appeal, 'recalling the younger set of our scholars to a more careful consideration of Longfellow, especially his "Hyperion." That curious medley of romance and autobiography was German literature for the ordinary American of the '40's and '50's.... It influenced the New England mind profoundly; it used to be a Harvard classic "before the war." In my judgment its influence was far more pervasive than that of Longfellow's other early writings; it set the fashion for German literature *of a certain kind*. Its very limitations explain to us the old-fashioned American ignorance of the greater German literature: Lessing, Goethe, and so on down to Heine. I hope that some of our younger set may be moved to make a careful study of Longfellow's German studies' (*Nation*, LXXXVI [January 9, 1908], 32). This appeal had its response, it is hardly necessary to add, in the studies of Hatfield, Long, Pochmann, and others.

[2] See Pochmann et al., *German Culture in America* (Madison, 1957), pp. 388-408 for a summary discussion of Poe's knowledge of the German language and his indebtedness to German stories, particularly to Hoffmann's – subjects on which critics have divergent opinions. For a detailed study of the critical reception and influence of Hoffmann both in England and the United States, see Henry Zylstra's 'E. T. A. Hoffmann in England and America' (unpubl. diss., Harvard Univ., 1940). An older study of the relationship of Poe to Hoffmann is 'The Influence of E. T. A. Hoffmann on the Tales of Edgar Allan Poe' (*Studies in Philology*, III [1908]), where the author, Palmer Cobb, examines the indebtedness of Poe, the 'Germanic dreamer,' to German literature for his material and technique. Cobb

alized in *Blackwood's* as early as 1824, just two years after his death, have continued their appeal to readers of English, as is evidenced by this recent volume of ten tales, which, after its initial appearance in 1946, was published again in 1959 in two editions, one clothbound and the other paperbound. Another volume, *Tales from Hoffmann* (New York), edited by J. M. Cohen and containing five stories, was published in 1951, the same year in which a Heritage Press edition of *Tales of Hoffmann* (New York) made its appearance. *Story of a Nutcracker; A Free Version from the Tale by Hoffmann*, by Sir Desmond MacCarthy and Bryan Guiness, was also published in both London and New York. The perennial appeal in the United States of Hoffmann's tales is further demonstrated by the inclusion of *The Cremona Violin* in Kesten's anthology, *The Blue Flower*, by the same story in Lange's collection, *Great German Short Novels and Stories*, in both instances in a translation first published in 1885 by J. T. Bealby, and by *The Mines at Falun*, newly translated by Peggy Sard, in Flores' *Nineteenth-Century German Tales*.

Of all works of German literature of any era or any author, very few, if any, have so thoroughly become a part of the reading experience of Americans as have the tales of the Grimm brothers, Jakob and Wilhelm.[1]

concludes that Poe, as a magazine editor, was attracted to German literature in general by the articles on this subject and by translations from the German which appeared in numerous English and American periodicals, and specifically to Hoffmann by an article by Walter Scott which had appeared in the *Foreign Quarterly Review* for July, 1827; that since Poe was able to read German, Hoffmann's tales were available to him in the original as well as in translation; that at least five of Poe's stories reveal indubitable influence of Hoffmann; and that, although Poe borrowed motifs, his style remained unaffected by Hoffmann's influence.
[1] Since the *Kinder- und Hausmärchen*, as they were entitled in the original, have had such an important and distinguished history in Germany as well as in England and the United States, it is worth reviewing briefly the record of their publication. First published in Berlin in 1812, Volume One of the *Kinder- und Hausmärchen* contained eighty-six tales; three years later, in 1815, Volume Two appeared with an additional seventy tales, making a total of one hundred and fifty-six in the two volumes of the first German edition. The second edition, revised and enlarged, contained one hundred and sixty-one tales and nine other pieces designated *Kinderlegenden*. Each successive edition offered additional tales as well as some deletions until the definitive seventh edition, published in Göttingen in 1857, comprised a total of two hundred and one tales and ten legends. The *Jubiläums-Auflage*, edited by Reinhold Steig and published in the centennial year of the appearance of the first edition of Volume One, was the thirty-third edition of the 'Grosse Ausgabe.' The initially

Since their first appearance in English translation, the tales, in collections that include just a few stories to those that include nearly all of those contained in the definitive German edition of 1857, have attracted numerous translators, some of the principal ones of which are represented by volumes published in the United States between 1945 and 1960.

The earliest translation of Grimms' *Märchen* to reappear after 1945 is that by Lucy Crane, first published in London by Macmillan in the year 1882. The same publisher reissued Miss Crane's translation in *Household Stories from the Collection of the Brothers Grimm* in the Children's Classics Series in 1949 and again in 1954. Translations by Miss Crane are included, along with those by two additional important translators, Mrs. Edgar

reserved but increasingly enthusiastic reception accorded the publication of the Grimms' *Märchen* in Germany is illustrated by the fact that between 1912 and 1935 a total of two hundred and fifty German editions appeared. (Wilhelm Schoof, *Zur Entstehungsgeschichte der Grimmschen Märchen; Bearbeitet unter Benutzung des Nachlasses der Brüder Grimm* [Hamburg, 1959], pp. 190-192).

In the year 1825, between the appearance of the second and third editions of the main collection, the Grimm brothers published a *Kleine Ausgabe* of fifty tales, which, by the year of the centenary, 1921, had achieved its fiftieth edition; this too was edited by Steig. (For an account of the inception of the original Grimm collection and its amplification in subsequent editions, and a tabular classification of the additions and deletions of the first seven editions, see T. F. Crane's 'The External History of the *Kinder- und Hausmärchen* of the Brothers Grimm,' *Modern Philology*, XIV [February, 1917], 577-610; continued in XV [June, 1917], 65-77; concluded in XV [October, 1917], 355-383.)

The Grimms' *Märchen* were introduced into English by means of a two-volume collection, selected and translated by Edgar Taylor and first published in London; Volume One, containing thirty-one stories, appeared in 1823, and Volume Two, with twenty-four stories, in 1826. A second, one-volume edition of Taylor's selection was published in 1839 with the title *Gammer Gretel; or German Fairy Tales, and Popular Stories from the Collection of MM. Grimm, and Other Sources*, containing a total of forty-two stories. The stories selected by Taylor for inclusion in the first two editions of the tales in English translation have determined the contents of many successive collections of Grimms' *Märchen* published in England and the United States. Taylor's selections, reprinted numerous times, contained a few narratives that were not translations from the Grimms, and excluded others that were in the original collection which Taylor felt obliged to omit, as he wrote in his preface, 'in deference to the scrupulous fastidiousness of modern taste, especially in works likely to attract the attention of youth.' As early as 1826 the first American edition of the tales, consisting of Volume One of what subsequently became Taylor's standard English translation, was published in Boston with the somewhat garbled title revealing the difficulties presented to those unfamiliar with Gothic type: *German Popular Stories Translated from the Rinder* [sic] *und Hans* [sic] *Märchen, Collected by M. M. Grimm from Oral Tradition*.

Lucas and Marian Edwardes, in a collection published as one of the Rainbow Classics (Cleveland, 1947). Mrs. Lucas' translations, first published in London in 1900, were included, along with those of other translators, in another volume issued in a popular edition, a special edition, and a deluxe edition by Grosset (New York, 1945). The selection by Marian Edwardes, first published by Dent in 1901, formed the basis of a revised edition of this work published in 1949 in Everyman's Library by Dent in London and Dutton in New York, which contains forty-seven tales and eliminates those originally included by Edwardes from sources other than the collection by the Grimm brothers. Appearing in 1949 in the series entitled The Children's Illustrated Classics, and reissued again in 1951, this collection boasts, in the Publishers' Note: 'No tale is now included in the present volume that is not "authentic Grimm."' The work of still another principal translator of the tales, Margaret Hunt, whose translations of two hundred and ten narratives in *Grimms' Household Tales* published in two volumes in London in 1884, was 'revised, corrected and completed' by James Stern for *Grimm's Fairy Tales, Complete Edition*, published in New York by Pantheon Books in 1944, just one year prior to the opening date of the present study. Some fifteen other collections of the tales, of which the majority contain just a few stories while others consist of retold versions rather than translations, were issued by a number of publishers and, along with the volumes mentioned above, were intended primarily as books for children. The international, perhaps supranational, association elicited by the tales is illustrated by *Snow White and Other Stories from Grimm; Retold by Jeanne Cappe* (New York, 1957), which is a translation from the French by Marie Ponset. The extremely popular motion pictures, 'Snow White and the Seven Dwarfs' and 'Hansel and Gretel,' are still another avenue of currency for the Grimm brothers' tales in the United States. That the tales have been fully adopted into the family of American children's stories is further implied by the fact that they have been retold or edited by persons who know little or no German and whose chief interest is not their historical and national origin or their value as genuine folk-tales, but their perennial appeal to American children.

In the United States, apparently to a somewhat greater degree than in Germany, the Grimms' *Märchen* have been relegated to the field of children's literature.[1] It is not to be denied that one of the purposes of the Grimms' original publication was to provide stories for children. This contention is illustrated not only by the Grimms' choice of a title for the collection, but also by the fact that they presented one of the first copies of the first volume of the tales, finished just a few days before Christmas in the year 1812, to the wife of Achim von Arnim – whose husband's patient urging was primarily responsible for the brothers' decision to postpone the first printing no longer – with the inscription: 'An die Frau Elisabeth von Arnim für den kleinen Johannes Freimund.'[2] But that the Grimm brothers intended the publication of their collection to be more than an anthology of stories for children can be confirmed not only by the scholarly interests of the brothers but also by the notes and comments, certainly of no interest to children, appended to the first volume,[3] and later by the separate volume of commentary by the

[1] Several editions of the *Kinder- und Hausmärchen* which reflect an adult, sometimes scholarly, interest in the tales, has been published recently in Germany together with scholarly studies and analyses of the tales, of which the following incomplete list offers some indication: *Die Kinder- und Hausmärchen der Brüder Grimm*; *Vollständige Ausgabe in der Urfassung*, ed. Friedrich Panzer (Wiesbaden, 1956 and 1961); *K-HM, Historische Ausgabe*. [Beigedruckt: 1. Vorgeschichte der Märchen, 1805-12, 2. Grimm: Urhandschrift der 1812 veröffentlichten Märchen] (Berlin, 1948); *K-HM, In der ersten Gestalt* (Mit einem Nachwort von Walter Killy) (Frankfurt am Main, 1962); Wilhelm Schoof, *Zur Entstehungsgeschichte der Grimmschen Märchen* (Hamburg, 1959).
[2] See Johannes Bolte and Georg Polívka, *Anmerkungen zu den Kinder- und Hausmärchen der Brüder Grimm*, IV (Leipzig, 1930), 427-428.
[3] The importance, from the beginning, of the 'Anmerkungen' for the Grimms, as contrasted with concern which von Arnim had expressed as to the potential appeal of the volume to children, is pointed up by an exchange of correspondence between them immediately after the first volume had been printed. Arnim wrote: 'Eben habe ich von Reimer für meine Frau Euer Märchenbuch erhalten, es ist gar schön gebunden und soll ihr am Christabend beschert werden, ich habe es bei Savigny versteckt und auch wegen des goldnen Schnitts nur etwas blättern können, ich sag Euch im Namen meines Kindes herzlichen Dank, es ist ein recht braves Buch, das sicher lange gekauft wird.... Eins hätte ich Euch noch geraten, wenn ich die Einrichtung des Buches gekannt, Vorrede und Zusätze in einem Journale, jetzt in dem Euren zu geben und zu den Märchen einige Blätter von Eurem Bruder radieren zu lassen, der Mangel an Kupfern und die umgebende Gelehrsamkeit schliessen es jetzt eigentlich vom Kreise der Kinderbücher aus und hindern die allgemeinere Verbreitung. Es sollte mich sehr wundern, wenn nicht ein Leipziger Speculant die unterhaltendsten

Grimms on the tales, which was published in 1822. In fact, the Grimms allegedly later regretted using the word *Kinder* in their title. Nevertheless, in the United States, judged by the number and nature of their editions, the tales are almost exclusively the property of children.

An important exception to this pattern is furnished by a significant recent publication of the Southern Illinois University Press, *The Grimms' German Folk Tales* (Carbondale, Ill., 1960),[1] an entirely new and in-

Märchen herausnehme und mit Bildern begleitet nachdruckte....' Jakob and Wilhelm, in their reply about two weeks later, explained: 'Der Anhang, den Du wegwünschest, ist zu unsern Kindermärchen gekommen 1) weil ich nicht einsehe, warum die Leute, die ihn nicht lesen mögen, ihn nicht überschlagen können;...2) dieser Anhang schützt das Buch gegen viel Angriffe und macht eine Art Respekt von dem Inhalt; ich bin selbst überzeugt, dass es eine nicht unansehnliche Classe von Lesern eigentlich um des Anhangs willen kauft. 3)... 4) ähnliche Anmerkungen hat doch auch Herder zu seinen Volksliedern ohne Schaden gegeben; die englischen Percy und Scott haben ihrer noch viel mehr und unmittelbar unter dem Text....' (Quoted in Reinhold Steig's *Achim von Arnim und die ihm nahe standen, Dritter Band, Achim von Arnim und Jakob und Wilhelm Grimm* [Stuttgart and Berlin, 1904], 251-253). And just one year later, in a letter to von Arnim dated January 28, 1813, Jakob wrote: '...dass Du das Märchen vom Fischer und auch das vom Mahandelboom nicht für rechte Kindermärchen hältst, fiele mir meinerseits unmöglich. Der Unterschied zwischen Kinder- und Hausmärchen und der Tadel dieser Zusammenstellung, auf unserm Titel, ist mehr spitzfindig als wahr, sonst müssten streng genommen die Kinder aus dem Haus gebracht, wohin sie von jeher gehört haben, und in einer Cammer gehalten werden. Sind denn diese Kindermärchen *für Kinder* erdacht und erfunden? ich glaube dies so wenig, als ich die allgemeinere Frage nicht bejahen werde: ob man überhaupt für Kinder etwas eigenes einrichten müsse?...' (Steig, III, 269).

[1] A second important volume that invests Grimms' *Märchen* with interests other than those associated with children's literature, while not published in the United States yet of sufficient importance to be mentioned here, is *Grimms' Other Tales* (London, 1956), a new selection made by the folklorist and curator of the Lippe Folk Museum, Wilhelm Hansen, and edited and translated by Ruth Michaelis-Jena and Arthur Ratcliff, in an edition limited to five hundred copies. The fifty stories here translated, it is explained in the introduction, are 'other tales' in that they 'are little known in the sense that some were published by the Grimms in their first edition of *The Household Tales* (1812) but later omitted and not translated by Taylor (1823); others were printed only in the Grimm's very full notes, available to scholars in the standard edition of Bolte-Polivka; yet others came from the original manuscript given by the Grimms to Clemens Brentano and afterwards known as the Oelenberg MS (edited by Lefftz, and now out of print); and the remainder are still in manuscript among the Grimm Papers in the keeping of the University of Tübingen, though some have been printed at hazard in various German folklore periodicals. None is included in the definitive [German] edition of *The Household Tales* [nor in Taylor's classic English translation]; and one may well venture to think that all will be new to the common reader in the English-speaking world.'

dependent translation, by Francis P. Magoun, Jr., of Harvard University, and Alexander H. Krappe, of the two hundred tales and the ten *Kinderlegenden* which comprise the 1912 Jubilee-edition of Reinhold Steig. Magoun, in the brief Foreword to the volume, emphasizes, in contradiction to prevailing sentiment, the mature, adult quality of the tales, which are described as 'Wilhelm Grimm's final achievement of one of the noblest monuments of German prose':

> Originally composed by intelligent, keen-witted German peasant folk and told for mutual entertainment by grown-ups for grown-ups, these famous folk tales are, contrary to popular notion, not essentially for younger children, to whom, in fact, only a few are likely to appeal. A limited number, perhaps some twenty or thirty commonly included in almost innumerable select translations especially designed for children, have, to be sure, achieved notable success among children;... The tales will, as a whole, appeal essentially to grown-ups with a taste for a good story well told. In the diction, style, and development of the various narratives there is nothing childish or juvenile, still less anything mannered or from the point of view of the original teller anything archaic.

Individual stories from the Grimms' *Märchen* have appeared in many forms, again primarily, but not exclusively, for children's use, the most popular being 'Snow White' and 'Hansel and Gretel.' The special popularity of these two stories can doubtless be traced to the well-received Walt Disney motion picture production of 'Snow White and the Seven Dwarfs' (1937) and the Michael Meyer film production of 'Hansel and Gretel' (1954), based on the opera of the same title by Engelbert Humperdinck and Adelheid Wette. These motion pictures provide evidence of an added dimension of the currency of these tales in the United States. The latter tale was published in 1952 by the Limited Editions Club as *The Story of What Happened to Hansel and Gretel* (New York) in a translation by P. H. Muir. One of the tales was included in several anthologies, such as Hermann Kesten's *The Blue Flower* and

---

Of particular use for further study are the Notes which, with the translated English title, provide the German title and the source of each tale.

In The Allison-Shelley Collection is copy number 50, signed by the illustrator, Gwenda Morgen, as well as the Original Materials (so labeled) of this volume, including the wood engravings and other illustrations, an unmarked set of the page proof, both a marked and an unmarked set of the galley proof, together with correspondence on the terms of agreement for publication and proof for advertising material.

Marjorie Fischer's *Strange to Tell*. Many of the children's books contain adaptations, condensations, or simply borrowings of themes from the tales; others have been made into plays; still others are picture books or books called forth by the motion pictures mentioned above. Very recent evidence of persistent interest in these fairy tales and the brothers who collected them is provided by the cinemascopic motion picture 'The Wonderful World of the Brothers Grimm' (1961), based on 'Die Brüder Grimm' by Hermann Gernster. Certainly more Americans are acquainted with the work of Jakob and Wilhelm Grimm, even if quite indirectly and unconsciously, than with that of any other German writers.[1]

[1] Wayland D. Hand, in 'Die Märchen der Brüder Grimm in den Vereinigten Staaten' (in *Brüder Grimm Gedenken 1963: Gedenkschrift zur hundertsten Wiederkehr des Todestages von Jacob Grimm*, ed. Ludwig Denecke and Ina-Maria Greverus, Hessische Blätter für Volkskunde, No. 54 [Marburg, 1963], pp. 525-544), examines the reception and influence which the tales of the Grimm Brothers have had in this country. He finds that, although large numbers of Americans have long been acquainted with the tales, it is nevertheless quite contradictory 'dass gerade in Amerika, wo innerhalb der letzten zwei Jahrzehnte durch die weltbekannten Disney-Zeichenfilme die Grimmschen Märchen einen ihrer glänzendsten Erfolge erzielt haben, der durchschnittlich gebildete Amerikaner wenig gewusst hat von den Schöpfern und Gestaltern der Märchenwelt,...' Popular American acquaintance with the collectors themselves, he points out, was first achieved only a few years ago when the motion picture 'The Wonderful World of the Brothers Grimm' was seen by a large segment of the American population.

An interesting and illuminating chapter on the recent history of the original manuscript of the Grimms' fairy tales is contained in the *Collector: A Magazine for Autograph and Historical Collectors* (LXVI, 1 [January, 1953], 1-3), where the editor of the periodical, Miss Mary A. Benjamin, reported that the manuscript had come into her possession and was offered for sale at $ 75,000. The collection is believed to be the original manuscript that came into existence as the Grimm Brothers gathered and wrote down the tales, one by one, between the years 1806 and 1810. Reportedly the end of many of the tales is marked by the word 'mündlich' indicating the manner in which the tales had been gathered. The manuscript had been given by Jakob Grimm to his friend Clemens Brentano who in turn presented it to the Abbot of the Cistercian Monastery at Oelenberg in Alsace-Lorraine sometime prior to 1840. According to the article in the *Collector* the present Abbot of the monastery personally brought the manuscript to the United States to be sold by Miss Benjamin. 'The original manuscript,' she reports, 'consists of 113 pages of small, close writing, in perfect state of preservation. Sixty-six pages are in the hand of Jacob; 32 in that of Wilhelm, and 15 in four other unidentified hands. In terms of stories, there are all told forty-seven. Twenty-seven are by Jacob, 14 by Wilhelm, and 6 are in the hands of unknowns.... The importance of the present manuscript lies in the fact that it is *the first, and only known form* [sic] of the Grimms' manuscripts of their notable work.' In a later issue of the same periodical

Another kind of fairy tale, the art tale or *Kunstmärchen*, is represented by the publication of Wilhelm Hauff's *Dwarf Long-Nose* (New York, 1960), a translation by Doris Orgel of – to use the words of Phyllis McGinley in the Preface – 'his most famous tale,... a story as well-known to children in Germanic countries as "Snow White" or "Sleeping Beauty."' In the brief Preface she points up a contrast of Hauff with the Grimm brothers: 'Perrault was a collector, as was Lang and as were the Brothers Grimm. There is something about the robust and earthy quality of primitive folk tales which seems to defy imitation. That Hauff managed it is a tribute to his odd talent and perhaps only his extreme youth accounts for his ability to create stories as artless and spellbinding as if they had been handed down to him from generations of cottagers.' Another of his stories, 'The Story of the Haunted Ship,' was included in Marjorie Fischer's anthology, *Strange to Tell*, in an older translation by S. Mendel. Hauff, whose stories had appeared in English translation in abundance in the last two decades of the nineteenth and the first decade of the twentieth century,[1] has, since that time and until these recent appearances, seldom been represented in English translation, either in the reappearance of earlier versions or in the appearance of new ones.

Eduard Mörike – like Hauff, a Swabian – wrote only two notable prose works, an autobiographical novel *Maler Nolten* and a *Novelle* entitled *Mozart auf der Reise nach Prag;* it is in his poetry that he attained

(LXVII, 7, 8 [July-August, 1954], 1-2) Miss Benjamin reported that the original manuscript of the Grimms' fairy tales – to which nothing that 'has appeared on the American market since the original manuscript of Lewis Carroll's "Alice in Wonderland" sold at an auction for $ 50,000 can compare – has been sold. Dr. Martin Bodmer, the distinguished collector from Geneva, Switzerland, was the purchaser.'

[1] The appearance of a number of translations of Hauff's works during these decades coincides with the increase in the number of critical studies and analyses of his works during the same period. In an article entitled 'Washington Irvings Einfluss auf Wilhelm Hauff: Eine Quellenstudie' (*Euphorion*, XX [1913], 459-471), which analyzes one facet of the literary crosscurrents between America and Germany in the early nineteenth century, Otto Plath observed: 'In den letzten beiden Jahrzehnten hat sich die Literatur über Hauff mehr als verdoppelt. Im "Euphorion" und anderen bedeutenden literarischen Zeitschriften Deutschlands, sowie in den "Publications of the Modern Language Association of America" und der "Americana Germanica" hier in unserem Lande finden sich eine ganze Anzahl Aufsätze und kürzere Berichte über diesen beliebten Schriftsteller des deutschen Volkes und seine literarischen Erzeugnisse,...' (p. 459).

the high position he maintains in German literature today. Yet in spite of his prominence as a lyric poet it is primarily through his *Novelle* that he is represented in English translation. To be sure, translations of a few of his poems have appeared in anthologies of German poetry, but generally no more than six, and more often only one or two, are included in any one volume. Even in so recent an anthology as J. Wesley Thomas' *German Verse from the 12th to the 20th Century in English Translation* (Univ. of N. Car. Stud. in Germ. Langs. and Lits., No. 44 [Chapel Hill, 1963]), Mörike is represented by no more than six poems. Flores' anthology, it is true, contains twenty of his poems. His story of a day in Mozart's life first appeared in English when a translation by Florence Leonard was included in the seventh of the twenty volumes comprising the eclectic and monumental series entitled The German Classics of the Nineteenth and Twentieth Centuries: Masterpieces of German Literature Translated into English (ed. Kuno Francke and William Guild Howard [New York, 1913-14]). *Mozart on the Way to Prague*, in a translation and with an introduction by Walter and Catherine A. Phillips that had first been published in London in 1934, was republished in New York in 1947. Flores' volume contains the same story in a new translation by Mary Hottinger.[1]

Another important literary figure of nineteenth-century Germany, generally regarded as its greatest lyric poetess, has had an even more limited introduction in English translation than Mörike. Her poems having been included in almost negligible numbers in only a few anthologies of translations, Annette von Droste-Hülshoff may be said to be virtually unknown in this country. Again, as in the case of Mörike, her famous *Novelle*, *The Jew's Beech-Tree*, first appeared in the seventh volume of The German Classics in a translation by Lillie Winter. It is this same story, in a translation by E. N. Bennett first published in Bennett's anthology, *German Short Stories* (London, 1934) and reprinted

---

[1] Another recent translation of the story by Leopold von Loewenstein-Wertheim, under the title *Mozart's Journey to Prague* (London, 1958), appeared in England where apparently a 'discovery' of Mörike has occured as evidenced by the publication of a biography (*Eduard Mörike: The Man and the Poet* by Margaret Mare [London, 1957]) and a volume of his poems (*Poems by Eduard Mörike, Translated by Norah K. Cruickshank and Gilbert F. Cunningham* [London, 1959]).

in Lange's *Great German Short Novels and Stories*, by which she is represented in the United States during the period under survey.

In contrast to Mörike and Droste-Hülshoff, who distinguished themselves as literary artists through both poetry and prose, Adalbert Stifter found literary expression solely in stories and novels. But like Mörike and Droste-Hülshoff, Stifter has fared poorly in the number of translations published in the United States, although a few more translations of his works have been published in England.[1] On the one-hundredth anniversary of the first publication of *Der heilige Abend*, originally published in 1845 and later rewritten and incorporated in *Bunte Steine* as *Bergkristal*, a translation by Elizabeth Mayer and Marianne Moore entitled *Rock Crystal, A Christmas Tale* was published in New York and subsequently reprinted in Pick's *German Stories and Tales* (New York, 1954). A new translation of *Das Heidedorf* by Helen Stoddard Reed also appeared recently (see *The Library of Congress Author Catalog, 1948-1952*). Interestingly enough, three translations of *Brigitta* appeared in a period of three years: one by Edward Fitzgerald independently (London and Emmaus, Pa., 1957), one by Herman Salinger in Flores' *Nineteenth-Century German Tales* (New York, 1960), and the third by Ilsa Barea in Spender's *Great German Short Stories* (New York, 1960).

The stature and importance of Heinrich von Kleist in the history of German literature certainly cannot be accurately gauged from the very few translations into English of his works published either in England or the United States. As a reference to Morgan's *Bibliography* will show, Kleist was very little known in either England or the United States, judged by the number of translations available. In the United States prior to the period under consideration he had been represented only through the translations of four of his dramas and two of his stories, all of which had appeared in anthologies or periodicals.

---

[1] For an exhaustive bibliography of works on Stifter published in the United States and England as well as of English translations of Stifter's works from 1850 to 1960, see 'Stifters Werk in Amerika und England: Eine Bibliographie,' *Vierteljahrsschrift des Adalbert-Stifter-Instituts des Landes Oberösterreich*, IX (1960), 39-42, by Walter A. Reichart and Werner H. Grilk, and 'Nachtrag zu Stifters Werk in Amerika und England: Eine Bibliographie' (*ibid.*, pp. 129-132) by Eduard Eisenmeier.

It is significant, then, that during the period under survey Kleist was actually introduced to American readers as a writer of *Novellen* with the publication of translations of all eight of his stories under the title of *The Marquise of O— and Other Stories* (New York, 1960), with a Preface by Thomas Mann written just shortly before his death. The translator of the stories, Martin Greenberg, by describing in the Introduction his own acquaintance with this obscured figure from Germany's literary history, summarizes general American acquaintance with Kleist and his relative position among readers in the United States: 'The first time I read anything by Heinrich von Kleist was some thirteen years ago. Till then I knew his name vaguely as that of a German dramatist of the early 19th century, one of those obscure classic writers whom nobody reads or seems to know much about outside his own country.' This first complete collection in English of his stories commemorates, as it were, the sesquicentenary of Kleist's death in 1811. Critical reviews of the volume were almost unanimous in their acclaim, warmly welcoming the good translations in modern English of the stories of a writer 'whose eight plays,' one critic wrote, 'have established him as the Shakespeare of Germany.' Noting his negligible position in the United States, the same critic further commented: 'Though isolated translations of some of his works have appeared periodically, dating as far back as 1844, Kleist's impact in America has been restricted to a few devout scholars' (Bernard V. Valentine, 'Dark Side of Drama,' *Sat. Review*, XLIII [December 10, 1960], 24). Exploring the reason that Kleist was long accepted only with serious reservations both in his own country as well as in English-speaking areas, the same reviewer concluded: 'Only a post-Freudian mind would be adequately responsive to the psychological undercurrents of Kleistian situations'; and this statement concurs with Greenberg's opinion expressed in the Introduction: 'Like Stendhal, like Georg Büchner, Kleist was an avant-garde writer in the true sense of the term; he was not only ahead of the literary fashions of his time, he was not only ahead of his generation, he was ahead of his age. Another century, and a new age, needed to roll around for him to come into his own.' Before the appearance of this significant collection, one of Kleist's stories, *The Earthquake in Chile*, had been published in two general anthologies, in Kesten's *The Blue Flower*, in a translation by Roman Brown, and in Lange's *Great German Short Novels and Stories*, in a translation by Lange himself; in the very year the complete collection appeared, the same story, by still another translator, Michael Hamburger, was included in Spender's *Great German Short Stories*. An entirely new translation by Charles E. Passage of Kleist's masterpiece, *Michael Kohlhaas*, was included in Flores' anthology; this was the first appearance of the story in English translation in more than four decades. Within the sixteen years surveyed in the present study, four of Kleist's stories were published in translation for the first time, and the translation of his stories engaged the efforts of five different translators. Such attention he had never before received in this country.

Furthermore, two of Kleist's dramas also saw publication between 1945 and 1960, and in addition, two others of them have appeared as recently as 1962. *Prinz Friedrich von Homburg*, translated into English only twice before, appeared in 1956 as *The Prince of Homburg*, in a translation and with an introduction by Charles E. Passage – whose translations of Schiller's dramas were mentioned in a preceding chapter – in the Library of the Liberal Arts. Also translated only twice before, Kleist's *Das Käthchen von Heilbronn, oder die Feuerprobe* was translated most recently by Arthur H. Hughes and published in 1960 as *Katie of Heilbronn, 1808; or Trial by Fire: A Great Historical Drama of Knighthood*. *Der zerbrochene Krug*, generally regarded as one of the greatest comedies in German literature, had been translated into English in its entirety only once until the year 1958 when B. Q. Morgan completed his translation of the play into English verse; Morgan's translation remained unpublished until 1961 when *The Broken Pitcher* appeared as Number Thirty-One of the University of North Carolina Studies in the Germanic Languages and Literatures (Chapel Hill). Having appeared first in *Poet Lore* magazine in 1949, John T. Krumpelmann's translation of this comedy was published in 1962 by Frederick Ungar Publishing Company, the firm responsible, as noted before, for the appearance of so many works from the German, including Schiller's plays. Ungar, also in 1962, published Kleist's *Amphitryon*, never before available in English, in a translation by Marion Sonnenfeld.

The fact that recent English translations of four of Kleist's dramas were published in the United States since 1954 – one of them for the first time – together with the first complete collection of his stories in English is indicative of a rather exceptional reception accorded a German writer in this country. Seriously neglected by almost all translators for nearly a century and a half, his works, both narrative and dramatic, became available to an almost overwhelming degree within just a few years. It is clear that Kleist's present currency in the United States has never been exceeded, equaled, or even approached previously.

While recognition and critical reception of the plays that are held to have established their author as 'the Shakespeare of German drama' were belated, both in his own country and in the United States, the recent publication of his dramas in this country is indicative not only of a new interest in Kleist, but is parallel to a continuing and, in some cases, a new or growing interest in other German dramatists of the nineteenth century. Like Kleist, two other dramatists of the early nineteenth century, namely Christian Dietrich Grabbe and Georg Büchner, were granted only a very limited introduction in the United States until after 1945. Others, such as Franz Grillparzer and Friedrich Hebbel, whose works had earlier appeared in English translation, were represented in the period under consideration through new editions and translations.

Grabbe, who until 1952 was represented in English translation solely by one poem in Longfellow's *The Poets and Poetry of Europe* (1845), and none of whose dramas had ever been published in English translation, was introduced to American readers when Eric Bentley included his *Jest, Satire, Irony*, translated by Maurice Edwards, in *From the Modern Repertoire: Series Two* (Denver, 1952; 2d ptg., Bloomington, Ind., 1957). Büchner, long ignored as a literary figure in Germany itself, was first translated into English ninety years after his death, when, in 1927, his three plays were published in New York[1] in a translation by Geoffrey

---

[1] For a study of the reception of Büchner in the United States and the significance of the first American publication in German (1886) of his drama, *Dantons Tod*, to that reception, see Ralph P. Rosenberg's 'Georg Büchner's Early Reception in America,' *JEGP*, XLIV (1945), 270-273. Rosenberg finds that the early reception of Büchner both in Germany and in the United States presents parallels: '...the early reception of Büchner in America has gone through a phase similar to his early reception in Germany. In first calling attention to

Dunlop. These translations were republished in New York in 1952. In addition to this separate volume devoted to Büchner's plays, his dramatic works were also included in four other volumes, edited by Eric Bentley. *Danton's Death*, translated by Stephen Spender and Goronwy Rees, appears in *From the Modern Repertoire: Series One* (Denver, 1949; 4th ptg., Bloomington, Ind., 1962); the same drama, in a translation by John Holmstrom, is included in Volume Five (1957) of *The Modern Theatre*, a series comprising six volumes of modern drama primarily from the United States and Europe, edited by Eric Bentley and published by Doubleday from 1955 to 1960. Volume One (1955) of the series contains Büchner's *Woyzeck*, translated by Theodore Hoffman. *Leonce and Lena*, translated by Bentley himself, appears in his *From the Modern Repertoire: Series Three* (Bloomington, Ind., 1956). *Lenz*, Büchner's *Novelle* based on the life of the eccentric *Sturm und Drang* dramatist, translated by Goronwy Rees, is one of the selections in Spender's *Great German Short Stories*. Although this recent 'flood' of works by Büchner may, superficially, seem due to the promotion of one person, namely Eric Bentley, who is also responsible in such a great measure for translations of Brecht and several other German authors that have been published in the United States, recent interest in Büchner extends beyond Bentley. Evidence of this fact is provided not only by the republication of the volume containing his plays, and the appearance of his short

Büchner, the German-American socialists played the same role in America as did the socialists in Germany.' It is this association with the socialists, Rosenberg proposes, that aroused antagonism against him in the circle of more conservative critics; this, in turn, allegedly accounts for Büchner's very late recognition, not only in this country but in Germany as well. Until recently it had been assumed that Büchner's associations with non-German cultural and literary forces had been confined almost exclusively to France; his knowledge of English literature, it had been believed, was limited to his interest in Shakespeare. This view has been broadened by Rudolf Majut who, in one article, explored Büchner's relationship to English thinkers and scientists ('Georg Büchner and Some English Thinkers,' *MLR*, XLVIII [1953], 310-322), and who, in a second essay, surveys Büchner's encounters and associations with English poets and novelists, including Chaucer, Shakespeare, Young, Byron, Bulwer Lytton, Scott, and Dickens ('Some Literary Affiliations of Georg Büchner with England,' *MLR*, L [1955], 30-43). In a still more recent article Karl S. Guthke traces a reference in *Dantons Tod* to still another probable association with English literature ('Georg Büchner und William Mudford?' *Archiv für das Studium der neueren Sprachen und Literaturen*, CLXLVIII [1961-62], 170-171).

story in Spender's anthology, but also by the still more recent publication of a volume entitled *Georg Büchner: Complete Plays and Prose* (New York, 1963) – the first complete edition of his works in English – translated by Carl Richard Mueller, and published as a Mermaid Dramabook, one of a series by Hill and Wang comprising plays by both classical and contemporary playwrights. In the Introduction the translator summarizes the recent realization of the stature and status of this once forgotten nineteenth-century German literary figure who, in his short lifetime,

> ...wrote three plays, two of them so extraordinary that they have served as the impetus for literary movements down to the present day's Theatre of the Absurd. Theodore Hoffman has recently listed them as Naturalism, Social Realism, Psychological Irrationalism, Expressionism, and Existential Theatre. He is the seemingly inexhaustible source of modern drama and has been universally extolled by the leaders of the aforementioned movements. And yet, though he was far ahead of his own time, and though he sank into virtual oblivion after his death, until his rediscovery by the first of the great Naturalist playwrights, Gerhart Hauptmann, he is still in advance of our own age. Only time will demonstrate what new movements he will father for future generations.

The publication of Ferdinand Raimund's *The Spendthrift: A Musical Fairy Tale in Three Acts* (New York, 1949), introduced American readers to the Viennese playwright, whose dramatic works have had a perennial appeal in his own country and have been quite regularly revived on the Vienna stage, but who is scarcely known beyond the boundaries of Austria, certainly not in the United States.[1] 'This first English edition of any of Raimund's works,'[2] as asserted by the translator and adaptor, Erwin Tramer, in the Preface, was published for the very purpose of acquainting 'the English-speaking public with this great

---

[1] It is worthy of note that, on the German stages that came into existence following the great influx of German immigrants into the United States after 1848, Raimund's plays in the original were performed in impressive numbers. But the apparently successful performances in German by German-Americans failed to inspire any performances in English on the American stage or any published translations of his plays for English-reading Americans. A study entitled 'The Reception of Raimund and Nestroy in England and America' by O. Paul Straubinger (in *Österreich und die angelsächsische Welt*, ed. Otto Hietsch [Vienna, 1961], pp. 481-494), clearly confirms the fact that Raimund has been accorded almost no reception at all in this country, while in Austria both Raimund and Nestroy enjoy a continuing popularity that 'can be attributed largely to local tradition and sentiment' (p. 490).
[2] This is essentially accurate, although Morgan's *Bibliography* (no. 7306a) records a translation of *Der Alpenkönig* (1850?).

dramatist, so undeservedly neglected for over a century.' In fact, as Tramer further asserts, 'there seem to be only two [previously] published translations [of Raimund's works], both of *Der Verschwender:* one into Czech, as *Marnotratník,* and one entitled *La Malŝparulo,* which is Esperanto, the language so many know of and so few know.'

Recognition in the United States of another Austrian dramatist, Franz Grillparzer, has been accorded not only belatedly but also to a relatively limited degree.[1] Indeed, even today, although his name may have become familiar, however slightly, to American readers, even that familiarity may be due solely to the persistent devotion of two scholars whose energetic efforts have been responsible exclusively for the appearance of recent translations of ten of Grillparzer's dramas. As late as 1907 Gustav Pollak, in the Preface to his study, *Franz Grillparzer and the Austrian Drama* (New York, 1907), claimed for his volume 'no higher merit than that of being, strange to say, the first attempt to

[1] Arthur Burkhard, in *Franz Grillparzer in England and America* (Vienna, 1961), establishes quite conclusively that Grillparzer and his plays are, indeed, little known in the United States and less so in England, although his study furnishes evidence of the 'staging of seven of Grillparzer's plays in more than one hundred performances in all sections of the country from New York to San Francisco, from St. Paul to New Orleans' (p. 20). In this volume, Burkhard presents, in addition to an annotated bibliography of works on Grillparzer in England and America, an account of the performances of Grillparzer's plays in the two countries, together with a detailed discussion of Grillparzer's works in English translation. Chapter 3 of this volume, entitled 'Grillparzer in English Translation,' is an expansion of the subject treated by the same author under the identical title in *Österreich und die angelsächsische Welt* (ed. Otto Hietsch [Vienna, 1961], pp. 411-417). In comparing the nature of the reception accorded to Grillparzer in the United States with that accorded him in England, Burkhard concludes in the first-mentioned study: 'America may have rendered Grillparzer greater service on the stage than England; in the field of criticism, however, the British output, though not always so voluminous, is discreet and discriminating' (p. 11). Ernest Reinhold, in 'The Reception of Franz Grillparzer's Works in England during the Nineteenth Century' (unpubl. diss., Univ. of Michigan, 1956), after an analysis of articles and reviews in British periodicals, translations, scholarly publications, and stage productions, concludes that indifference toward Grillparzer, which characterized the nineteenth-century British attitude, has ended. 'The present ...century has corrected earlier misunderstandings and revised scholarly opinions of his works. Though not a popular success as in German-speaking countries, Franz Grillparzer is being recognized in England as the greatest dramatist after Schiller' (*Dissertation Abstracts,* XVII [Ann Arbor, 1957], 146). Also examining the British reception of Grillparzer during the nineteenth century, O. Paul Straubinger, in 'Grillparzer's Reception in England' (*Moderne Sprachen,* IV [Nov.-Dec., 1959], 20-25), confirms 'with regret that the interest which has been shown was largely academic' (p. 25).

acquaint American and English readers with the dramatist and the man. The translations are, as far as I am aware, the first English renderings, "Sappho" alone excepted, of any of the beauties of the original.' Although Pollak is in error, strictly speaking, in believing his translations to be the very first in English of Grillparzer's dramas,[1] his claim is, generally speaking, correct; and even he supplies only selections in translation. Pollak translated *König Ottokars Glück und Ende* most fully, with some twenty-two hundred lines from a total of nearly three thousand of the original German; his selections for translations are much shorter from other dramas: *Sappho, Das goldene Vliess, Ein treuer Diener seines Herrn, Des Meeres und der Liebe Wellen, Weh dem, der lügt, Esther, Libussa, Die Jüdin von Toledo*, and *Ein Bruderzwist in Habsburg*. And even Pollak's interest, although manifested by the publication of his volume in this country, seems to reflect not so much a genuine American interest in Grillparzer as a zealous conviction, originating within his own Austrian background, to proclaim among 'an English-speaking audience not only the potency of Grillparzer's own genius, but also the peculiar fascination inherent in the work of two other authors who have shed lustre on their Austrian fatherland.... German in speech and training, they are yet Austrian to the core.' Accordingly, the first two chapters treat Ferdinand Raimund and Ludwig Anzengruber, 'two dramatists in particular, unknown to the English-speaking world, [who] have touched the German heart with all the magic power of genius,' and who, with Grillparzer, reveal 'the native genius of Austrian poetry.' As a further indication of the nationalistic piety with which Pollak was inspired and motivated, his book is dedicated 'to the memory of my parents who sleep in Austrian soil.'

The sesquicentennial year of Grillparzer's birth in 1941 passed virtually without popular notice in the United States, while in Germany and Austria

---

[1] In 1879, *Medea*, translated by F. W. Thurstan and S. A. Wittmann, was published in London (see Morgan's *Bibliography*, no. 3102); Thomas Carlyle had also translated a few lines of *König Ottokar* in an essay entitled 'German Playwrights,' which originally appeared in 1829 in the *Foreign Review*, No. 6, and which was subsequently reprinted in his *Critical and Miscellaneous Essays Collected and Republished* (London, 1840; see *Bibliography*, no. 3100).

it elicited a number of written tributes to his memory.[1] And aside from the work of one translator, Herman L. Spahr, whose translation of *The Ancestress* (Hopeville, Ga.) was published in 1938, no English translations of Grillparzer's dramas would be available today, were it not for the work of Henry H. Stevens and Arthur Burkhard. Beginning in 1938, these two scholars have translated into English verse no fewer than ten of Grillparzer's dramas. The record of their translation activity can best be observed by listing the translations, all of which, with a single exception, were published by The Register Press in Yarmouthport, Massachusetts:

> *Hero and Leander*, tr. Henry H. Stevens, 1938.
> *King Ottokar, His Rise and Fall*, tr. Henry H. Stevens, 1938.
> *Thou Shalt Not Lie*, tr. Henry H. Stevens, 1939.
> *Family Strife in Hapsburg*, tr. Arthur Burkhard, 1940; republished, 1949.
> *A Faithful Servant of His Master*, tr. Arthur Burkhard, 1941.
> *Libussa*, tr. Henry H. Stevens, 1941.
> *Medea*, tr. Arthur Burkhard, 1941; revised, 1956.
> *The Guest-Friend* and *The Argonauts* (bound together), tr. Arthur Burkhard, 1942.
> *The Golden Fleece* (*The Guest-Friend*, *The Argonauts*, and *Medea*), tr. Arthur Burkhard, 1942.
> *A Dream is Life*, tr. Henry H. Stevens, 1946.
> *The Golden Fleece*, '1947 reprint of the original [1942] edition'; 'Printed in Germany by F. Bruckmann KG., Munich, Bavaria.'
> *Family Strife in Hapsburg*, tr. Arthur Burkhard, reprint of the 1940 edition, 1949.
> *Sappho*, tr. Arthur Burkhard, 1953.
> *The Jewess of Toledo* and *Esther*, tr. Arthur Burkhard, 1953.
> *Medea*, tr. Arthur Burkhard, 'Third revised edition,' 1956.
> *Hero and Leander*, (newly) tr. Arthur Burkhard, 1962.
> *King Ottokar, His Rise and Fall*, (newly) tr. Arthur Burkhard, 1962.

In addition to these translations, there is another, unpublished translation of *Hero and Leander* by B. Q. Morgan, which, like a number of his other

---

[1] For an exhaustive bibliography of Grillparzer, which contains more than five hundred items, which spans a fifteen-year period encompassing the anniversary year, and which includes literature about Grillparzer, complete and individual editions of his works, as well as translations of his works into eight foreign languages (Bulgarian, Czech, English, French, Dutch, Italian, Romansch, and Swedish), see O. Paul Straubinger, 'Grillparzer-Bibliographie: 1937-1952,' *Jahrbuch der Grillparzer-Gesellschaft, Dritte Folge/Erster Band* (Vienna, 1953), pp. 34-80.

translations of German dramas, exists in typescript in Morgan's personal possession and as a microfilm in the library of Columbia University (see *The National Union Catalog... 1958-1962*). Only two of Grillparzer's non-dramatic works have ever appeared in English. *The Poor Musician* translated by Alfred Remy, together with 'My Journey to Weimar,' from Grillparzer's autobiography, also translated by Remy, appeared in Volume Six of The German Classics. Other than the translations by Stevens and Burkhard, mentioned above, *The Poor Fiddler*, translated by E. B. Ashton (pseudonym of Ernst Basch) and included in Kesten's anthology, *The Blue Flower*, was the only published work of Grillparzer's to appear during the period under survey.

Unlike Franz Grillparzer, Friedrich Hebbel has never had any single champion in the United States, and although his works had earlier appeared in English translation in more impressive numbers than Grillparzer's, he is less well represented by translations of his works published in the United States between 1945 and 1960, when none of his poetry and only one of his plays appeared in print.[1]

If no single translator or team of translators has concentrated on Hebbel's works, there are nonetheless two publications which together were responsible for the appearance early in the century of six different

---

[1] A comparison of the recognition accorded Hebbel and Grillparzer, both among German-speaking and English-speaking audiences, is drawn by Ronald Peacock who writes: 'Hebbel is a lesser artist than Grillparzer; but such is the magnetic hold of abstract ideas over the German mind that his countrymen have always accounted him the more important poet. Those who accuse Grillparzer of shallowness because they cannot find in his art a religion or a "Weltanschauung" turn with relief to Hebbel's profundities; and the name of "Grübler" – the man who broods and broods – that Hebbel earned for himself loses on their lips any critical reservation it might imply and becomes simple homage. Perhaps it is the rank given by his countrymen that explains why he has been translated into English and assigned his niche in the Everyman Library, whilst Grillparzer remains comparatively unknown' (Ronald Peacock, *The Poet in the Theatre* [New York, 1946], p. 64). The volume of the Everyman Library to which Peacock refers contains three of Hebbel's dramas, *Gyges and His Ring*, *Herod and Mariamne*, and *Maria Magdalena*, and was first published in 1914.

See Walter A. Reichart, 'Hebbel in Amerika und England: Eine Bibliographie,' *Hebbel Jahrbuch 1961* (Heide in Holstein, 1961), pp. 118-135, for a listing of all the translations and printings of Hebbel's works (in periodicals, anthologies, and including school editions) published in the United States and England, and of the critical studies of Hebbel's work, from 1862 to 1961.

translations of five of his works. In *Poet Lore, A Magazine of Letters*[1] appeared *Agnes Bernauer*, translated by Loveen Pattee (volume 20 [1909]), *Judith*, translated by Carl van Doren (volume 25 [1914]), and *Maria Magdalena*, translated by Paula Green (volume 25 [1914]). Volume Nine of The German Classics also contained two of Hebbel's dramas and one of his stories, plus some of his miscellaneous writing: *Maria Magdalena*, translated by Paul Bernard Thomas, *Siegfried's Death*, translated by Katherine Royce, and *Anna*, translated by Francis H. King. The only work of Hebbel to be published in the United States during the sixteen years surveyed here was an English verse translation of his drama *Herod and Mariamne* (Univ. of N. Car. Stud. in Germ. Langs. and Lits., No. 3 [Chapel Hill, 1950]), asserted by the translator, Paul H. Curts, to be 'probably the greatest German drama of the nineteenth century.' That a drama of this import has been so neglected, both among the reading public – it had been translated only once before, in 1912 – and in the theatre, even in Germany, is explained by Curts in his Introductory Note: '*Herod and Mariamne* will never enjoy wide popularity with the masses. To appreciate Hebbel the audience must think as well as feel, and that is not the mood in which most people attend the theatre.' Perhaps this comment also explains the reason that this single drama of Hebbel's to appear in this country was published under academic auspices. Two additional dramas of Hebbel's were translated by B. Q. Morgan, *Agnes Bernauer* and *The Nibelungs*, but they have remained unpublished, existing as microfilms of Morgan's typescript copies, deposited in 1958 in the library of Columbia University (see *The National Union Catalog... 1958-1962*). On the other hand, a new translation of *Maria Magdalena* by Carl Richard Mueller has been published at San Francisco in 1962, which date is beyond the limits of this study, possibly suggesting some very recent renewal of interest and possibly hinting of an attempt to correct the previous neglect of Hebbel in the United States.

---

[1] The extent to which this magazine has been responsible for the influx of German literature in English translation in the United States can be ascertained by consulting the bibliography presented by Hermann Barnstorff in 'German Literature in Translation Published by Poet Lore, 1891-1939,' *MLJ*, XXV (1941), 711-715.

Writers of the Later Years

German literature of the later nineteenth and early twentieth centuries in English translations that appeared after 1945 is represented, to a somewhat greater degree than has been noted heretofore, in general anthologies of German or other continental literature. This is due to the fact that the *Novellen* of Gottfried Keller, Theodore Storm, and Conrad Ferdinand Meyer have been less frequently published as separate volumes, as is also the case with the plays of Arthur Schnitzler and Frank Wedekind. Further reason for this phenomenon is that both literary forms, the *Novelle* and the play, like poetry, naturally lend themselves to inclusion in anthologies.

At first thought, the recent publication of a work by Friedrich Gerstäcker in English translation may be somewhat surprising, for although during his lifetime and until the turn of the century he was quite popular in this country – understandably, since the scene of a number of his stories is laid in the United States, and he himself lived here from 1837 to 1843[1] – his popularity here since that time has waned and few translations of his works have been published in the United States in the present century. The two translations of his works that have appeared since 1945 hardly presage any revival of American interest in Gerstäcker, especially since both reflect special circumstances. *California Gold Mines* (Oakland, California, 1946), with a foreword by Joseph A. Sullivan, was published in an edition limited to five hundred copies as the sixth volume of the California Centennial Series. The text consists of selections from an undated edition by Harper of *Travels Round*

---

[1] For an account of Gerstäcker's first American visit, see George H. R. O'Donnell, 'Gerstäcker in America, 1837-1843,' *PMLA*, XLII (1927), 1036-43. Gerstäcker also visited the United States on two subsequent occasions, both times much more briefly than on the first occasion, once while on a journey around the world from 1849 to 1852, and nearly two decades later while on another extended trip from 1867 to 1868. Gerstäcker's picture of America as revealed in his numerous volumes is examined by A. J. Prahl in 'America in the Works of Gerstäcker,' *MLQ*, IV (1943), 213-224. More recently Bjarne Emil Landa, in 'The American Scene in Friedrich Gerstäcker's Works of Fiction' (unpubl. diss., Univ. of Minnesota, 1952), has presented a fuller study of Gerstäcker's portrayal of America, concluding that 'the vision of America rendered in Gerstäcker's fiction is obtained principally through the medium of German immigrants' (*Dissertation Abstracts*, XII [Ann Arbor, 1952], 424).

the World, itself a translation of Gerstäcker's *Reisen*. This volume was preceded in 1942 by his *Scenes of Life in California* (San Francisco), which is a translation by George Cosgrave, not directly from the German original, *Kalifornische Skizzen* (1856), but from a French version by Revilliod, *Scènes de la vie californienne* (1859). Gerstäcker's most popular story, *Germelshausen*, was newly translated by Alexander Gode-von Aesch and published by Barron's Educational Series (Great Neck, N.Y., 1958). The frequent use of *Germelshausen* as a school text doubtless accounts for the comparatively wide acquaintance of Americans with this story. It was not long after the Broadway musical 'Brigadoon' opened at the Ziegfeld Theatre on March 13, 1947, that a letter to the editor appeared in the 'Drama Mailbag' of the New York *Times* which pointed out the similarity of the plot to that of Gerstäcker's *Germelshausen* which, the writer of the letter revealed, she had been required to read as a student in a German class.[1]

Still quite popular today in Germany, especially among children and young people, is Karl May, who, like Gerstäcker, was a prolific author of exotic adventure stories and tales of travel, but who, unlike Gerstäcker, has never been known in the United States in spite of the fact that the plots of many of his stories are laid in this country among the American Indians. As a matter of fact, as far as can be determined, none of his works in translation had ever been published in the United States or in England before the year 1955 when *In the Desert*, translated earlier by F. Billerbeck-Gentz and subsequently edited by M. A. de Becker and C. A. Willoughby, was published simultaneously in Bamberg and New York. As recently as 1936 one American, in a popular article entitled

[1] Written by Beth Herber, this letter appeared together with a reply elicited from the author of 'Brigadoon,' Alan Jay Lerner, in which he labels the similarity of his plot to that of Gerstäcker an 'unconscious coincidence,' asserting that 'legends of disappearing towns can be found in the folklore of many, many countries' ('Reader Questions Origin of "Brigadoon" and Gets Author Lerner's Reply,' New York *Times* [Mar. 30, 1947], Sec. 2, p. 7). However, John T. Krumpelmann, in 'Gerstäcker's *Germelshausen* and Lerner's *Brigadoon*,' *MDU*, XL (1948), 396-400, where he undertakes a comparative study of the two works, concludes that in spite of much wide divergence in treatment of the theme, 'internal evidence indicates that the author of this musical play had *Germelshausen* well in mind when he was composing *Brigadoon* and that he may also have had some knowledge of Gerstäcker's *Die versunkene Stadt*' (p. 400).

'Karl May: Germany's James Fenimore Cooper' – one of the very few articles on May ever to appear in an American periodical – reported that prior to her trip to Germany the previous year, she had never heard of Karl May, yet in Germany, this author's 'dozen or more books about the American frontier... have had a sale in the German language alone of over six million volumes,' ranking Karl May as a 'best-seller, a rating which he has had for three generations.' This account she closed with an enthusiastic, if illogical, endorsement: 'I recommend the books... not only because they are good stories, but because despite the subject matter and the painstaking effort at accuracy they remain so essentially un-American, so German and as such romantic in their point of view.'[1] If she is correct in her observation that May's treatment of so thoroughly American a subject as the Indians of the West remains un-American, then it might well be excepted that American readers would find his works artificial and therefore unwelcome.[2]

[1] Helen Appleton Read, *A-GR*, II (June, 1936), 4-6. Explaining that at one time schoolboys were punished for reading May's books because they were 'supposed to distract the mind of the student from more serious matters and engender a dangerous *Wanderlust*,' and because 'they were credited with impairing the taste for good literature,' Mrs. Read offers the following reason for the fact that in Germany 'today there is definite vogue for Karl May. Perhaps it can be explained on the grounds that the books extol the heroic attitude towards life and the ideal of comradeship which are the twin *leitmotivs* of the present [Nazi] *Weltanschauung* in Germany. But as a matter of fact, Karl May enthusiasts tell me that no explanation is necessary other than the simple fact that the books continue to be among the best adventure stories that have been written in the German language and that therefore their appeal is perennial.' Claiming that Cooper's Leatherstocking Series, 'as celebrated in Germany as it is in America,' provided the inspiration for May's stories of the American frontier, Mrs. Read further points out: 'It must not be forgotten at this point that Goethe was responsible for the great vogue in Germany for the so-called "Indianische Romantik." James Fenimore Cooper was his avowed favorite American author – a preference which, in view of the respect accorded any opinion expressed by the sage of Weimar, became an esthetic canon. Furthermore, his advice that anyone using similar material should model his work on the Leatherstocking Series accounts for the Cooperesque formula which Karl May adopted.'

[2] In reference to May's unhappy treatment of America in his many novels, Klaus Mann, in an article entitled 'Dream-America,' *Accent*, VIII(1947-1948), 173-184, considers two German-writing novelists who 'conjured up a dream land they chose to christen "America"' (p. 175): Franz Kafka and Karl May. Contrasting Kafka, 'a genius,' to May, whom he refers to as 'an unusually cheap and puerile story-teller,' Mann attacks May for his stories of America in which 'there is hardly a single detail ...that is not a complete and ludicrous misrepresentation' (p. 178), and in which 'the Dream-America he presents is not only a

Although universally recognized as of incomparably greater stature than Gerstäcker or May, the Swiss writer, Gottfried Keller, in spite of all the panegyrics honoring him, not only by German critics and scholars but also by Americans, has achieved a very limited reception in the United States among readers of English, for his works have never been widely translated into English. Called 'the greatest narrative writer that Switzerland has produced' (by Wolf von Schierbrand in the Preface to *Seldwyla Folks: Three Singular Tales* [New York, 1919]),[1] 'the great-

gross falsification but also a vicious insult' (p. 180). May's stories, Mann claims, 'nourished' the imagination of the young Hitler: 'The Third Reich marked Karl May's ultimate triumph, the ghastly realization of his puerile and immoral dreams. It is according to his ethical and aesthetic standards that the Austrian house-painter, nourished in his youth by Old Shatterhand, attempted to re-build the world. He and his henchmen were desperadoes in the good old Karl May tradition – perverted romanticists, infantile, criminal, irresponsible. Hopelessly estranged from both reality and art, those reckless fantasts and murderous adventurers were ready to sacrifice all civilization and common sense on the altar of "heroism" – the evil, atavistic kind of "heroism" preached and dramatized by their literary master and predecessor, Karl May of Saxony' (p. 179).

[1] Von Schierbrand, as early as 1919, explored reasons for Keller's obscurity in English-speaking areas, which to be sure, provided only a partial answer for that decade and subsequently: 'The question may well be asked how it is that the literary lifework of such a man as Gottfried Keller has for so many years been denied the most sincere form of homage, that of translation, by the whole non-German-speaking world. There may be additional reasons for this seeming neglect, but I believe the chief one lies in the fact of the unusual difficulty of the task. To cast the thoughts and conceits of an individualistic writer into another vehicle of speech is in itself no easy matter. But in the case of Gottfried Keller it is especially so. For the man ... was a Swiss, not by any manner of means a German. And not only is the subject matter of his lyrical and epical output strongly tinged with Helvetism, but his very language as well. The Swiss-German vernacular is more than a mere dialect; it is almost a tongue of its own. On all but the few solemn and formal occasions of life the Swiss expresses himself in what he terms "Schwyzer-Dütsch," which is indeed scarcely understood by persons habituated to German proper, and even when the Swiss author perforce drops into the latter he uses so many peculiarly Helvetian terms and modes of speech, so many archaic saws, his whole method of handling the language is so different that to reshape what he says into another tongue without doing violence to the spirit, the soul, the flower and thus marring the translation irretrievably and doing gross injustice to the original becomes doubly hard.' That Keller is not known in this country was decried already during his lifetime, as evidenced by a twelve-page, double-column article on Keller entitled 'A Swiss Novelist' by Helen Zimmern, reprinted from *Frazer's Magazine*, (Vol. CI [1880], pp. 459-465), in *Littell's Living Age* for May 8, 1880 (Vol. CXLV, pp. 368-379), and in *Appleton's Journal* for June, 1880 (New Series, Vol. VIII, pp. 368-379), in which the author exclaims: 'Has it ever occurred to one person in twenty to find out whether Switzerland boasts a contemporary literature?... Better still, who has read Gottfried Keller?'

est of the German-Swiss poets' and 'one of the most original minds in nineteenth century German letters' (by B. Q. Morgan in the Introduction to *A Village Romeo and Juliet* [New York, 1955]), and regarded (by George Lukács) as the greatest German narrator since Goethe, Keller, as a writer who elicits such epithets, has been accorded a relatively limited reception in the United States until quite recently. Before 1945 translations of only a few of his poems had found their way into anthologies, few of his individual stories were available in recently published editions, and only a single chapter from *Der Grüne Heinrich* had been translated as a sample to readers of English of Keller's qualities as a novelist – a meagre sampling, in view of the fact that the Fränkel-Helbing edition of his *Sämmtliche Werke* (Bern, 1931-1948) fills twenty-two volumes. During the period under study several of his stories, all previously translated, appeared in anthologies: *Spiegel, the Kitten* in Kesten's *The Blue Flower; The Virgin as Nun* in Marjorie Fischer's *Strange to Tell; The Naughty Saint Vitalis* in Lange's *Great German Short Novels and Stories;* and *A Little Legend of the Dance* in Spender's *Great German Short Stories*. A new translation of *Meret* by Mary Hottinger is included in Angel Flores' anthology. In 1953, *Legends and People*, a volume strikingly illustrated by Joseph Low and published by Story Classics (a division of Rodale Press), contained *Spiegel the Cat*, based on a translation by E. B. Ashton (pseudonym of Ernst Basch) and taken from Kesten's anthology; *Clothes Make the Man*, based on a translation by Käthe Freiligrath Kroeker; also three of the *Sieben Legenden: Eugenia, The Virgin and the Devil*, and *The Virgin as Knight*, all translated by Martin Wyness, whose translations of all seven of the legends had been published in both London and New York in 1911. The most frequently translated of Keller's works has been *Romeo und Julia auf dem Dorfe*; a translation, entitled *A Village Romeo and Juliet*, by Paul Bernard Thomas with the collaboration of B. Q. Morgan, was published in 1955 and again in 1960 by Frederick Ungar – apparently the same translation which about forty years earlier appeared in Volume Fourteen of The German Classics, where according to Morgan's *Bibliography*, both Thomas and Morgan had already collaborated on the translation although the volume itself mentions only Thomas. Most significant for a fuller appreciation of Keller in the United States is the appearance of the first translation of his massive developmental novel, *Green Henry*, translated by A. M. Holt and published by Grove Press in 1960, more than a century after its author finished the first version of this his first novel. Reaction to the work, as indicated through reviews, was generally favorable. One reviewer wrote: 'Beyond showing in an unobtrusively convincing manner how a character is formed, it spreads before the reader a multitude of remarkable persons and a wealth of universal experience. The warmth Keller poured into his books has not cooled off; the colors he used have not faded' (E. S. Pisko in the *Christian Science Monitor*, Jan. 26, 1961, p. 5).

Keller's compatriot and contemporary, Conrad Ferdinand Meyer, has been even less well known in the United States, and the sixteen years surveyed in the present study reveal little that has been published to acquaint American reading audiences with him. Indeed, no separate volume of a work or works by Meyer appeared between 1945 and 1960, and of the anthologies examined, only one, Lange's *Great German Short Novels and Stories*, contained a single story of his, *Plautus in the Convent*, a translation by William Guild Howard that first appeared in Volume Fourteen of The German Classics.[1]

[1] Meyer, despite his obscurity in English translation, continues to be the subject of scholarly attention, as evidenced by several recent American and British studies. Heinrich Henel, in his study of *The Poetry of Conrad Ferdinand Meyer* (Madison, 1954), reveals that apparently even in Switzerland and Germany attention to Meyer has been only peripheral, for 'there is no critical edition of Conrad Ferdinand Meyer's *Gedichte*, and a large mass of poems and preliminary versions has never been published.... The definitive fifth edition of the *Gedichte* contains only 231 poems, but a serious study of Meyer's work must take account of a body of poems about four times as large which is available only in manuscript' (p. vii). A complementary volume is W. D. Williams' study of *The Stories of Conrad Ferdinand Meyer* (Oxford, 1962), in the Preface to which the author confirms that also in England, as in the United States, Meyer has attracted but little attention: 'Conrad Ferdinand Meyer is one of the neglected masters of the short story. His work has long been the subject of some critical attention on the Continent but has not been at all widely noticed in this country. There are some signs that English readers are beginning to acquire some familiarity with the work of German writers of this and the last century, for so long inexplicably and unjustifiably neglected, and we may look forward to a new understanding in this island of the manifold and varied splendours achieved in German in the short-story form. Certainly, in any such awakening, Meyer's stories will play their part, ...' Another recent, American, study is Stuart Alyn Friebert's 'A Chronicle of Conrad Ferdinand Meyer's Life with a

Theodor Storm, a North German contemporary of Switzerland's Keller and Meyer who, like them, was both a lyrical poet and a writer of prose, has been translated only slightly more often than Meyer, but not nearly so frequently as Keller; and were it not for the rather numerous translations of one of his stories, *Immensee*, he would scarcely even have been represented in English at all. The number of English translations of this one work of Storm's is doubtless related to the fact that *Immensee*, like Gerstäcker's *Germelshausen*, had long been a perennial classroom favorite and had been introduced to many Americans in one or another of numerous textbook editions.[1] Morgan's *Bibliography* indicates that prior to 1945 translations of only two of his stories, *Der Schimmelreiter* and *Immensee*, had ever been published in the United States. And Storm's most popular story accounts for his being represented in English translation on two occasions between 1945 and 1960, when *Immensee*, in a literal translation by Guenther Reinhardt, was published in 1950 by Barron's Educational Series, and again, when the same story, in an older translation by C. W. Bell, first published in London in 1919, was included in Lange's anthology of German stories. In 1956 two of Storm's stories appeared in an English version for the first time: *Viola Tricolor, The Little Stepmother*, translated by B. Q. Morgan, and *Curator Carsten*, translated by Frieda M. Voigt, published in one volume by Friedrich Ungar.

Comparatively wide interest in the United States in Gerhart Hauptmann

Collection of His Comments on His Own Works' (unpubl. diss., Univ. of Wisconsin, 1958), which consists, in addition to an account of Meyer's life, of a chronologically arranged collection of his remarks concerning his own works.

[1] The relationship between the extensive classroom use of the story, American acquaintance with the name of Theodor Storm, and the number of times the story has appeared in English is suggested by comments of Matthew Taylor Mellon in the Translator's Note to his translation of *Immensee* (New York, 1937): 'Although the name of Theodore Storm is certainly not one of the greatest in German literature, it is perhaps almost as well known in America as that of Goethe and Schiller. This is because his little novels, particularly *Immensee*, have been used for years as required reading in German classes. Thousands of students have plodded their way through its pages at the rate of thirty lines a day, yet few have retained any connected idea of the story. It is my hope that this translation may awaken in some a desire to reread the German original, ...' Mellon's volume is 'dedicated to the memory of Heinrich Unverhau, friend and teacher, with whom I first read *Immensee*.'

and his works, stimulated at least partially by his first personal visit to America in 1894, was intensified upon his receiving the Nobel Prize in 1912,[1] and was revived by another visit to the United States in February and March, 1932, for the American observance of the Goethe Centennial. The record of Hauptmann's critical and popular reception in this country has been investigated in detail by Edith Cappel in 'The Reception of Gerhart Hauptmann in the United States' (unpub. diss., Columbia Univ., 1952), a study of the critical opinion and evaluation of Hauptmann as reflected in newspapers, books, and periodicals over a period of fifty-five years, between 1892 and 1947. Noting that Hauptmann has failed 'to achieve in America that recognition as a world literary figure which Europe, as early as 1922 [sic], had accorded him in the Nobel Prize award,' Miss Cappel summarizes the record of American interest in Germany's winner of the Nobel Prize as follows:

> Interest in Hauptmann and his work varied greatly between 1894 and 1947, the high points being marked by the production or publication of his works, or events of importance to the poet, such as the Nobel award in 1912, his sixtieth anniversary in 1922 and his visit to America in 1932. The low point was reached twice – during World War I, when the publication of Lewisohn's *Dramatic Works* almost alone kept Hauptmann alive in this country, and during World War II, when his ambiguous attitude toward the Third Reich subjected him to attack by American critics. During the Thirties and Forties scholarly studies far outweighed the popular newspaper and periodical notices which had been numerous in the early decades. (Quoted from *Dissertation Abstracts*, 13 [1953], 89-90).

The 'low point' reached during the Second World War, referred to by Miss Cappel, is confirmed by an authoritative bibliography of Hauptmann in America, in which the publication of only one translation is listed in the year 1936, none in the years 1937, 1938, and 1939, one in 1940, two in 1941, none in 1942, one in 1943, and none in the concluding

---

[1] Hauptmann, the fourth of six Germans to win the Nobel Prize Award in Literature, was granted this distinction 'principally for his rich, versatile, and prominent activity in the realm of the drama' (inscription with the Nobel Prize Award in Literature, 1912, quoted in Annie Russel Marble, *The Nobel Prize Winners in Literature, 1901-1931* [New York, 1932], p. 133). The other Germans to whom the same award has been presented are Theodor Mommsen (1902), Rudolf Eucken (1908), Paul Heyse (1910), Thomas Mann (1929), and Hermann Hesse (1946).

year of the bibliography.[1] This record stands in sharp contrast to that of earlier years such as 1912, for which five publications of translations are listed, 1914 with seven, or 1917 with six. The greatest single achievement that provided the American reading public an acquaintance with the multifarious facets of Hauptmann's dramatic art was the publication of Ludwig Lewisohn's edition of *The Dramatic Works* (1912-1929) in nine volumes.[2]

Apparently in the case of Hauptmann, there was little correlation between publication of translations and stage productions of his works as records of his popularity in the United States. Important years of his success on the American stage were reached in 1899-1900 and 1906-1907 when *The Sunken Bell*, in an acting version prepared by Charles Henry Meltzer, was presented in a number of cities, with E. H. Sothern playing the role of Heinrich, and Julia Marlowe portraying Rautendelein.[3]

---

[1] See Walter A. Reichart, 'Fifty Years of Hauptmann Study in America (1894-1944): A Bibliography,' *MDU*, XXXVII (1945), 1-31. Consisting of some 700 items, the bibliography is devided into three sections, the entries in each arranged chronologically: 1. American reprints in German, 2. American translations, and 3. Writings about Hauptmann and his works. This bibliography is extended to June, 1962, by Reichart in 'Hauptmann Study in America: A Continuation Bibliography,' *MDU*, LIV (1962), 297-310.

[2] *The Dramatic Works of Gerhart Hauptmann (Authorized Edition)*. On the title page of Volumes One through Seven also appears: Edited by Ludwig Lewisohn, Professor in the Ohio State University. In Volume Eight appears: Translated by Willa and Edwin Muir. No editor or translator is mentioned on the title page of Volume Nine. Volumes One through Eight were published in New York by B. W. Huebsch, Volume Nine by The Viking Press.

[3] For an account of the reception of this dramatic success, see John J. Weisert's 'Critical Reception of Gerhart Hauptmann's "The Sunken Bell" on the American Stage,' *MDU*, XLIII (1951), 221-234. For other studies of Hauptmann's plays produced in the United States, see John C. Blankenagel, 'Early Reception of Hauptmann's *Die Weber* in the United States,' *MLN*, LXVIII (1953), 334-340; and E. H. Dummer, 'Gerhart Hauptmann and the Chicago Stage,' *A-GR*, VI (December, 1939), 17-19. Walter A. Reichart, in 'Gerhart Hauptmann's Dramas on the American Stage,' *Maske und Kothurn: Vierteljahrsschrift für Theaterwissenschaft*, VIII (1962), 223-232, surveys the record of performances of Hauptmann's dramas in German and English in the United States from 1894, when a performance of *Hannele* 'first brought the name of Gerhart Hauptmann before the American public,' to 1924, when 'Eva LeGallienne revived *Hannele* in a series of special matinées at the Court Theatre, but aroused little interest.' Reichart points out that, when Hauptmann visited the United States for the Goethe Centennial in 1932, impressive tributes were paid to him, 'yet the enthusiasm that greeted Hauptmann in New York, Washington, Baltimore, and Boston

Hauptmann seems not to have recovered from the 'low point' of his popularity in the United States, for from 1945 to 1960 only two independent volumes of Hauptmann's works were published in this country.[1] A single paperbound volume containing *The Weavers, Hannele*, and *The Beaver Coat*, newly translated by Horst Frenz and Miles Waggoner, with an introduction by Frenz, was published in 1951 by Rinehart in an edition circulated largely as a college text. This volume was republished in 1959.[2] A translation by B. Q. Morgan of *The Heretic of Soana*, previously published in 1923, appeared in 1958 with an introduction by Harold von Hofe, republished by Friedrich Ungar. Two additional translations by B. Q. Morgan, both unpublished, are recorded as microfilms of typewritten copies: 'The Weavers: A Drama of the Eighteen Forties' and 'The Beaver Coat: A Thieves' Comedy in Four Acts' (see *The Library of Congress Catalog... 1958-1962*). Hauptmann's short story, *Bahnwärter Thiel*, which had been available in English only once before (in Cerf's anthology of 1933), appeared again in the same English version by Adele S. Seltzer in Lange's anthology.

Arthur Schnitzler, quite popular in the United States during the first several decades of this century,[3] is virtually forgotten by contemporary

---

was largely academic. Universities, scholars and literary men hailed him as a great dramatist, but not a single professional stage presented his work in the theatre.'

[1] Even the centennial year of Hauptmann's birth (1962) aroused but little interest in the United States beyond strictly academic circles. Walter A. Reichart, in a plenary summary of the American activities evoked by the centenary, concludes: 'World War II partially silenced the public acclaim of Hauptmann's work, but *literary historians and scholars* [italics mine] continue to recognize Hauptmann as the representative and most eminent German dramatist since Grillparzer and Hebbel' ('Gerhart Hauptmann: His Work in America,' *A-GR*, XXIX [December, 1962-January, 1963], 4-6, 31). See John J. Weisert's 'The Hauptmann Centenary in America,' *A-GR*, XXIX (April-May, 1963), 11-12, for an account of American publications and commemorative activities evoked by the centennial anniversary of Hauptmann's birth.

[2] It is noteworthy that in 1961, just a year beyond the closing date of this study, a paperbound volume, published by Bantam Books and presumably intended for popular circulation, offered these same three plays together with *Drayman Henschel* and *Rose Bernd*, all translated by Theodore H. Lustig (*Five Plays* [New York, 1961]).

[3] For a detailed examination of Schnitzler's impact in the United States during the first three decades of this century see Beatrice M. Schrumpf's 'The Reception of Arthur Schnitzler in the United States' (unpubl. M. A. thesis, Columbia Univ., 1931). This study establishes that, beginning with 1899, when *Freiwild* was presented in the Irving Place Theatre in

popular reading audiences. The shock of his frank treatment of sex, which doubtless accounted for much of the earlier popular attention he attracted, seems dated to current American readers and theatre-goers and is no longer effective. Although many of his works had been translated, they are, for the most part, now out of print in this country. Were it not for Eric Bentley's effort, even fewer of Schnitzler's works would be currently available, for Bentley's anthologies, *From the Modern Repertoire*, are, as he explains in the Preface to *Series One*, 'a sampling of that remarkable modern repertoire which lies buried in libraries.' It is in *Series One* (1949) that *Round Dance* appears, a translation by Keene Wallis of Schnitzler's *Reigen*. Eric Bentley's own translation, entitled *La Ronde*, of the same work is included in another of the translator's anthologies, Volume Two (1955) of *The Modern Theatre*. Fragments of Bentley's version of *La Ronde* are contained in a paperbound volume entitled *Stories of Scarlet Women*, published in 1955 by the Avon Book

New York City, Schnitzler's reception slowly increased until 1911 when, with the publication of Granville Barker's translation of *Anatol*, the first real notice of the author took place; the nature and extent of his reception vacillated until about 1919 'when we have a falling away in popularity. In the following years Schnitzler "came back," so to speak, and from 1925, when *Fräulein Else* brought new enthusiasm, until the present [1931] his fame has increased almost uninterruptedly' (p. 46). Miss Schrumpf further concludes that 'until approximately 1925 Schnitzler was known chiefly as a play-writer, and primarily as a writer of one-act plays.... In the past five years, however, the tables seem to have turned and Schnitzler is more widely known for his novelettes and short stories' (p. 48). Exploring the factors which determined her conclusions she observes: 'American readers like the deftness of Schnitzler's style and they realize that Schnitzler achieves in a novelette more than many a writer does in a long novel. This of necessity involves a compact, terse style, which results in a book which one can not easily put aside until it is finished' (p. 48).

The study contains a lengthy listing of school editions of Schnitzler's works, translations of his works into English, productions of Schnitzler's plays on stage and screen, articles concerning Schnitzler himself, the principal reviews of works and plays produced, reports of interviews, articles written by Schnitzler for American publication, translators of Schnitzler's works, principal Schnitzler critics, Schnitzler's publishers in the United States, periodicals in which translations from Schnitzler were published, works frequently published, and comparison of the dates of publication of his works in Germany with the dates of first publication of the same works in the United States. A much more recent, but brief survey of Schnitzler's reception in the United States is provided by Herbert Foltinek's 'Arthur Schnitzler in Amerika' (in *Österreich und die angelsächsische Welt*, ed. Otto Hietsch [Vienna, 1961], pp. 207-214), which contains a bibliography of the most important critical articles on Schnitzler published in the United States from 1912 to 1958.

Company. *Anatol* appears in *From the Modern Repertoire: Series Three*, in the English version by H. Granville-Barker, first published in 1911 and long out of print, a version that Morgan calls 'clever, but not Schnitzler' (*Bibliography*, no. 8475). *A Farewell*, translated by Beatrice Marshall, is also included in the Modern Library anthology edited by Lange. The single separately published work of Schnitzler's to appear between 1945 and 1960 is *Casanova's Homecoming* (translator not given), published in 1947 by the Sylvan Press, in 1948 by Avon Book Company, and again in 1949 by the Citadel Press, with illustrations by Rockwell Kent.

Although the passing of time has adversely affected Schnitzler's position in the United States, there is evidence of some renewed scholarly interest in the man and his work. A recent survey by Herbert Foltinek entitled 'Arthur Schnitzler in Amerika' (in *Österreich und die angelsächsische Welt*, ed. Otto Hietsch [Vienna, 1961], pp. 207-215) shows that between 1950 and 1958 three doctoral disertations, one master's thesis, one volume of Schnitzler's correspondence (with Georg Brandes), and six articles appeared in the United States. Very recently an entire volume devoted to studies of Schnitzler made its appearance under the title *Studies in Arthur Schnitzler* (ed. Herbert W. Reichert and Herman Salinger, Univ. of N. Car. Stud. in Germ. Langs. and Lits., No. 42 [Chapel Hill, 1963]).

Like the name of Schnitzler, that of Frank Wedekind is not popularly known in the United States today. Although very few of his plays had been published in England, he had been better represented by published translations of his plays in this country, particularly during the second decade of the century. At one time his plays were also performed on the American stage, but the most recent productions since the Second World War have been less than successful. Very recently, after *The Awakening of Spring* had been presented at the Pocket Theatre in New York City, one critic, referring to the earlier 'shock value of the play' concludes that as 'conveyed in Wedekind it has the quality of a museum piece.' The same critic advises: 'There are plays of historic stature that would better be left on the library shelves or confined to study in drama classes. Such a one is Frank Wedekind's "The Awakening of Spring,"...' (Lewis

Funke, 'Theatre: Wedekind's "The Awakening of Spring,"' New York *Times*, May 13, 1964, p. 50).[1] The 'dated' quality of his works seems to have dimmed, if not obliterated, his name in America – a land for which Wedekind treasured a personal feeling of kinship (originating, undoubtedly, from the fact that his father was a naturalized American citizen and the additional fact that he himself, although born in Hannover, was named Benjamin Franklin Wedekind, which he later abbreviated to Frank).[2]

During the years surveyed in the present study several new translations of previously translated works of Wedekind were published. A volume entitled *Five Tragedies of Sex*, published simultaneously in New York and London in 1952, contained translations by Stephen Spender and F. Fawcett, with an introduction by Lion Feuchtwanger, of *Spring's Awakening, Earth-Spirit, Pandora's Box, Death and the Devil,* and *Castle Wetterstein* – all, except the last, previously rendered into English by other translators; in fact, the first four of these plays constituted an earlier volume entitled *Tragedies of Sex*, which was translated by S. A. Elliot and published in both New York and London in 1923. In addition to *Castle Wetterstein*, another work of Wedekind to be given an initial appearance in English during this time is *The Solar Spectrum (Those Who Buy the Gods of Love); An Idyll from Modern Life, 1893–1894*

---

[1] The adapters of the play, Arthur A. Seidelman and Donald Levin, it should be noted, altered the names of the characters to suggest an American background. Funke comments that 'there is also a suggestion that the locale has been shifted to this country, though that never did seem clear,' to which he adds: 'In any event, whatever the reasons may have been for the changes, they have done nothing to change the fact that "The Awakening of Spring" has been passed by time.'

[2] For an account of Wedekind's family background and his parents' experience in the United States, see Oskar Seidlin, 'Frank Wedekind's German-American Parents,' *A-GR*, XII (August, 1946), 24-26. Like Frank Wedekind, his father, Friedrich Wilhelm, was a physician. His first son, born in the United States, was named Armin, reminiscent of the 'Old Country.' The second and third sons were born in Germany and given names recalling the Wedekinds' years of residence in the 'New World': Benjamin Franklin and William Lincoln. Frank Wedekind's daughter Kadidja made her home in the United States after Hitler's rise to power. Seidlin points out that 'although the great dramatist never came to the United States, he liked to fancy himself as an American citizen (which, of course, he was not), peopled many of his plays with tourists from America (Der Kammersänger, Karl Hetman, der Zwergriese), and showed an eccentric predilection for such American-Indian names as Mine-haha and the like' (p. 26).

(1958?; publisher unknown), translated by Dietrich Faehl in collaboration with Eric Vaughn. *The Marquis of Keith* likewise received its first publication in English during these years, having been translated by Beatrice Gottlieb, in Bentley's *From the Modern Repertoire: Series Two*. A new translation of *Spring's Awakening*, Bentley's own version, appears in Volume Six of *The Modern Theatre*, edited by Bentley. An older translation of Wedekind's short story, *The Burning of Egliswyl*, by Friedrich Eisemann is contained in Lange's collection of German stories. Wedekind's play, *Der Kammersänger*, which appeared as *The Court Singer*, translated by Albert Wilhelm Boesche in Volume Twenty of The German Classics, formed the basis of a one-act opera, *The Tenor* (Bryn Mawr, Pa., 1956), by Hugo Weisgall, with the libretto by Karl Shapiro and Ernst Lert.

During the period of years between 1945 and 1960, as the preceding survey shows, German literature of the nineteenth century was well represented through the publication of translations in the United States. Poetry, particularly that of the Romanticists, was the least well represented, and when it did appear, it was generally under academic auspices. An important, notable exception was the publication of Flores' *Anthology of German Poetry from Hölderlin to Rilke in English Translation*, which, having been issued as a paperbound volume, presumably was intended for popular consumption.

Those writers who were chiefly lyric poets appear least often; others, such as Eichendorff and Mörike, who also produced stories, were generally represented by their prose. But beyond doubt, it was the short story and the tale which dominated the picture of Romantic German literature in the United States. A number of these stories appeared singly in anthologies, others were published as separately bound books. The drama, too, made its impact on the publishing profile, particularly with the plays of Grillparzer. Of special significance was the initial appearance of two plays by authors who had never before been translated into English, Grabbe and Raimund.

From the later nineteenth century several authors, once well received in the United States, seem to be fading from American popular interest, the most important of which is Hauptmann, the only author of his era to have once gained such intensity of American attention as to stimulate a nine-volume edition of his dramas in English – a phenomenon doubtless related to international attention focused on Hauptmann as Germany's fourth winner of the Nobel Prize Award in Literature. Schnitzler and Wedekind have been left behind by even more audacious contemporary American and non-American writers; whether there will be a new evaluation of their works, probing beyond the once immediate appeal of sexual frankness to an appraisal of their art, remains to be seen.

6

THE TWENTIETH CENTURY

The preceding chapters have shown that much, although not all, of German literature written before the beginning of the twentieth century and published in English translation in the United States between the years 1945 and 1960 appeared under academic auspices; moreover, much of the critical reception of German literature of earlier centuries owed its origin specifically to Germanists in universities. To be sure, popular American reception of the poetry of Heine or the tales of the Grimm Brothers, for instance, during the decades of the mid-twentieth century appears indisputable. Yet such important German literary figures as Schnitzler or Hauptmann, although once widely welcomed in this country, today seem safely interred for American posterity chiefly in libraries and universities rather than persisting as part of the experience of the general reader or theater-goer of today.

Reception of German literature of the twentieth century, however, presents a somewhat different picture. In the first place, a much larger number of writers is represented by translations of their works published in the United States. Whereas the whole of German literature of the entire nineteenth century was represented by only approximately twenty literary figures published in translation, there are some two hundred authors of twentieth-century German literature of whose works at least one, and in a number of cases many, appeared in English translation during the years under examination. It is generally true, of course, that any contemporary scene presents a much more multifarious aspect than that same era later displays when viewed with historical perspective. Literary figures that once loomed large in their own era, and indeed may have dominated it for a few years, have frequently passed into oblivion with the dawn of a new era or the maturation of a new generation. Vivid examples of this phenomenon are August von Kotzebue and August Wilhelm Iffland whose plays dominated not only the German stage but also the attention of readers during the last decade of the eighteenth and the first decades of the nineteenth century. Even abroad, in the United States and in England, Kotzebue's plays were received with overwhelming enthusiasm and their author hailed by Sheridan as the 'German Shakespeare.' Now, however, the names of Kotzebue and Iffland have long since been forgotten and are mentioned in histories of literature and literary chronologies chiefly for the sake of completeness. A similar re-evaluation of twentieth-century German literature is bound to be made by future generations under different cultural constellations. Indeed, the process of re-examination for the first decades of the present century has already been in progress for some time, relegating some writers to oblivion and elevating others to new or more permanent importance. It is certainly true that quite a few contemporary writers currently enjoying a popular reception will in time be judged severely and found with little or nothing of significance to offer generations that have succeeded them; certainly reading audiences of the year 2000 will accord a much more limited reception to works written just before, during, and immediately following the Second World War than is the case at present, with the result that a much smaller number of German writers than at present will eventually represent, through translations of their works, the first half of the twentieth century to American readers.

Secondly, German writers of the twentieth century demonstrate perhaps a greater association with the American scene than those of any previous time. Never before have so many German authors visited the United States, traveled across this country, and, particularly during the Second World War, made their home here. Such personal association undoubtedly left its trace upon the literary sensitivity of many of them, developing an unprecedented degree of understanding of the American scene. The political and economic importance of the United States has made America a kind of experience to which many German writers feel compelled to react either positively or negatively, either consciously or unconsciously.

Thirdly, while academic patronage, particularly among Germanists, is responsible for the appearance in the United States of some of the translations from twentieth-century German literature, these auspices account for the appearance of a relatively smaller number than was the case with the translations of literature of preceding centuries. This fact is hardly surprising, and doubtless parallels in the literary history of other cultures might well be found. Surely it is contemporary literature, whatever the era, that generally presents the greatest and broadest popular appeal, and older literature (again, generally speaking) becomes more and more the property of scholars and students. This is true of a literature within its own culture, such as American literature in the United States or German literature in Germany, as well as of literature in translation in another country, such as American literature in Germany or German literature in the United States.

As with earlier centuries treated in the preceding chapters, lyric poetry of the twentieth century is the literary genre represented by the least number of volumes to be published in English translation in the United States, although considerably more of twentieth-century German lyric poetry than that of any earlier era has become available in American-published translations. The publication of several anthologies devoted exclusively to German poetry of the present century, as well as the appearance of separate volumes of poems by individual poets, such as Rilke and George, account for this phenomenon.

In addition to *An Anthology of German Poetry from Hölderlin to Rilke in English Translation* (Garden City, N.Y., 1960), edited by Angel Flores, which was mentioned in the discussion of the nineteenth century, and which includes five lyric poets of the twentieth century (Stefan George, Christian Morgenstern, Hugo von Hofmannsthal, Georg Trakl, and Rainer Maria Rilke), two further anthologies, devoted exclusively to lyric poetry of this century made their appearance in the

United States between the years 1945 and 1960. The one, entitled *Twentieth-Century German Verse* (Princeton, 1952), translated and edited by Herman Salinger, contains forty-three poems of twenty-one poets of the present century. The other, entitled *New Young German Poets* (San Franscisco [sic], 1959), contains forty-one poems of ten poets who, as the editor and translator, Jerome Rothenberg, points out in the Introduction, 'were all born between the outbreak of the First World War and the first years of Nazi rule,' and who 'are part of the generation that's come of age over the ruins of Hitler's psychotic Reich.' They include authors who recently have become quite well known, as well as others who have remained relatively obscure: Karl Krolow, Paul Celan, Helmut Heissenbüttel, Walter Höllerer, Klaus Bremer, Heinz Piontek, Ingeborg Bachmann, Günter Grass, Ernst Jürgen Dreyer, and Hans Magnus Enzensberger. Another volume, entitled *The Penguin Book of German Verse* (Baltimore, 1957), is essentially an anthology of German lyric poetry in the original from the beginning down to the present time with only plain prose translations of each poem.[1]

As far as could be determined, no single volume devoted exclusively to twentieth-century German short stories or tales in English translation

---

[1] More recently, but beyond the period under consideration, four volumes, all bilingual anthologies, have been published in the United States. *Modern German Poetry: 1910–1960* (New York, 1962), edited and with an introduction by Michael Hamburger and Christopher Middleton, is a collection of more than one hundred and fifty poems by fifty-six poets, translated by various translators. *Contemporary German Poetry: An Anthology* (Norfolk, Conn., 1962) contains some one hundred poems by thirty-nine poets, all translated by the editor of the anthology, Gertrude C. Schwebell, and accompanied by an introduction by Victor Lange. Another volume of German poetry, entitled *Twenty German Poets: A Bilingual Collection* (New York, 1962), edited, translated, and introduced by Walter Kaufmann, appeared as a volume in the Modern Library, with half of the poets from the eighteenth and nineteenth centuries (from Goethe to Nietzsche) and the remainder from the twentieth century. Numerous other anthologies of contemporary lyric poetry of international scope contain representative selections from German poets. In many such collections Rilke and Hofmannsthal are very often included; sometimes they alone represent the entire body of lyric poetry written in German in this century even though, paradoxically, neither of them was of German nationality. In another recent volume of German poetry, *German Verse from the 12th to the 20th Century in English Translation* (Chapel Hill, 1963, Univ. of N. Car. Stud. in Germ. Langs. and Lits., No. 44), J. W. Thomas presents poems of more than thirty German poets; the section of the anthology devoted to 'The Modern Poets' offers poems by Nietzsche, George, Hofmannsthal, and Rilke.

was published in the United States during the sixteen-year period following the Second World War. However, three chronologically more comprehensive collections of German stories published during this time also included selections from modern German literature. Victor Lange's *Great German Short Novels and Stories* (New York, 1952), a volume in the Modern Library, includes five twentieth-century authors among the seventeen writers of stories that comprise the collection. This volume under Lange's editorship, replacing an earlier volume of the same title edited by Bennett Cerf and published in the same series in 1933, shows certain trends in the more recent estimate of twentieth-century German authors. In Lange's collection Jakob Wasserman, Stefan Zweig, and Arnold Zweig have been dropped; Frank Wedekind, Heinrich Mann, and Franz Kafka have been added; and Arthur Schnitzler, Gerhart Hauptmann, and Thomas Mann have been retained. More than half of the writers represented in Robert Pick's *German Stories and Tales* (New York, 1954) are from the twentieth century. Stephen Spender's *Great German Short Stories* (New York, 1960) presents the largest number of modern German story-writers in any single collection of German stories; of the seventeen authors that make up his anthology, thirteen are twentieth-century representatives.

There are, of course, numerous anthologies of stories from various countries in which German literature is also well represented. An example of such a volume is *The Best of Modern European Literature (Heart of Europe): An Anthology of Creative Writing in Europe, 1920-1940*, edited by Klaus Mann and Hermann Kesten, a collection first published in New York in 1943 and republished in Philadelphia two years later, which contains mostly very short selections, including some poetry, arranged according to the authors' nationality. Thus Kafka and Rilke are included in the section devoted to writers from Czechoslovakia, whose 'independence of literary nationalism is as typical of Czech letters as their preoccupation with human inferiority, death and ultimate restitution' (Christopher Lazare, in the Introduction [p. 495] to the section 'Czechoslovakia'). Here seven authors from Austria, fifteen from Germany, and two from Switzerland are included among a total of some one hundred and forty writers from twenty countries of Europe.

Another example of an anthology of twentieth-century stories of international scope in which German literature is represented is *Short Novels of the Masters* (New York, 1948), edited by Charles Neider, which contains Kafka's *The Metamorphosis*, in the translation by A. L. Lloyd, and Thomas Mann's *Death in Venice*, translated by H. T. Lowe-Porter. Still another example, from the many anthologies of similar nature, is *Strange to Tell; Stories of the Marvelous and Mysterious* (New York, 1946), edited by Marjorie Fischer and Rolfe Humphries, which is a collection of sixty-eight stories from European literature of several centuries and which includes, from German authors of the twentieth century, Rilke, Thomas Mann, Kafka, Arnold Zweig, and Feuchtwanger. Just as works by Rilke and Hofmannsthal are often included in anthologies of poetry, in anthologies of modern prose (and particularly those designed as text books) Kafka and Thomas Mann are represented most frequently, a fact which is indicative of the stature and international recognition these writers have gained.

As with twentieth-century prose fiction, so also in the case of modern German drama in English translation no single anthology was published in the United States from 1945 to 1960, although a number of volumes in which German drama is included did make their appearance here. Eric Bentley's two series of anthologies of dramatic literature from several countries have been significant in making available translations of two twentieth-century German dramatists. The three volumes entitled *From the Modern Repertoire* (1949-1956) and three volumes of *The Modern Theatre* (1955-1960) contain five different dramas by Brecht and two by Sternheim. Brecht is the playwright most frequently chosen to represent modern German drama in anthologies that contain plays by dramatists of various countries.

The multifarious nature of twentieth-century German literature, viewed, as it must be, without the perspective of historical distance from which future generations examining this period will benefit, complicates any attempt at orderly arrangement or fixed classification of authors, schools, or even genres. Not a few modern literary artists have created works in more than one genre; Rilke, Hesse, Benn, to mention only a few, wrote poetry and prose, Hofmannsthal and Brecht wrote poetry, prose, and drama. This phenomenon, while not unique in modern literature, makes it difficult to classify certain authors, as they are represented in English translations published in the United States, as poets, or novelists, or playwrights. Therefore a generally chronological order, taking cognizance of major literary affiliations, is presented below.

Rilke, perhaps more than any other modern German poet, has enjoyed an enthusiastic, broadly international recognition. His reception in the United States has been of such comparatively great proportions that his name may well be the first, or only, name of a recent German poet that immediately comes to mind among non-specialists in literature. Not only was Rilke responsible in a large measure for the revival of German poetry at the beginning of this century, but his importance to modern poetry beyond the confines of German-speaking areas, and especially in the United States and England, is today generally recognized and gratefully acknowledged.

Even before 1945, the beginning year of the present study, much of Rilke's work had been translated into English, indicating something of the extent of his currency and reception in the English-speaking world by that time.[1] As early as 1939 one critic, himself a poet of renown, in a review of a British translation of Rilke's *Duino Elegies* by J. B. Leishman and Stephen Spender reprinted in the United States (New York, 1939), could write: 'With the appearance of this translation of "Duino Elegies," which, with the "Orpheus Sonnets," form the final flower of his work,

---

[1] The British Germanist, H. M. Waidson, in an article entitled 'Zeitgenössische deutsche Literatur in englischer Übersetzung,' *Deutschunterricht für Ausländer*, VIII (1958), 65-71, investigates 'welche Möglichkeit das breitere englische Publikum hat, welches nur Englisch liest, die zeitgenössische deutsche Dichtung kennenzeulernen,' and attemps to establish 'ein ungefähres Bild der deutschen Literatur des 20. Jahrhunderts, welche zumeist in der Zeit seit 1945 dem englischen Leser geboten worden ist' (p. 65). In relation to Rilke's reception in England he writes: 'Lyrik zu übersetzen fordert eine solche Hingabe und Geduld, dass man kaum erwarten dürfte, dass vieles auf diesem Gebiet gemacht werden könnte. Dennoch hat sich das Werk Rilkes schon vor 1939 in England eingebürgert' (p. 65). Concerning Rilke's influence upon English literature he refers to Stephen Spender's contention 'dass Rilke's Werk von den meisten englischen Dichtern der Zeit auf so eingehende Art betrachtet worden ist wie das Werk selbst von T. S. Eliot,' and adds, 'Dichter, die in den dreissiger Jahren eine führende Rolle spielten, wie W. H. Auden, Edith Sitwell oder Spender, haben bestimmt viele Anregungen von Rilke empfangen' (p. 66).

the bulk of Rilke's poetry is now available in English,...' (W. H. Auden, 'Rilke in English,' *New Republic* [Sept. 6, 1939], pp. 135-136).[1] The extent of the currency, reception, as well as influence of Rilke's works in the United States at the beginning of the Second World War is at least partially summarized by the same critic's comment: 'Not the least interesting phenomenon of the last four years has been the growing influence of Rilke upon English poetry: indeed, Rilke is probably more read and more highly esteemed by English and Americans than by Germans, just as Byron and Poe had a greater influence upon their German and French contemporaries than upon their compatriots' (*ibid.*, p. 136). It is somewhat paradoxical, if not unique, in the history of inter-cultural literary relationships that a poet who himself had had little interest in, or no feeling of sympathy with, or even an overt repulsion toward, another country should become, in that same country, one of the most revered literary artists. Such is the case with Rilke and America. ' "America," ' one critic points out, 'is Rilke's favourite word for those tendencies in modern civilization which he is most afraid of and repelled by – ...'[2] Throughout his lifetime and until

[1] Julius Wirl, in 'Englische Übertragungen von Rilkes erster *Duineser Elegie*, (in *Österreich und die angelsächsische Welt*, ed. Otto Hietsch [Vienna, 1961], pp. 432-453), undertakes a detailed comparative study of this Leishman-Spender English rendition of the first part of Rilke's poem cycle with that by Virginia and Edward Sackville-West (London, 1931), and with a third by Nora Wydenbruck (in *Rilke: Man and Poet* [New York, 1950]). Wirl points out: 'Keines deutschsprachigen Dichters Werk an der – zeitlich grosszügig bemessenen – Jahrhundertwende ist so oft ins britische und ins amerikanische Englische übertragen, keines auch mit so heissem Bemühen von Angelsachsen gedeutet und paraphrasiert worden wie das Rilkes. Im besonderen gilt das von seinen beiden der Form und dem Gehalt nach in sich geschlossensten Verswerken, den *Duineser Elegien* und den *Sonetten an Orpheus*' (p. 433).
[2] See Eudo C. Mason's *Rilke, Europe, and the English-Speaking World* (Cambridge, Eng., 1961), from which this quotation is taken (p. 161), for a discussion of 'Rilke's Real Quarrel with the English-Speaking World' – the title of one of the chapters. Mason quotes from Rilke's literary works, from his personal correspondence, and from reminiscences of acquaintances to establish that Rilke came to 'regard America as representing, so to speak, the diabolic principle in his world, ...' (p. 162) but that 'the word "America" had become for Rilke a designation rather for a code of values and a mental attitude which were repugnant to him than for a country or a people' (p. 161). Rilke himself reveals his attitude toward America in a letter of November 13, 1925, to his Polish translator, Witold Hulewicz, in which, explaining the meaning of his *Duino Elegies*, he declares: 'Noch für unsere Grosseltern war ein "Haus," ein "Brunnen," ein ihnen vertrauter Turm, ja ihr eigenes Kleid, ihr

about a decade after his death, comparatively little interest in Rilke was evident in the United States; yet interest here grew and a full recognition of his genius developed so that today it is in America that several of the most important collections of Rilke manuscripts and materials are deposited, and it is here that a number of the leading Rilke scholars reside and that important Rilke studies have been produced.[1] Few German poets have experienced a currency in the United States as widespread as Rilke.

An authoritative bibliography of English translations of Rilke's works lists a total of nineteen separate volumes published in the United States to the year 1945,[2] the earliest of which was a volume entitled, simply,

Mantel: unendlich mehr, unendlich vertraulicher; fast jedes Ding ein Gefäss, in dem sie Menschliches vorfanden und Menschliches hinzusparten. Nun drängen, von Amerika her, leere gleichgültige Dinge herüber, Schein-Dinge, *Lebens-Attrapen* ... Ein Haus, im amerikanischen Verstande, ein amerikanischer Apfel oder eine dortige Rebe, hat *nichts* gemeinsam mit dem Haus, der Frucht, der Traube, in die Hoffnung und Nachdenklichkeit unserer Vorväter eingegangen war' (*Rainer Maria Rilke: Briefe, Zweiter Band, 1914 bis 1926*, ed. Karl Altheim [Wiesbaden, 1950], p. 483).

[1] Klaus W. Jonas, in 'Rainer Maria Rilke in Amerika,' *Börsenblatt für den deutschen Buchhandel*, Frankfurt edition, No. 82 (Oct. 11, 1963), pp. 1064-1065, states: 'Es gibt kaum ein Land, das weniger Anziehungskraft auf Rilke ausgeübt hat als Amerika. Dem Dichter, der diesen weiten Kontinent nie betreten hat und ihn daher nur von Hörensagen kannte, schien Amerika die Quintessenz alles dessen zu sein, was er im Tiefsten verabscheute. Er glaubte, hierzulande alle Tradition, die ihm so heilig war, zu vermissen, ja geradezu totale kulturelle Ebbe vorzufinden, die ihm im Innersten zuwider war. Wie aber hat dieses Land auf Rilke und sein Werk reagiert? Es ist eine nicht zu leugnende Tatsache, dass Amerika zur Zeit seines Todes, im Dezember 1926 – von ganz wenigen Ausnahmen abgesehen –, keinerlei Vorstellung mit seinem Namen verband. Als einzige amerikanische Zeitung, die von seinem Hinscheiden überhaupt Notiz nahm, widmete die New York *Times* "dem österreichischen Dichter und Freund Rodins" einen Nekrolog von kaum hundert Worten' (p. 1864). In this article Jonas discusses primarily the important Rilke archives found in America, such as the von Mises collection in the Houghton Library at Harvard University and the Rilke collection at Yale University.

[2] See *Rilke in English: A Tentative Bibliography* (Cambridge, Mass., 1947), compiled by Richard von Mises in collaboration with B. J. Morse and M. D. Herter Norton, and copyrighted by Herbert Steiner, late Professor of German at The Pennsylvania State University, since superseded by relevant sections of the *Katalog der Rilke-Sammlung Richard von Mises*, comp. and ed. Paul Obermüller and Herbert Steiner, with Ernst Zinn (Frankfurt am Main, 1966). The very extensive bibliography of Rilke by Walter Ritzer, *Rainer Maria Rilke Bibliographie* (Vienna, 1951), contains only a few references to translations of Rilke's works published in the United States. This gap in Ritzer's work is filled by Adolf E. Schroeder's 'Rainer Maria Rilke in America: A Bibliography, 1926-1951' (*MDU*, XLIV [1952], 27-38), which provides 239 items, including not only translations but also biographical and critical books and articles that appeared in this country from the year of Rilke's death to the twenty-fifth anniversary of his death.

Poems: Rainer Marie Rilke, translated by Jessie Lemont and published in New York in 1918. In 1943 a much expanded volume of Rilke's poems by the same translator was published by Columbia University Press; two years later, in 1945, Lemont's translations of the *Sonnets to Orpheus* and the *Duino Elegies* were published in a single volume by the Fine Editions Press.

All of C. F. MacIntyre's translations of Rilke's poetry have been published by the University of California Press. His translation, together with an introduction and notes, of *The Life of the Virgin Mary* appeared in 1947. His translations of *Selected Poems* (Berkeley) were published in 1956 as the second edition of a volume that had first been published simultaneously in England and the United States in 1940 under the title *Fifty Selected Poems*; a third edition appeared in 1958 and has been reissued subsequently. MacIntyre's translation of the *Sonnets to Orpheus* was published in 1960, followed one year later by his translation of the *Duino Elegies*.

Ludwig Lewisohn, well known especially for his important work on Goethe already treated, is one of several translators of German authors whose translations of Rilke's poems appeared for the first time during the period surveyed here: *Thirty-One Poems by Rainer Maria Rilke* (New York, 1946). Another 'new' translator is Harry Behn whose translations of the *Duino Elegies* (Mount Vernon, N.Y.) were published in 1957. Stephen Spender's translation of *The Life of the Virgin Mary* was reprinted from the British edition in New York in 1951.

A sixth translator of Rilke's poetry actively represented in this period is the prolific British translator of the German poet, J. B. Leishman, many of whose translations, first published in England, were reprinted in the United States. The first of these to appear during the period under survey was the poem cycle *From the Remains of Count C. W.* (New York, 1953). His translations and introduction comprise a volume entitled *Rainer Maria Rilke: Poems, 1906 to 1926* (Norfolk, Conn., 1957). Leishman's translations also constitute the volume entitled *Rainer Maria Rilke: Selected Works; Volume II: Poetry* (Norfolk, Conn., 1960), which contains the whole of *The Book of Hours, Requiem, The Life of Mary*, the *Duino Elegies* and the *Sonnets to Orpheus*, together with selections from other of Rilke's poems. The companion volume *Rainer Maria Rilke: Selected Works; Volume I: Prose*, first published six years earlier, in 1954, and republished simultaneously with the volume of poetry, contains selected short writings, all translated by Miss G. Craig Houston, including *The Lay of the Love and Death of Cornet Christoph Rilke*.

The latter work, in a translation by Leslie Phillips and Stefan Schimanski that was published independently in London in 1948, appeared in the United States the following year (Forest Hills, N.Y., 1949). This same short work also appeared independently as *The Song of the Life and Death of the Cornet, Christoph Rilke* (n.p., 1950), translated by Howard Steven Strouth. *The Lay of the Love and Death of Cornet Christopher Rilke* (New York, 1959) was also published in a revised edition of a translation, first published in 1932, by Mrs. M. D. Herter Norton, who has been referred to by one critic as 'die aktivste Förderin amerikanischer Rilke-Forschung,' and who, the same critic declares, can 'den Ruhm für sich in Anspruch nehmen, mehr als jeder andere Übersetzer für die Verbreitung von Rilkes Werk in Amerika geleistet zu haben.'[1] Mrs. Norton's translation of *The Notebooks of Malte Laurids Brigge* was published in 1949 by W. W. Norton and again in 1958 by Capricorn Books. She had been a collaborator with John Linton on the first English translation of the same work which had appeared in 1930 under the title *The Journal of My Other Self*.

Rilke's autobiographical story, *Ewald Tragy*, did not appear in English until 1958 when a translation by Lola Gruenthal was published simultaneously in London and New York. Even in German its circulation had been quite restricted, for it was first published in an edition limited to ninety-five copies for members of the Münchner Gesellschaft der Bücherfreunde as the annual presentation for 1927/28; it was republished in German in the United States in the year 1944 (Verlag der Johannespresse, New York). A translation of Rilke's *Rodin* by Jessie Lemont and Hans Trausil, first published in the year 1919, was republished by the

---

[1] See Klaus W. Jonas' 'Rilke und Amerika,' *Etudes Germaniques*, IX (1954), 55-59, from which the quotation is taken (p. 56), for a brief discussion of Rilke's reception in the United States and the persons and publications largely responsible for his reception. Essentially the same article appears under the same title in *German Life and Letters*, VIII (1954), 45-49.

Fine Editions Press in 1945. Among a few other miscellaneous publications in English of Rilke's prose works is a volume of five short essays translated by Carl Niemeyer and published under the title of *Five Prose Pieces* (Cummington, Mass., 1947), of which 271 copies were printed; four of these essays had been previously published as *Primal Sound and Other Prose Pieces* (Cummington, Mass., 1943) in an edition limited to 175 copies.

Prior to 1945 two separate volumes of Rilke's letters in English translation had been published in the United States. During the next sixteen years, from 1945 to 1960, no fewer than seven individual volumes of his correspondence appeared in English through American publishers, the most impressive being a two-volume edition of *Letters of Rainer Maria Rilke*, translated by Jane Bannard Greene and M. D. Herter Norton, Volume One (New York, 1945) covering the period from 1892 to 1910, and Volume Two (New York, 1948) covering the period from 1910 to the poet's death in 1926. Mrs. Norton's translations of Rilke's letters to a single correspondent, F. X. Kappus, from 1903 to 1908, originally published in 1934 as *Letters to a Young Poet*, were republished in a revised edition under the same title in 1954. The Philosophical Library published two volumes of his letters: *Letters to Benvenuta* (New York, 1951), translated by Heinz Norden, with an introduction by Louis Untermeyer, and *Rainer Maria Rilke: His Last Friendship* (New York, 1952), containing ten letters of Rilke to Mrs. Nimet Eloui Bey, a young Egyptian woman whom he met just three months before his death, together with a lengthy study of the relationship by Edmond Jaloux, all translated from the original French by William H. Kennedy. Two additional volumes of Rilke's voluminous correspondence made their appearance in the United States: *The Letters of Rainer Maria Rilke and Princess Marie von Thurn and Taxis* (Norfolk, Conn., 1958), translated and with an introduction by Nora Wydenbruck; and *Selected Letters* (Garden City, N.Y., 1960), edited by Harry T. Moore.

Even a cursory survey indicates, from the number of translations of his works that continue to be published in the United States, both as independent volumes and in collections and anthologies, that the reception of Rilke in this country continues unabated down to the present day. The paucity of genuine lyric poetry produced in Germany during the era of national Socialism and the Second World War may by contrast have heightened the effect of his poetic voice. Yet, as new poets arise in Germany today, Rilke continues to hold the attention of persons appreciative of poetic genius. The extent of American interest in Rilke has indeed been, and continues to be, extraordinary.

Rilke's contemporary, Hugo von Hofmannsthal, another of the leading literary artists of the early twentieth-century writing in German, was also, like Rilke, active in several different genres. Lyricist, dramatist, storyteller, and essayist, his significance in modern literature is recognized far beyond the confines of German-speaking areas. Particularly for his libretti for operas by Richard Strauss he is widely known internationally. Yet for all his importance in the development of modern German literature, his reception in the United States has been proportionately more restricted than Rilke's. While representative selections from his works, particularly his lyrical poetry and his narrative prose, have frequently been included in various anthologies, very few independent volumes of Hofmannsthal's works in English translation have been published in the United States. If the translations of his libretti are excluded, the list of American-published works of this Austrian poet is noteworthy for its shortness. The greatest attempt at presenting his works in English to American reading audiences was initiated only quite recently when Pantheon Books, which has done much to support German literature in the United States by the publication of English translations, produced a volume entitled *Hugo von Hofmannsthal: Selected Prose* (New York, 1952), containing selections from the body of his prose fiction and his essays, translated variously by Mary Hottinger and Tania and James Stern, with an introduction by Hermann Broch. Appearing as Number 33 in the Bollingen Series, this volume, although not originally announced as such, has now come to serve as the first of three that constitute a series known as The Selected Works of Hofmannsthal. Volume Two appeared nearly a decade after Volume One, in 1961, as *Poems and Verse Plays*, a bilingual edition edited, with an introduction, by Michael Hamburger and with a preface by T. S. Eliot. Volume Three, *Selected*

Plays and Libretti,[1] published in 1963, is likewise edited by Michael Hamburger. Except for these three collections and the publication of the libretto *Arabella; A Lyrical Comedy in Three Acts* (New York, 1955), no other independent volumes of Hofmannsthal's works in English translation were published in the United States during the period under survey.[2] There is a translation by B. Q. Morgan of *Death and the Fool: A Short Play in Verse* which, along with the several nineteenth-century dramas mentioned in the preceding chapter, exists in typescript in the possession of the translator and of which a microfilm was made in 1958, as noted previously about other works in translation, at the instigation of Eric Bentley, at Columbia University (see *The National Union Catalog ... 1958-1962*). Hofmannsthal is also represented, as already mentioned, in anthologies of poetry and short stories, examples of which are his *A Tale of the Cavalry*, translated by James Stern, in Stephen Spender's *Great German Short Stories* and his *An Episode in the Life of the Marshal de Bassompierre*, translated by Mary Hottinger, in Robert Pick's *German Stories and Tales*. Certainly Hofmannsthal has not enjoyed an American reception commensurate with his importance to modern German letters.

Hofmannsthal's early friend and the leader of the literary circle of which Hofmannsthal was a member for several years, Stefan George, is little known in the United States and were it not for the efforts of two translators, very few of his works would be currently available to readers of English. His poetry is included in relatively few anthologies, and still fewer separate volumes of his work in English translation have been

---

[1] This volume contains, besides his early drama, *Electra*, and his comedies, *The Cavalier of the Rose* and *Arabella*, all of which became libretti for operas of Richard Strauss, Hofmannsthal's play, *The Salzburg Great World Theatre*, his comedy, *The Difficult Man*, first produced by Max Reinhardt, and his last tragedy, *The Tower*, with a note on this work by T. S. Eliot.

[2] It may be noted that the correspondence between Hofmannsthal and Strauss, a selection from which had been published before the beginning of the period under consideration (*Correspondence between Richard Strauss and Hugo von Hofmannstahl: 1907-1918* [New York, 1927]), appeared in its approximate entirety under the title *A Working Friendship: The Correspondence between Richard Strauss and Hugo von Hofmannsthal* (New York, 1961), translated by Hanns Hammelmann and Ewald Osers with an introduction by Edward Sackville-West.

published in the United States. In fact, according to an authoritative bibliography[1] only one such volume had appeared prior to the beginning year of this study; it was entitled *Stefan George: Poems* (New York, 1943), and was translated by Carol North Valhope (pseudonym of Olga Marx) and Ernst Morwitz, whose purpose, they proclaimed, was 'to acquaint the English-speaking reader with a world of poetry and thought that is as significant for cultural development as that of Goethe and Nietzsche' (p. 254). This volume of George's poems, like the three volumes of Hofmannsthal's works, was published by Pantheon Books. The efforts of the same two translators are responsible for the appearance of the very significant and only other independent volume of George's works in English. *The Works of Stefan George* (Univ. of N. Car. Stud. in Germ. Langs. and Lits., No. 2 [Chapel Hill, 1949]) contains 'a complete translation of the seven volumes of verse which constitute the main work of Stefan George,' and is the only complete translation of George's works ever to appear anywhere.

Karl Wolfskehl, another member of the *George Kreis*, whose home for a time was their place of meeting, has essentially never been known in the United States except among scholars and, more specifically, among Germanists, for whom his work has also been the subject of very limited attention. Even in anthologies his name seldom appears and his death in 1948, after living in exile in New Zealand since 1938, went virtually unnoticed in America. The first and only volume of his writing to appear in English translation anywhere was entitled *1933, A Poem Sequence* (New York, 1947), a translation, made by the same team of translators that provided English versions of George's poetry, of a group of poems that first appeared in Berlin as *Die Stimme spricht*.[2]

Like Wolfskehl, Kurt Tucholsky was forced into exile with the growth of Naziism in Germany, taking up residence in Sweden; and again

---

[1] Georg Peter Landsmann's *Stefan George und sein Kreis: Eine Bibliographie* (Hamburg, 1960) presents an exhaustive list of the works of George and those of the *George Kreis* and includes all translations of George's poetry in anthologies and periodicals to the year 1960.

[2] A bibliography of Karl Wolfskehl's works and of critical writings on him and his works is provided by Walter Euler and Hans-Rolf Ropertz in a volume prepared under their editorship entitled *Karl Wolfskehl* (Volume 4 of *Agora: Eine humanistische Schriftenreihe*, ed. Manfred Schlösser and Hans-Rolf Ropertz [Darmstadt, n.d.]).

like Wolfskehl, he is virtually unknown in the United States, being represented in English translation only by a single volume entitled *The World Is a Comedy: A Tucholsky Anthology* (Cambridge, Mass., 1957), translated and edited by Harry Zohn. Tucholsky, whose life and literary productivity invite comparison with those of Heine, remains, in contrast, almost undiscovered in this country even in academic circles.

Another German poet who has attracted much more attention than either Wolfskehl or Tucholsky in both Germany and the United States is Gottfried Benn,[1] although it was not until 1960, four years after his death, that the first and to date only independent volume of his work in English translation appeared. This publication is entitled *Primal Vision: Selected Writings*, and is edited by E. B. Ashton (pseudonym of Ernst Basch), whose introduction deals directly with the question, so important to readers of the post-Nazi era, of Benn's ambiguous position in the Third Reich and his often questioned relation to Naziism.[2] Until,

---

[1] Edgar Lohner's *Gottfried Benn Bibliographie, 1912-1956* (Wiesbaden, 1958) indicates the extent of the publication of Benn's works, both lyric poetry and prose, in German and in translation (English, French, Italian, Swedish, Danish, Yugoslavian, Spanish, and Japanese). His bibliography also shows the critical attention paid to Benn through critical articles and reviews published in Germany and in other countries, including the United States.

[2] Even today Benn – like several other German writers such as Ernst Jünger who remained in Germany and openly or by their presence seemingly endorsed Naziism, or like Ernst Wiechert, who undertook a kind of 'innere Emigration' – has not been 'cleared' by all critics and readers from his 'adaptation to the Nazi regime.' A most recent vivid example of the degree to which this question still remains alive is provided by an article in a popular magazine: 'Writers who were able to adapt themselves, and their work, to the Nazi regime have had no trouble adapting themselves to present-day conditions in Germany. The late Gottfried Benn became "Kommissarischer Leiter" of the Poetry Section of the Prussian Academy of Arts, and a director of the Union of National Writers, yet he was accorded the highest honors in Adenauer's Germany.' After quoting from the now famous letter of appeal of 1933 from Klaus Mann, exiled in France, to Benn, accommodated within Nazi Germany, the author of the article continues: 'And Gottfried Benn's reply was made in the form of an open letter entitled "Answer to the Literary Emigrants," a reply which embodied such statements as "I personally declare for the new state," and "What is here at stake is not new forms of government but a new vision of the birth of man." This bombast was featured by Goebbels in the press and on the air' (Kay Boyle, 'A Voice from the Future,' *Holiday*, XXXVI, iv [Oct., 1964], 20-22). As another example an article in another popular magazine can be cited: 'Some [writers], like Gottfried Benn and Ernst Jünger, took refuge in what Benn called "the aristocratic form of emigration."... Benn saw more clearly, and withdrew

and since, the appearance of this volume all English translations of Benn's works appear either in periodicals or anthologies, such as Stephen Spender's *Great German Short Stories*, in which Benn's *The Conquest* is included in a translation by Christopher Middleton.

These six literary figures – Rilke, Hofmannsthal, George, Wolfskehl, Tucholsky, and Benn – are the only ones who, primarily as lyric poets, represent German literature of the twentieth century between 1945 and 1960 to American readers through the publication of individual volumes of their works in the United States in English translation. To be sure, only one of the six – George – wrote lyric poetry almost exclusively; yet all of them may be referred to essentially as lyric poets since it is in this genre that they have attained their greatest stature, achieved their widest recognition, and made their most significant contribution to German letters.

Like Rilke and, to a lesser degree, Hofmannsthal in the field of modern German poetry, so Franz Kafka and Thomas Mann are the two writers of prose fiction in twentieth-century German literature most widely known in the United States. Not only do translations of their works appear in numerous anthologies but their novels and stories also appear in English translation in book form in such impressive numbers that, measured by this criterion alone, and not to mention the extent to which their works have been the subject of attention in critical studies and popular articles, Kafka and Mann enjoy the greatest currency and are the most widely received of all German writers of fiction in the United States during the sixteen years under survey.

Kafka, again like his compatriot Rilke, was during his lifetime and for

---

first into obscurity of style, then into silence. But the sheer fact of his presence in Nazi Germany seemed to destroy his hold on reality. After the war he set down some of his recollections of the time of night. Among them, we find an incredible sentence. Speaking of pressures put on him by the regime, Benn says: "I describe the foregoing not out of resentment against National Socialism. The latter is now overthrown, and I am not one to drag Hector's body in the dust." One's imagination dizzies at the amount of confusion it must have taken to make a decent writer write that. Using an old academic cliché, he makes Naziism the equivalent of the noblest of Homeric heroes' (George Steiner, 'The Hollow Miracle: Notes on the German Language,' *Reporter*, XXII, 4 [Feb. 18, 1960], 36-41).

the first few years after his death almost unknown among American readers, and, to pursue the parallel still farther, although he never visited this country, America became for him a point of reference to which his artist-temperament was forced to respond. But here the parallel ceases. While for Rilke America represented, as noted previously, the epitome of everything negative to him as an artist, for Kafka America became a kind of magical, imaginary place of escape from himself and his native city of Prague, a land 'der freien Lüfte' (to use Kafka's phrase from the opening paragraph of his fragmentary novel, *Amerika*).[1] Although America attracted the interest and attention of Kafka, Kafka himself, on the other hand, attracted attention in America only slowly and somewhat belatedly. Until 1930, when *The Castle* appeared in this country as the first translation into English of any of his works in book form to be published here, he was virtually unknown to American readers, and it was five years later when Werner Neuse assertedly became 'the first American to introduce Kafka to the reading public in the United States: his essay was published in one of the "little magazines [!]," *Books Abroad*, in the summer issue of 1935.'[2] *The Trial*, for example, first published in German in 1925, did not appear in English until 1937. Likewise, *Amerika* was first published in German in 1927, only three years after the author's death, but it was not until more than a decade

---

[1] See Klaus Mann's 'Dream-America,' *Accent*, VIII (1948), 173-184, for a discussion of Kafka's 'escape from imprisonment' by means of his *Amerika*, where, like his hero Karl Rossmann, Kafka was 'carried away, as it were, by the free winds of heaven, the powerful, tonic breath of Dream-America' (p. 184).

[2] See Klaus W. Jonas' 'Franz Kafka: An American Bibliography,' *Bulletin of Bibliography*, XX (1952), 212-216 and 231-233, for a list of 'American publications by and about Franz Kafka,' i.e., writings of Kafka in English translation published in the United States, and criticism of Kafka that appeared in periodicals and books published here. This bibliography has been extended to the year 1958 in a supplement under the same title by Ann Benson (*Bulletin of Bibliography*, XXII [1958], 112-114).

Apparently Jonas, in speaking of Neuse's introduction of Kafka to Americans, was referring to critical essays, for, as noted above, *The Castle* had been available in English by 1930. And two years earlier Kafka had made his initial appearance in English in one of the most important of the little magazines when in Volume 11 of *transition* (February, 1928) 'The Sentence,' translated and adapted by Eugene Jolas, appeared as the first English translation of any of Kafka's work anywhere; this translation was republished in New York the following year (1929) in a volume entitled *Transition Stories*.

later, in 1938, that it appeared in English translation. In the intervening years, however, American interest in Kafka has grown tremendously. There are several recent bibliographies of Kafka, all of which provide statistical evidence of the almost unprecedented appeal this once obscure writer has since made to readers and critics in the United States.[1]

Kafka's works were introduced to readers in this country through British translations by Willa and Edwin Muir, who performed the function for Kafka that Mrs. H. T. Lowe-Porter did for Thomas Mann. Their translation of *The Castle*, noted above, reprinted from the British edition, introduced Kafka to Americans in English and became the first of a number of translations that they undertook subsequently, including *The Trial*, originally published in New York in 1937 and republished in 1941, and *Amerika*, published in New York in 1940, likewise all reprints of British editions. During the period 1945 to 1960 their translation of *The Castle*, which had been reissued in a second edition, with a homage by Thomas Mann, in New York in 1941, was republished in 1954 and again in 1956 in a definitive edition containing additional material translated by Eithne Wilkins and Ernst Kaiser. Also republished was their translation of Kafka's other two novels: *The Trial* (1945 and 1957), revised and with additional materials translated by E. M. Butler, and *Amerika* (1946, and by a different publisher, 1955), with a preface by

---

[1] Three particularly useful bibliographies of Kafka, in addition to those by Jonas and Benson (see above, p. 128, n. 1), have been prepared by Angel Flores. The first, *Franz Kafka: A Chronology and Bibliography* (Houlton, Maine, 1944), presents a list of works by Kafka published in the original German, in English translation, and in translations in other languages, as well as a list of criticism of Kafka that appeared in Germany, the United States, England, and other countries. A comparison of this bibliography with another by Flores of more than a dozen years later, 'Bibliographical Index of the Works Available in English' and 'Biography and Criticism: A Bibliography' (in *Franz Kafka Today*, ed. Angel Flores and Homer Swander [Madison, 1958], pp. 251-285), and with a third by the same Kafka critic, 'Franz Kafka: Bibliography and Criticism – A New, Up-to-Date Bibliography' (in *The Kafka Problem*, ed. Angel Flores [New York, 1963], pp. 455-477) indicates quite graphically the extent of interest in Kafka and his works that has developed not only in the United States but also throughout the world. Two additional important and detailed bibliographies of Kafka have appeared: Rudolf Hemmerle's *Franz Kafka: Eine Bibliographie* (Munich, 1958), and Harry Järv's *Die Kafka-Literatur* (Malmö-Lund, 1961). An analysis of the earlier Kafka criticism by American scholars and reviewers is provided by Ann Benson in 'The American Criticism of Franz Kafka, 1930-1948' (unpubl. diss., Univ. of Tennessee, 1958).

Klaus Mann and an afterword by Kafka's close friend, Max Brod, who, by flagrantly but justifiably disobeying the directive to destroy Kafka's manuscripts, is responsible for preserving such an important contribution to twentieth-century German letters. Other translations of Kafka's works by the Muirs that were published in the United States as separate volumes for the first time after 1945 include a volume entitled *The Great Wall of China: Stories and Reflections* (1946), which contains, in addition to the title story, three longer stories, fifteen very short stories and fables, and aphorisms; *Parables* (1947), translated by the Muirs together with Clement Greenberg; *The Penal Colony: Stories and Short Pieces* (1948); and a collection published in The Modern Library entitled *Selected Short Stories of Franz Kafka* (1952).

While the Muirs have been more prolific than any other translators of Kafka, theirs have by no means been the only translations. Particularly more recently, as interest in Kafka has mounted, other translators have devoted their attention to collections of his writings as well as to individual stories for inclusion in anthologies. Ernst Kaiser and Eithne Wilkins have translated a collection of his writings, including the rather famous letter to his father, entitled *Dearest Father: Stories and Other Writings* (1954). Tania and James Stern have translated another collection which also takes its title from one of the stories it contains, *Description of a Struggle* (1958). The same translators are responsible for the appearance in English of *Letters to Milena* (1953), edited by Willy Haas. A. L. Lloyd's translation of *Metamorphosis*, originally published in London in 1937, was republished in New York in 1946. *The Diaries of Franz Kafka*, edited by Max Brod, have been translated by Joseph Kresch (Volume I: 1910-1913 [New York, 1948]), and Martin Greenberg, with the co-operation of Hannah Arendt (Volume II: 1914-1923 [New York, 1949]).

In contrast to Kafka, Thomas Mann had direct personal experience with the United States. For him this country was not 'Dream-America' but rather a land of reality in which he spent fifteen important later years of his life – an experience he shared with a number of German writers who, unwilling to compromise with Hitler's Naziism, chose to make their home in other countries. And, again unlike Kafka, Mann became known in the United States during his lifetime, and by the time of his death, although he was no longer living in this country, he had achieved the full range of his popularity here. One critic, writing in commemoration of Mann's seventieth birthday in 1945, claimed: 'Never has a foreign writer been acclaimed so spontaneously in America nor has any literary work in translation enjoyed such sudden popularity. ... his new publications were heralded with an enthusiasm and praise such as had never before been bestowed upon a foreign writer' (Walter A. Reichart; see below, p. 132, n. 1). But like Kafka, Mann received only limited attention here until about the end of the third decade of this century when the award of the Nobel Prize for Literature in 1929 stimulated recognition more commensurate with the extent of his popularity already established in Germany. Although by that time all of his major works already published in German had also achieved American publication (*Royal Highness*, 1916; *Bashen and I*, 1923; *Buddenbrooks*, 1924; *Death in Venice and Other Stories*, 1925; *The Magic Mountain*, 1927; *Children and Fools*, 1928), the dates of their publication here illustrate the somewhat delayed reception of Mann in the United States. In the case of *Buddenbrooks*, for example, American reading audiences had been forced to wait nearly a quarter of a century for an English translation. Mann's first visit to this country in 1934 occasioned the further acquaintance of Americans with this German author of important new novels and stories that had been appearing in translations published by Alfred A. Knopf, the New York publisher responsible for the American publication of English translations of not only many German works but also of other non-American writing. Several important recent bibliographies devoted exclusively to Mann – one of nearly two hundred pages and another, still more recent, of some three hundred pages – present dramatic evidence of the extent of Mann's extraordinary worldwide reception,[1] to which the reception accorded him in the United States, as evidenced

---

[1] Klaus W. Jonas' *Fifty Years of Thomas Mann Studies: A Bibliography of Criticism* (Minneapolis, 1955) presents more than three thousand items. Hans Bürgin's *Das Werk Thomas Manns* (Frankfurt am Main, 1959) is particularly useful for its careful listing of editions of Mann's works in German and of translations published in thirty-one countries. Bürgin's list of translations has been reproduced and extended to 1964 in a paperbound volume entitled *Thomas Mann: Erinnerungen an meinen Vater, von Golo Mann; Thomas Mann in Übersetzungen: Bibliographie*, published by Inter Nationes in Bonn in 1965.

by the American publication of his works in English translation and the publication of voluminous writings about him and his works by Americans, is no exception and of which it forms no small part.[1]

By the year 1945 Thomas Mann had already lived in the United States for about seven years, having resided briefly in Princeton, New Jersey, and subsequently in Pacific Palisades, California. His open opposition to the Nazi regime, expressed in his writings and public addresses, and accentuated by his residence here, doubtless contributed toward the interest generated by his literary productivity, so that after his arrival in the United States and even after 1952, by which time he had once more made his home in Europe, his works received American publication in English translation essentially simultaneously with, or immediately following, their publication elsewhere in the original German.[2] The years from 1945 to 1960 are marked not only by the appearance of translations of his new works but also by the republication of translations of earlier works and by the publication of collections of his writings and the inclusion of his shorter works in anthologies.

The first of Mann's works to appear as a separate volume in English translation for the first time during the sixteen years surveyed in the present study was *The Tables of the Law* (New York, 1945) in a translation by Mrs. H. T. Lowe-Porter, the American woman, Pennsylvanian by birth and herself a poet, whose translation of *Buddenbrooks* in 1924 became the first of many of Mann's works she was to provide subsequently in English; as Mann's official translator, she, more than any other person,

---

[1] For an exhaustive bibliography of about five hundred works by and about Thomas Mann that had appeared in the United States down to 1945, see Walter A. Reichart's 'Thomas Mann: An American Bibliography,' *MDU*, XXXVII (1945), 389-408. Herman Ramras, in 'Main Currents in American Criticism of Thomas Mann' (unpubl. diss., Univ. of Wisconsin, 1949), presents an analysis of Mann criticism produced by American scholarship. Other more limited bibliographies of Mann in America are provided in a number of American studies of Mann, of which Joseph Gerard Brennan's *Thomas Mann's World* (New York, 1942 and 1962) can be cited as one example.

[2] Two of Mann's novels in the original German were first 'published' in the United States. In 1947 *Doctor Faustus* was 'reproduced from typewritten copy' and 'the first issue of 50 copies, numbered and signed by the author, was published in the United States in order to secure American copyright.' Similarly, in 1951, the first issue of 60 copies of *Der Erwählte* was published in this country (see *The Library of Congress Author Catalog, 1948-1952*).

is linked with the history of Mann's reception among American readers. Her translations of his Joseph-tetralogy were published together and complete for the first time in 1948, although the individual volumes had appeared earlier (*Joseph and His Brothers*, 1934; *Young Joseph*, 1935; *Joseph in Egypt*, 1938; *Joseph the Provider*, 1944). Each of the first three volumes had achieved multiple editions prior to the 1948 publication of the four volumes in one. In the same year appeared *Doctor Faustus: The Life of the German Composer Adrian Leverkühn as Told by a Friend*. Three years later, in 1951, *The Holy Sinner* was published as Mrs. Lowe-Porter's final translation of Mann. After Mann had left the United States and made his residence in Kilchberg, near Zürich, Switzerland, a translation of *Die Betrogene*, by a new Mann translator, Willard R. Trask, was published as *The Black Swan* (1954). Mann's last novel and his final major work, *Confessions of Felix Krull, Confidence Man: The Early Years*, appeared in a translation by another new Mann translator, Denver Lindley, in 1955 and was reissued as a paperbound volume in 1957.

During the years from 1945 to 1960 several new collections of Mann's works were also published in the United States, in most cases stories and other writings that had appeared previously either as separate books or together with other shorter works. *The Thomas Mann Reader*, published in 1950 and reissued in 1957, and selected, arranged, and edited by Joseph Warner Angell, contains some of his short novels and stories, excerpts from his longer novels, and some of his literary and political essays. *Death in Venice and Seven Other Stories*, published in 1954 and reissued ten times by 1960, is an expansion of a collection of a different translator, first published in 1925 as *Death in Venice and Other Stories*, which had contained, beside the title story, only two other stories, *Tristan* and *Tonio Kröger*.

Three of Mann's long novels were also republished between 1945 and 1960. Mrs. Lowe-Porter's translation of *The Magic Mountain*, originally published in 1927, attained its ninth edition in 1946 and its tenth in 1953, the latter containing Mann's essay 'The Making of The Magic Mountain,' which had first appeared in the *Atlantic Monthly* in January, 1953. *The Beloved Returns: Lotte in Weimar* reappeared in 1957. *Buddenbrooks* was issued in a paperbound edition in 1952, and *The Transposed Heads* in 1959. Stories by Mann have also been included in many general anthologies published in the United States.

In addition to the works of fiction by Mann, a number of volumes of his literary and political essays were published in the United States, as well as a volume of his letters. Few German authors, and, particularly few other modern German writers, have been received in America as enthusiastically and by such a large reading audience, nor has any other twentieth-century German writer been the subject of so much critical attention.

Hermann Hesse, Thomas Mann's junior by only two years, was also a recipient of the Nobel Prize for Literature, and, as in the case of Thomas Mann's reception in the United States, it was this award in 1946 which called attention in this country to Hesse, who had by this time established a wide reputation not only in Germany and Switzerland but also in the Scandinavian countries, particularly in the East European countries, and also in Japan. But in contrast to Thomas Mann, Hesse received the award relatively late in his life (in 1946 he was sixty-nine years old), resulting in an extremely belated recognition in America that even down to the present day has remained quite limited. Even after 1946, according to reliable and exhaustive bibliographies,[1] no unusual increase

---

[1] Numerous bibliographical studies of Hesse have been produced since 1927 when Ernst Metelmann's 'Hermann Hesse,' *Die schöne Literatur*, XXVIII (1927), 299-312, appeared as the first. For a brief discussion of the bibliographical studies that appeared up to the year 1957, see Joseph Mileck's 'Hesse Bibliographies,' *MDU*, XLIX (1957), 201-205. Of special importance for the present work is Klaus W. Jonas' 'Hermann Hesse in America,' *MDU*, XLIV (1952), 95-99, which, while making no claim to completeness, presents a list of English translations of Hesse's works published in periodicals or as independent volumes, and provides a list of American critical studies of Hesse. Jonas' 'Additions to the Bibliography of Hermann Hesse,' *Papers of the Bibliographical Society of America*, XLIX (1955), 358-360, extends his list by three years with twelve items. A most extensive Hesse bibliography, interestingly enough the product of scholarship in America where Hesse has had such a limited reception, is Joseph Mileck's *Hermann Hesse and His Critics; The Criticism and Bibliography of Half a Century* (Chapel Hill, 1958, Univ. of N. Car. Stud. in Germ. Langs. and Lits., No. 21), which presents a comprehensive indication of the extent of Hesse's reception throughout the world, including the United States, by providing a list of some 1000 items about Hesse. For a very recent bibliography of Hesse studies, see the exhaustive work by Otto Bareiss, *Hermann Hesse: Eine Bibliographie der Werke über Hermann Hesse, Teil I* (Basel, 1962), *Teil II, Zeitschriften- und Zeitungsaufsätze* (Basel, 1964).

of American interest in Hesse developed, if judged by the total number of English translations published in this country, although the number of studies in scholarly journals began to increase significantly after 1946.

The time lapse between the appearance of his works in German and their publication in the United States in English translation has been for the most part quite extraordinary when considered in light of the great attention focused upon him in other countries. *Das Glasperlenspiel*, for example, which first appeared in Switzerland in 1943 and which, chiefly, earned for Hesse the Nobel Prize, was first published in the United States and England only six years later, in 1949, as *Magister Ludi*, with the subtitle *The Nobel Prize Novel: Das Glasperlenspiel*, in a translation by Mervyn Savill. In 1957 this same British translation was republished by a different American publisher. *Siddhartha*, first published in Berlin in 1922, remained unavailable to readers of English until nearly three decades later when Hilde Rosner's translation was published in the United States (New York, 1951 and 1957). Similarly, Hilde Rosner's translation of *Die Morgenlandfahrt* as *The Journey to the East* was first published in the United States in 1957, two and one-half decades after its original appearance in Berlin in 1932. Two others of Hesse's works, on the other hand, did receive relatively prompt publication in America. *Demian, The Story of a Youth*, translated by N. H. Friday, was published in New York in 1923, just four years after its original German publication in Berlin in 1919. Doubtless because of the Nobel Prize award to Hesse, this same translation was republished in 1948 by Henry Holt and Company, with a foreword by Thomas Mann. *Steppenwolf*, translated by Basil Creighton, was published in New York, also by Holt, in 1929, only two years after its original appearance in Berlin in 1927. Creighton's translation was reprinted in 1947 by the same publisher and was reissued in 1957 by a second publisher, who also issued it as a paperbound book in 1960. Hermann Hesse, unlike Thomas Mann through the service of Mrs. H. T. Lowe-Porter, has not had a single 'authorized' American translator, nor has he had, in the same sense as Mann in Alfred A. Knopf, a single 'official' American publisher and promoter, although Holt has published more of Hesse's works in English translation than any other American firm.

The reception of Franz Werfel in the United States presents a number of interesting parallels with, as well as contrasts to, the reception accorded to certain of his contemporaries and compatriots. Like Thomas Mann, Heinrich Mann, Bruno Frank, Bertolt Brecht, and other twentieth-century German literary figures, and unlike Hermann Hesse, who left Germany for Switzerland, Werfel joined the significant group of exiled German writers who made their home in the United States following the rise and spread of Naziism in Europe. The advantage of such personal association with the American scene in a foreign writer's appeal for a generous American reading audience is undeniable. On the other hand, no internationally important award, focusing international and also American attention on its recipient – such as the Nobel Prize awarded to Thomas Mann and Hermann Hesse – assisted Franz Werfel in gaining recognition in the United States. Yet down to the present, no other German writer of any era has ever succeeded in gaining such a wide currency and popular reception in this country as Werfel.

Well before his arrival in the United States in 1940[1] Werfel had become well known and widely read here for his novel *The Forty Days of Musa Dagh* which, first published in the original German in 1933, and published in an English translation by Geoffrey Dunlop in New York the following year, by 1935 had become one of the ten best selling works of fiction in the United States.[2] His lyric poetry, the genre with which Werfel had

---

[1] Werfel had visited the United States briefly on a previous occasion when he was still living 'the life of the Viennese intellectual elite with the usual journeys abroad' which '... led him to Germany, Switzerland, Czechoslovakia, his native country, to Italy, Palestine, Egypt, and even to far-off America' (Lore B. Foltin, 'Introduction: A Biography of Franz Werfel,' in *Franz Werfel, 1890-1945*, ed. Lore B. Foltin [Pittsburgh, 1961], p. 3).

[2] John R. Frey, in 'America and Franz Werfel,' *GQ*, XIX (1946), 121-128, states that this novel 'was a best seller in 1934, outselling supposedly every other book of that year' (p. 127). However, in Alice Payne Hackett's *Sixty Years of Best Sellers: 1895-1955* (New York, 1956), Werfel's novel is not listed among the ten best sellers in the year 1934; it is listed as number six of the best sellers in the year 1935. Frey provides no documentation for his statement, nor was I able to discover any evidence to support his claim. It may be of interest to note the list of ten best sellers (fiction) of 1935 and their authors:

    1. Lloyd C. Douglas, *Green Light*
    2. Ellen Glasgow, *Vein of Iron*
    3. Thomas Wolfe, *Of Time and the River*
    4. Rachel Field, *Time Out of Mind*

begun his literary career during the years that preceded the First World War, was and has remained practically unknown in this country, for until 1945 only a very few of his poems had been offered to American readers in English translation.[1] The appearance of Edith Abercrombie Snow's translations of fifty of his poems, selected from seven volumes of his poetry, and printed together with the original German in *Poems: Franz Werfel* (Princeton, 1945), has provided the only individual volume in English to represent Werfel's productivity as a lyric poet, and one is forced to conclude that Mrs. Snow was not referring to Werfel's reception in the United States when, in the Acknowledgments of her volume, she writes: 'Mr. Werfel was a great novelist and playwright, but it is as a poet that he will live longest.'

Likewise, as a playwright – an activity which dominated his major literary productivity during the second and third decades of this century – Werfel was less well known in the United States than in Europe, although nearly all of his dramas were published in America in English translation and several were produced in New York theaters. In the year 1926, for example, three of his dramas, *Goat Song* (with Alfred Lunt and Lynn Fontanne), *Schweiger*, and *Juarez and Maximilian*, were presented on the New York stage. The two dramas staged in New York after he had made his residence in this country, *Jacobowsky and the Colonel* (1944) and *Embezzled Heaven* (1944, with Ethel Barrymore), had reasonably successful runs but, in comparison with his popular success as a novelist, did not essentially extend his limited popularity as a playwright. In

    5. James Hilton, *Good-Bye, Mr. Chips*
    6. Franz Werfel, *The Forty Days of Musa Dagh*
    7. Thornton Wilder, *Heaven's My Destination*
    8. James Hilton, *Lost Horizon*
    9. Edna Ferber, *Come and Get It*
  10. Robert Briffault, *Europa*
(Hackett, p. 159).

[1] In the article noted above, John R. Frey lists a total of eleven poems by Werfel that had been translated into English and published in America prior to 1945. Nine of the eleven poems appeared in a volume entitled *Contemporary German Poetry: An Anthology* (New York, 1923), edited and translated by Babette Deutsch and Avrahm Yarmolinsky; of the other two, one appeared in the *Nation* (March 14, 1923) and the other in *Poet Lore* (December, 1926).

1958 a motion picture based on his *Jacobowsky and the Colonel*, released under the title *Me and the Colonel*, with Danny Kaye as Jacobowsky, was rated ninth of the ten best films of the year by the Committee on Exceptional Films of the National Board of Review.[1]

Werfel's greatest popular success in America, however, derived from his novels and primarily from *The Song of Bernadette*, first published in the original German in Stockholm in 1941 and one year later in New York in an English translation by Ludwig Lewisohn. The sale of almost half a million copies in 1942 made this novel the best selling work of fiction in the United States for the year; in 1943 it was still among the first ten best sellers of that year. The cumulative total sale of well over a million and a half copies by 1955 rate it as the one hundred sixteenth title in a list of three hundred and six books that have sold over one million copies in the sixty-year period from 1895 to 1955.[2] The 1943 motion picture of the same title, which was based on Werfel's novel and in which the actress Jennifer Jones started her film career, won five Academy awards. The stage version, on the other hand, originally dramatized by Walter and Jean Kerr for presentation in the theater of the Catholic University of America, proved unsuccessful on the Broadway stage in 1946 and closed after only three performances.

Werfel's novels were generally published in America in English translation soon after their appearance in the original German, with the result that very few of his works received their initial American publication after 1945, the year of his death. His last novel *Stern des Ungeborenen*, was first published in 1946 and made its appearance in America in the same year as *Star of the Unborn* in a translation by Gustave O. Arlt. During the years 1945 to 1960 a number of previously published translations of his works were reissued or republished, sometimes as paperbound volumes in inexpensive, widely available editions that attest to the unparalleled popularity attained by Werfel in the United States.

In addition to Franz Werfel, four other German writers have had at least one of their works of fiction[3] included among the ten best selling

---

[1] See Henry Hart's '1958's Ten Best,' *Films in Review*, X (1959), 1-4.
[2] See Hackett, pp. 174-177 and 17.
[3] Another German writer, Emil Ludwig, has been represented on the best seller list of books

books of a specific year, with two of the four attaining this distinction during the period of years surveyed in the present study.

Vicki Baum, born in Vienna, came to America in 1931 and became a citizen of the United States in 1938, and although she completed several works between 1945 and 1960, the year of her death, they were all written in English and cannot be considered a legitimate part of German literature in the United States. However, a motion picture entitled 'Weekend at the Waldorf,' which was based on a novel she originally wrote in German (*Menschen im Hotel*), was released in October, 1945. The translation of the novel, *Grand Hotel*, had in 1931 been the fourth best selling novel in America. The New York stage production of *Grand Hotel* in 1930-31 is reported to have grossed more than one and a quarter million dollars for thirteen months with nearly five hundred performances, making it, along with Brecht's *Threepenny Opera* and Werfel's *Jacobowsky and the Colonel*, one of the most successful German plays in New York, judged by the number of performances. *Grand Hotel* had also appeared as a motion picture in 1932.

Hans Fallada, the pseudonym of Rudolf Ditzen, received widespread attention in America in 1933, the year in which one of his very early novels, *Little Man, What Now?*, in a translation by Eric Sutton, achieved tenth place on the best seller list of fiction for the year. Of his two novels which achieved publication for the first time after his death in 1947, only one of them, *The Drinker*, translated into English by Charlotte and Albert L. Lloyd, was published in the United States (New York, 1952); it was reissued as a paperbound book in 1956. Fallada's best selling novel of 1933 was republished in 1957.

Almost paralleling the popular success of Werfel's *The Song of Bernadette*, Erich Maria Remarque's *All Quiet on the Western Front*, translated by A. W. Wheen, sold 300,000 copies the first year it appeared and thereby became the best selling work of fiction in 1929. By 1955 nearly a million and a half copies had been sold. Also like Werfel, but in

in America during several years, but in the non-fiction category. His *Napoleon* achieved second place in 1927 and fourth place in 1928; in 1930 his *Lincoln* became the sixth best selling non-fiction book; and his biography of a river, *The Nile*, was the ninth title on the best seller list in 1937 (see Hackett, pp. 143, 145, 149, and 163).

contrast to Hans Fallada, Remarque's popularity was not restricted to one widely circulated novel, since just two years later, in 1931, another of his war novels, *The Road Back*, also translated by A. W. Wheen, was again on the best seller list, this time in sixth place. When a third novel by Remarque, *Arch of Triumph*, translated by Walter Sorell and Denver Lindley, achieved seventh place on the list of best selling books in 1946, he became the first German author, preceding Annemarie Selinko, to achieve such widespread popularity following the close of the Second World War. During the period under survey his earlier novels continued to be reissued, while new works, appearing in English translation almost as soon as the German original, were published at an impressive rate: *Spark of Life*, translated by James Stern, appeared in 1952; *A Time to Love and a Time to Die*, translated by Denver Lindley, in 1954; *The Black Obelisk*, also translated by Denver Lindley, in 1957. The fact that several of Remarque's novels were made into successful motion pictures doubtless contributed to the popularity of his works in the United States.

Doubtless, too, the success of the motion picture 'Désirée' and the reception of the novel with the same title on which the film was based are related factors in making Annemarie Selinko (pseudonym of Annemarie Kristiansen) the only German writer to achieve by a single work a sales record equal to that attained with her novel *Désirée*. This novel, in third place on the list of best selling fiction for the year 1953, sold nearly one and three-quarter million copies by 1955, making it the best selling work ever translated from German into English and published in America, and the most recent of three books by German writers (with Werfel's *The Song of Bernadette* and Remarque's *All Quiet on the Western Front*) to have achieved total sales of more than a million copies.

Other German authors, whose writings have had a notable, although not spectacular, reception in the United States during the sixteen years surveyed in the present study, include, among others, Stefan Zweig, Lion Feuchtwanger, Theodor Plievier, and Heinrich Böll. There are, of course, many other twentieth-century German novelists, as the appended bibliography indicates, who, through the American publication of English translations of their works, have contributed significantly to the total currency and record of reception of German literature in the United States.

Drama as a literary genre, as has been noted in preceding chapters, has seldom had more than a limited appeal in the United States, for among American readers, in contrast to educated Europeans, the concept of drama as literature is restricted primarily to academicians and more specifically to specialists of literature. Relatively little drama, and even less German drama, finds its way through the printed page beyond the campus or academic community to the general American public. The stage performance of drama is surely a much more forceful and extensive means whereby a playwright may be granted recognition and eventually, in some cases, come to enjoy a generous reception and popular acclaim. Although the theater plays a much less significant role in the cultural life of American than that of Germany, Austria, or Switzerland, the stage performance of drama still remains the most important means – almost the exclusive means – whereby this literary genre receives recognition. In spite of the facts that there is comparatively meagre support for quality theater in the United States and that only a few American cities have developed what may justifiably be termed a vigorous theater community, nevertheless the performance of a play, generally speaking, provides the only assurance that a playwright or a specific work will ever become known or make any impact upon the cultural life of America beyond the classroom. While this is true of American playwrights and their plays, it is even more applicable to foreign playwrights whose plays must first await translation, often suffer from mistranslation or poor translation, and frequently are subjected to severe alterations and extensive adaptations for American audiences. Where the artistic creation of the literary artist must be subordinate to the commercial interest of the producer, comparatively few playwrights, desirous of recognition, can ignore the importance of financial success. A sophisticated view of theater as a significant art form, as one critic has suggested recently,[1]

---

[1] See Francis Hodge's 'German Drama and the American Stage' (in *The German Theatre Today: A Symposium*, ed. Leroy R. Shaw [Austin, Texas, 1963], pp. 69-88) for a discussion of the production of German plays in the United States with particular reference to what he terms 'educational theater,' i.e., university and college theaters and their importance to the eventual development of a new and more vital professional theater. 'The professional stage in America has become so infiltrated with university-trained people that a few years more

together with an adventurous attitude in the choice of plays, experimental staging, and the cultivation of a receptive audience must first be developed in order to provide an atmosphere in which the playwright can anticipate a more enthusiastic reception and his plays be assured anything more than obscurity.

It is hardly surprising, therefore, that only a few playwrights writing in German are known in the United States beyond essentially academic circles, since in contrast with the number of French plays produced on the American university or professional stage,[1] and in comparison with

will see it almost entirely in the hands of university products – playwrights, actors, designers, and directors' (p. 72).

[1] The comparatively much greater contemporary currency and reception of French culture in the United States, not only in the theater and in the literary realm but in the whole of American cultural life and activity, is discussed in a penetrating newspaper article by Wolfgang Leppmann entitled 'Vermisst wird das deutsche Kulturwunder: Warum der deutsche Einfluss in den Vereinigten Staaten nach wie vor weit hinter dem Frankreichs zurücksteht' (*Die Zeit*, May 31, 1963). Leppmann first confirms 'eine kulturpolitische Gegebenheit: die Vorherrschaft der französischen Sprache, Literatur und Kunst unter allen anderen kulturellen Strömungen, die aus dem Ausland auf Amerika einwirken.' Concerning the importance of the French language in the United States he writes: 'Relativ gesehen tritt das Primat des Französischen hingegen beim Vergleich mit einer anderen Kultursphäre hervor – der deutschen. Die Anzahl der Schüler und Studenten, die an amerikanischen Schulen und Hochschulen Französisch studieren zum Beispiel: sie ist rund doppelt so gross wie die derer, die Deutsch treiben.' Referring to the comparatively wide currency of French literature in the United States he finds it is 'nicht zu verwundern, dass viele Amerikaner glauben, die französische Literatur sei der Inbegriff aller schriftstellerischen Höhe und die deutsche selbst in englischer Übersetzung unlesbar oder nicht lesenswert.... Kurz, die französische Literatur ist drüben ungleich bekannter und beliebter als die deutsche.' And this preference for things French Leppmann finds in the area of painting, of philosophy, and of motion pictures. The reason, according to Leppmann, that German influence in the United States trails behind that of the French, lies 'an der Ungewissheit darüber, ob die deutsche Kultur nicht doch, wie drüben bisweilen angenommen wird, eher als ein historisches und weitgehend institutionalisiertes Faktum zu werten sei denn als eine tätig und täglich weiterwirkende Kraft.'

Another critic, examining the relatively slight recent importance of German literature in the United States offers this explanation: 'Ich glaube nicht, dass die geringe Einwirkung im wesentlichen auf die zwei Kriege und die Diskreditierung Deutschlands in der nationalsozialistischen Ära zurückzuführen ist, besteht doch auch in der Musik oder in der theoretischen Sphäre kein ähnliches Missverhältnis. Für bedeutsamer halte ich das, was Amerikaner zumeist als Mangel an Fleisch und Blut und konkreter Gestalt empfinden: die Neigung zur leidenschaftlichen Abstraktion, welche in der deutschen Literatur vielfach zum Ausdruck kommt. Das Urteil: ein deutscher Autor überlade sein Werk mit Theorie und körperloser Gedanklichkeit, ist drüben, auch wenn es einmal nicht zutrifft, längst zur

the number of American plays staged in various German cities, Americans have had few opportunities to attend performances of German dramas. Even university theaters in the past demonstrated only limited interest in German drama.[1] In summary, the fate of German drama in the

Gewohnheit geworden. Das ist das eine. Das andere ist ein wirklicher Mangel an schöpferischer Originalität im gegenwärtigen deutschen Schrifttum, der auch den Werken der glanzvolleren Zeiten deutscher Dichtung zum Nachteil gereicht, da den Ausländern vielfach erst die Zeitgenossen den Zugang zu den Werken ihrer Vergangenheit eröffnen. Gewiss spielt auch das Vorteil mit, dass die Deutschen – wie mir jüngst ein amerikanischer Professor sagte – ihre grossen Leistungen auf dem Gebiet der Gedankenschöpfungen vollbracht hätten, im Grunde aber kein künstlerisches Volk seien' (Peter Heller, 'Die deutsche Literatur aus amerikanischer Sicht,' *Welt und Wort*, XI [1956], 105-107).

In a relatively recent newspaper article Eric Bentley refers to Bertolt Brecht's apparent consciousness of the importance of French influence in the United States: 'In an IRT subway in 1945 Brecht had remarked to me that if only he were a Frenchman Broadway producers would be doing his plays. He added that since this couldn't be arranged, the next best thing would be to be applauded by Frenchmen, to have his plays successfully performed in Paris' ('How Brecht's "Circle" Came Full Circle,' New York *Times*, Mar. 20, 1966, p. x3).

[1] This situation, according to Francis Hodge, is changing today. In the survey mentioned above, Hodge presents the results of a study in which he compared the programming of representative university and college theaters in 1950 with that in 1961: 'A poll of 126 colleges and universities in 1950 revealed that forty-three schools produced nothing but Broadway successes, giving point to the old charge that the university theater is mainly an amateur adjunct of Broadway theater. Of the 403 productions reported, over 85 per cent were American and English plays, including about 8 per cent devoted to the Shakespearean repertory.... The significant point here is that less than 15 per cent were drawn from the Continental repertory. And who was represented by more than a single production in this category? Only one playwright was on the list from each of five dramatically significant countries: Spain (Sierra), Hungary (Molnár), Russia (Gogol), Norway (Ibsen), and Italy (Casella). France was represented by three: Molière, Rostand, and Anatol France. *No German playwright was listed*' (pp. 72-73). In 1961 '...the picture looked quite different. No school reported a program made up of Broadway successes; quite the contrary. All included at least one Continental European play. Of the 163 plays scheduled, 100 were American and English plays, this number including fourteen productions of Shakespeare, six of Shaw, and seventeen of new plays. Eight Classical Greek plays were also scheduled. The remainder – fifty-five plays or 34 per cent – were Continental. Here is the breakdown:

French	24 (7 Molière, 5 Anouilh, Beckett, Claudel, Ionesco)
Italian	7 (4 Pirandello)
German	13 (6 Brecht, 3 Dürrenmatt, Gresseiker, Schnitzler, Kaiser, and a stage version of a Kafka novel)
Miscellaneous	11 (Spanish, Norwegian, etc.)

...Next to Shakespeare and Molière, Brecht ties with Shaw as the most-produced playwright on the list. But we should also note that the German theater, in contrast with the English, French, and Greek theaters, is not represented by classical drama' (p. 74).

United States has been determined, firstly, by the absence of broad appreciation of drama as literature, secondly, by the lack of opportunity for many German playwrights to have their plays presented on the stage before the American public, and thirdly, by the failure of the academic community, to whom German drama as literature is familiar and by whom it is appreciated as such, to initiate German plays into the repertoires of the university theatre.

Of all playwrights of the twentieth century writing in German, the one who beyond doubt has made the greatest impact in the United States has been Bertolt Brecht. The record of his reception in America has been filled with paradoxes and strange inconsistencies. Like a number of other German literary artists, Brecht's reputation in Germany and indeed throughout Europe long preceded any extensive acquaintance with, to say nothing of appreciation for, his work in this country. According to one critic, 'in the United States, no tangible evidence of Brecht's fame can be found before 1933, when the *Dreigroschenoper* had its first American performance.' The same critic finds that 'the history of the reception of Brecht's plays, poems and critical writings on these shores is full of misunderstandings, partly grotesque. It can be divided roughly into three phases, the first one ending with Hitler's rise to power and Brecht's flight to Scandinavia, the second – that of gestation – encompassing the period between 1933 and 1947, and the third – that of fruition – spanning the years from 1948 to the present.'[1] His survey, then, focuses on the middle phase. A second critic examines the earliest phase, as it were, of Brecht's literary activity by studying his American plays which, except for one drama, had been completed by 1933.[2] A

[1] Ulrich Weisstein, in 'Brecht in America: A Preliminary Survey,' *MLN*, LXXVIII (1963), 373-396, treats the American publication and production of Brecht's plays, the meagre beginnings of American acquaintance with his dramatic theory, and the recognition of Brecht's talent as a poet, focusing 'on the one and a half decades in the course of which Brecht, slowly rising from obscurity, found his first American defenders, while his aims remained largely unfamiliar' (p. 374).
[2] In 'The American Plays of Bertolt Brecht,' *American Quarterly*, XV (1963), 371-389, Richard Ruland examines the plays by Brecht in which America serves as a setting or otherwise figures extensively. As Ruland notes, it is curious that Brecht had essentially finished his American plays before he joined other literary exiles in the United States, so that his treatment of America was not based on personal experience, just as was the case with

third important study traces the reception of Brecht's plays in the United States down to the present time, noting the paradox that 'American appreciation of Brecht developed only recently, although his greatest plays were written in the forties and the works now attracting attention in New York date from the twenties.'[1]

By 1945, the year with which the present study begins, Brecht had already been living in the United States nearly four years. Five of his works had been performed on American stages from New York and Philadelphia to San Francisco,[2] none of them proving outstanding successes, and several closing as failures after just a few performances. During the period from 1945 to the time of his death in 1956, nine more of his dramatic works were performed in forty-two productions, many

---

Kafka, noted previously. 'But in place of first-hand experience he had had what was surely the next most useful thing, a decade in Germany when America's influence dominated everybody and everything, the songs people sang, the dreams they dreamed, even the way they walked and held their shoulders.... What in Fitzgerald seems arrested adolescence was duplicated in a far more sophisticated Berlin as an exotic fad: Bertold Brecht became "Bert" and Georg Grosz "George"; sport, "Virginia" cigars and jazz became necessities of life; and American movies and novels helped people the arts with cowboys and Indians, Chicago mobsters and girls from the Salvation Army. It is this America that forms the backdrop for so much of Brecht's early work' (p. 372). More than contempt for Americans and their country, Rudolf concludes, Brecht's bitterness in these plays 'is a direct result of America's impact on Europe in the lustrous twenties and empty thirties; it reflects Brecht's disillusion with a Germany dominated by the influence of American capitalism. Like many Europeans, Brecht felt he had been sold out, but it is worth noting that his affection for the American people endured' (p. 388).

[1] May MacGinnis Roswell, in 'Bertolt Brecht's Plays in America' (unpubl. diss., Univ. of Maryland, 1961), noting the very slow recognition of Brecht in the United States, concludes that 'dullness, resulting from excessive Marxist didacticism and from attempts to follow Brecht's dramatic theories, has marred most productions of his plays in America' (quoted in *Dissertation Abstracts*, XXIV [1963], 749).

[2] For a useful list of American productions of Brecht's plays to 1956, see 'Brecht in America: Productions of Brecht's Plays in America up to the Time of His Death,' compiled by Walter Nubel, in Martin Esslin's *Brecht, The Man and His Work* (New York, 1961), pp. 340–351. In the same volume Esslin also provides 'A Descriptive List of Brecht's Works' (pp. 273–326) which furnishes 'brief outlines of the character and content of Brecht's writings, together with basic facts concerning the time of composition, first performance in the case of plays, and an indication of where they can be most readily found in published form' (p. 273). He also lists English translations. Full details about English and French translations of Brecht's plays are provided in John Willett's useful study, *The Theatre of Bertolt Brecht: A Study from Eight Aspects* (New York, 1960), pp. 21–61.

of which took place on the stages of colleges and universities. In fact, two of his plays which were subsequently produced individually the greatest number of times – *The Good Woman of Setzuan* and *The Caucasian Chalk Circle* – received their first American production not on the professional stage but on the university stage, the former at Hamline University in St. Paul, Minnesota, and the latter at Carleton College in Northfield, Minnesota, both in 1948. In addition, two of his less well-known plays were likewise first produced in America on university stages: *A Man = A Man* at the University of Michigan in 1952, and *The Exception and the Rule* at Dartmouth College in 1955. From the time of his death until 1960, the concluding year of this study (and indeed, down to the present time), Brecht continued to receive increased attention in American theatrical circles, although, beside the overwhelmingly successful production of *The Threepenny Opera*, which by the end of the year 1960 had been given more than seventeen hundred performances, only *The Good Woman of Setzuan* and *In the Jungle of Cities* were performed on the professional stage in New York City. As one critic has correctly observed, 'by a curious paradox, Brecht seems to have been performed more in the great country of capitalism than anywhere else except West (not East) Germany.'[1] It is curious that of the three works for the stage which Brecht wrote, at least for the most part, during the years in which he resided in the United States – *Die Geschichte der Simone Marchard*, *Schweyk im zweiten Weltkrieg*, and *Der kaukasische Kreidekreis* – two have never been produced on the American stage and have never been published in English translation, so that they remain unknown to American readers and theater-goers.

Another of the paradoxes evident in the record of Brecht's reception in the United States is the apparent disproportion between his fame and the relatively small number of his works published in America in English translation in readily available form. Since 1960, it is true, more of his works have become available to American readers than had been available previously, but between 1945 and 1960, only a few of his works had seen publication in the United States. This is to be explained by, and

[1] Esslin, p. 340.

once more confirms, the observation made previously that, firstly, there is relatively little appreciation in this country for drama as literature, and that, secondly, poetry, which he also published, seldom receives wide circulation in translation. Yet it is precisely in these two genres that Brecht made his major contribution to literature. Were it not for the stage productions of his plays it is safe to assume that Brecht would be a comparatively obscure figure in America, for the few widely available translations of his plays published by 1960 and the single volume of his poetry published in the United States would hardly have been sufficient to extend his name beyond academic circles. Yet, as one critic has noted, 'Bertolt Brecht has become fashionable in America.... More recent is the fame of the cocktail party variety; Brecht, like Kafka before him, is a name worth dropping these days.... Before long Brecht will follow Kafka into the company of European writers whose work has finally caught up with their American reputations.'[1] But if the number of Brecht's dramas and poems published in English translation is surprisingly small, his narrative prose is an 'unknown quantity.'[2]

The only narrative prose work to be published separately between 1945 and 1960 was *Threepenny Novel* (New York, 1956), a reprint of a translation by Desmond I. Vesey first published in 1938 under the title *A Penny for the Poor*. Fifty of Brecht's poems, in the original German facing English translations by H. R. Hays, make up the one volume of his poetry published in the United States, entitled *Bertolt Brecht: Selected Poems* (New York, 1947 and 1959). The only separately published and widely circulated volume of his plays published in this country during the sixteen years under survey was *Parables for the Theatre; Two Plays: The Good Woman of Setzuan and The Caucasian Chalk Circle*,[3] translated by Eric and Maja Bentley, first published in 1948 and republished in

---

[1] Ruland, p. 371.
[2] Ulrich Weisstein, in the article referred to above, concludes: '...the full recognition finally and deservedly bestowed upon Brecht the playwright in the United States has yet to be extended to Brecht the poet, while Brecht the writer of narrative prose remains an unknown quantity' (pp. 395-396).
[3] For an account of 'the adventures of Brecht's "Caucasian Chalk Circle" in the United States,' see Eric Bentley's article cited above, pp. 142-143, n. 1.

1957 with a number of subsequent printings. Although several of his dramas had indeed been translated, down to 1960 they existed only in typescript from which microfilms were made and deposited in the Columbia University Library. Eric Bentley, whose efforts to introduce and promote Brecht as well as other German writers in the United States have been unparalleled, has included five of Brecht's plays in two of his own series of drama anthologies. In the one, *From the Modern Repertoire* (Denver and Bloomington, 1949-1956), appear *The Threepenny Opera*, translated by Desmond Vesey and Bentley, *Galileo*, translated by Charles Laughton, and *Saint Joan of the Stockyards*, translated by Frank Jones. In the other, entitled *The Modern Theatre* (New York, 1955-1960) appear *The Threepenny Opera*, in the Vesey-Bentley translation, and *Mother Courage* and *The Measure Taken*, both translated by Bentley. The most comprehensive collection of Brecht's plays became available in the United States only in 1961 when Bentley's *Seven Plays by Bertolt Brecht* was published in New York.

No other German playwright has made an impact in America equal to that by Brecht, although a significant number of plays by German playwrights has been presented on the New York stage, demonstrating the cultural association, however tenuous, that links the dramatic and dramaturgic interests of the United States and Germany. New York performances of Werfel's *Jacobowsky and the Colonel*, adapted by S. N. Behrman, Fouqué's *Ondine*, adapted and translated by Jean Giraudoux and Maurice Valency, a stage version of Kafka's *The Trial*, adapted by Aaron Fine and Bert Greene, Schnitzler's *La Ronde*, adapted by Eric Bentley, and Stefan Zweig's version of Ben Jonson's *Volpone*, adapted by Ruth Lagner, all ran for more than one hundred performances, while other plays by these and other German playwrights were performed a lesser number of times. They include Werfel's *Embezzled Heaven*, Hochwälder's *The Strong Are Lonely*, and Schiller's *Mary Stuart*.

After Brecht, of all the dramatists writing in German, the Swiss playwright Friedrich Dürrenmatt has attracted the greatest contemporary attention in the United States. The selection of Dürrenmatt's *The Visit*, adapted by Maurice Valency, as the play to open the new Lunt-Fontanne Theatre in New York at Forty-Sixth Street and Broadway, formerly the

Globe Theater, on May 5, 1958, served to call attention, quite abruptly, to this new playwright. Until that time New York audiences knew him only by Maximilian Slater's adaptation of *Die Ehe des Herrn Mississippi* entitled *Fools Are Passing Through*, which was presented at the Jan Hus Auditorium just a month earlier as the first Dürrenmatt production on the New York stage. After sixty-four performances between May 5 and July 5, 1958, *The Visit* closed briefly but reopened the next season for another one hundred and twenty-six performances. In 1959 *The Visit* won the New York Drama Critics Circle Award as the best foreign play of the year. The next year Dürrenmatt's *The Jackass*, by contrast, proved quite unsuccessful, closing after only two performances.

The first English translation of any of Dürrenmatt's works was not published in the United States until 1955 when *The Judge and His Hangman*, translated by Therese Pol, first appeared. In 1958 *The Visit*, adapted by Maurice Valency, and in 1959 *The Pledge*, translated by Richard and Clara Winston, followed. Dürrenmatt's story, *Traps*, also translated by Richard and Clara Winston, was published in New York in 1960, and in the same year an adaptation of this work for the stage by James Yaffe was presented under the title *The Deadly Game* for thirty-nine performances. A shortened version of the same adaptation had been presented on television in 1958. Generated primarily by the Lunt-Fontanne production of *The Visit*, popular interest in Dürrenmatt developed rapidly so that within just a few years he emerged from obscurity to a playwright hailed by critics as one of Europe's best new writers. Certainly few, if any, other playwrights now living and writing in the German language have experienced an equally cordial reception in America.

Before 1960 Max Frisch, a second contemporary Swiss writer, was virtually unknown in the United States. Erwin Piscator's Dramatic Workshop presentation of Frisch's *A House in Berlin* in 1950 was apparently soon forgotten, and no further plays by Frisch were produced on the New York stage during the next decade. By 1960 two of his novels, both translated by Michael Bullock, had achieved American publication. *I'm Not Stiller* was published in 1958 and was followed one year later by *Homo Faber: A Report*. Frisch's first drama in English translation to be published in the United States, *The Chinese Wall*, appeared in 1961. Subsequently Frisch has also had a vogue on the American stage. By 1960 the popularity of Frisch and Dürrenmatt was unexceeded by that of any other representatives of contemporary German literature.

7

SUMMARY

The cultural heritage of the United States, related to that of the peoples of many other nations, has had particularly close associations with German culture. While indications of crosscurrents are evidenced in many areas, it is one aspect of the literary relations of the United States and Germany that has been the subject of the foregoing investigation. Since colonial days German literature has enjoyed in America a currency and reception of no small magnitude or significance. This study traces the currency of German literature in America during the sixteen-year period following the close of the Second World War. German literature from the Middle High German period down through the mid-twentieth century is measured in terms of its recent currency in the United States by an extensive bibliography of translations into English published in this country from 1945 to 1960.

From the Middle High German period works of the most important epic poets, Wolfram von Eschenbach, Gottfried von Strassburg, and Hartmann von Aue, and the chief lyric poet, Walther von der Vogelweide, are represented through recent translations into English published in the United States. These appeared, for the most part, under academic auspices and reflect primarily scholarly interests. The publication of a number of works by German mystics indicates an apparently increasing interest in the literature of mysticism. Only two literary figures, namely Lichtenberg and Lessing, represent the beginnings of the classical period of German literature.

The currency in English translation of the works of Goethe, the chief representative of German classicism, continues to be extensive. Of significance to the continuation of American interest in Goethe was the occurrence of the bicentennial anniversary of his birth, reinforcing the renewed devotion to his memory elicited by the centennial commemoration of his death seventeen years earlier. The publication of several volumes of his poetry, as well as new translations and new editions of earlier translations of his narrative prose, and, most notably, of his poetic drama, *Faust*, all attest to the continuing interest in Goethe as a universally acknowledged representative of worldly wisdom and literary genius.

Schiller, in contrast to Goethe, has had a much more restricted reception in the United States, especially as judged by the currency of translations of his works published here. Although, like Goethe, the bicentennary of his birth occurred during the period under survey, it failed to evoke in this country an interest sufficient to stimulate the publication of many of his works. The Broadway production of his historical tragedy, *Mary Stuart*, and the first volume of a series of translations by Charles E. Passage were the most significant events to interrupt the rather consistent pattern of Schiller's limited American reception outside of academic circles.

Although nineteenth-century German literature produced much lyric poetry of enduring merit, this genre has been represented by a meagre number of volumes of English translations. An exception to the restricted currency of nineteenth-century German poetry in the United States is the work of Heine. Although the centennial year of his death was marked by no unusual surge in the number of publications of his works, the abundance of such volumes to appear throughout the period under consideration provides evidence of his continued popularity in this country.

The short story (*Novelle*) and tale (*Märchen*) are the two genres most frequently found among English translations of German literature of the nineteenth century. Kleist was introduced as a story-teller in this country only after 1945. Interest in the tales of the Grimm Brothers extended beyond the traditional association with children's literature to publications intended primarily for adults. From the later nineteenth century the works of three persons were published most frequently: nonetheless, the recent currency of the works of Hauptmann, Schnitzler, and Wedekind, although still published here and occasionally performed on the American stage, reflects a decline in the popular appeal they formerly exerted in the United States.

German literature of the twentieth century, in comparison with that of preceding eras, has had the widest popular appeal in the United States. Lyric poetry appeared in relatively few separately published volumes, except for the works of Rilke, the currency of which is unsurpassed by those of any other German poet. Among the many German writers of narrative prose, Kafka and Thomas Mann are the two most widely known in the United States. The currency of Hesse's works in this country is quite limited and, were it not for the attention focused on him in 1946 when he was awarded the Nobel Prize for Literature, it is most probable he would be known here to an even more limited degree. The popularity of Werfel's works, already established in the United States before the opening year of this study, continued after his death. Remarque and Annemarie Selinko both wrote novels that were among the ten best selling books in years between 1945 and 1960. Modern German drama made its greatest popular appeal in the United States through Brecht, a number of whose plays were translated, and whose *Threepenny Opera* was the most successful German drama produced on the American stage. Toward the close of the period here surveyed, Dürrenmatt and, to a lesser degree, Frisch began to make an impact in the United States.

A number of authors who since 1960 have become quite well known in the United States, such as Günther Grass, Uwe Johnson, Siegfried Lenz, and possibly also Peter Weiss and Rolf Hochhut, had not yet had many, or any, of their works published in English translation in this country by the time of the closing year of the period investigated here. A study of the years since 1960 will doubtless reveal that new German writers have won American readers, that others previously introduced continue their appeal in the United States, and that still others have been forgotten by reading audiences here.

TITLE LIST OF GERMAN LITERATURE IN ENGLISH TRANSLATION PUBLISHED IN THE UNITED STATES, 1945-1960

The following list of titles, the significance of which as evidence of the currency of German literature in English translation in the United States during the period under consideration it has been the purpose of the preceding discussion to ascertain and assess, derives principally from published compendia such as the *Index Translationum*, the *National Union Catalog, A Catalog of Books Represented by Library of Congress Printed Cards*, the *Cumulative Book Index, Books in Print, Paperbound Books in Print*, and various publishers' catalogs and specialized bibliographies. Relatively rarely were actual copies of the volumes involved available for confirmation, correction, or amplification of data. The appearance, prior to completion of the manuscript of the present study, of the third edition of B. Q. Morgan's *A Critical Bibliography of German Literature in English Translation* with its *Supplement Embracing the Years 1928-1955* made it possible to compare the two lists, with the result that a few items were added to the following list and a number of others noted as missing from the *Supplement*; these are indicated by an asterisk after the date of the pertinent issue. Thus the following list supplements Morgan's *Bibliography* in two ways: by supplying omissions from the period 1945 to 1955 and by furnishing data for an additional five years. All in all, approximately 900 volumes are listed. Of the some 270 authors represented, including those whose works appear only in anthologies, more than 200 are responsible for one or more independently published volumes.

The list is arranged alphabetically by author. Authors employing a pseudonym are listed in the alphabetical order of their pen names with their real names in parentheses. An attempt has been made to record all editions of each work, but, without access to most of the volumes themselves as well as to publishers' records and other sources, it has not been possible to supply full information regarding separate printings of the same edition. Multiple dates indicate the presumption of reprintings, but these can not be regarded as complete; nor can their absence be considered warranty that reprintings did not occur. (For instances of the complexities involved in successive printings see MacNeice's and MacIntyre's translation of Goethe's *Faust* and the latter's translation of Rilke's poems.) No overt distinction is made between hard-cover and paperbound volumes. In cases where publishers' catalogs or other sources announced the appearance or projected appearance of a volume but where the exact date of publication was otherwise unavailable, the presumed date is given with a question mark and enclosed within parentheses. The list is limited strictly to books published in the United States, and there is no reference to the fact that some volumes are reissues of English publications as are others of earlier American ones. In a few instances it has been impossible to supply the German titles of works.

Following the general list of independently published translations is a title list of anthologies. First are listed those collections devoted exclusively to translations from the German, arranged alphabetically according to the name of the editor. The titles of the contents of collections of stories and dramas are given together with the names of authors and translators. In the case of volumes containing poetry, only the number of poems by each poet included is indicated. Finally, a few selective multinational collections of literature are included with the titles of translations from the German and the names of authors and translators contained in each volume.

While no effort has been spared to make the list complete, an absolutely complete listing, particularly one of broad scope, rarely is achieved. Doubtless this title list contains some errors and omissions. Certainly, however, the number of items listed here provides a reliable indication of the nature and extent of German literary works current in the United States from 1945 to 1960.

TITLE LIST OF TRANSLATIONS

AICHINGER, ILSE, 1921–
The Bound Man [Der Gefesselte] *and Other Stories;* tr. Eric Mosbacher. New York: Noonday, 1956.
See also Stephen Spender, *Great German Short Stories.*

ALBERS, JOSEF, 1888–
Poems and Drawings. New Haven: Readymade, 1958.

ALTENBERG, PETER (i.e., Richard Engländer), 1859-1919.
Alexander King Presents Peter Altenberg's Evocations of Love. New York: Simon and Schuster, 1960.

ANDERSCH, ALFRED, 1914–
Flight to Afar [Sansibar, oder der letzte Grund]; tr. Michael Bullock. New York: Coward-McCann, 1958.

ANDRES, STEFAN, 1906–
We Are God's Utopia [Wir sind Utopia]; tr. Elita Walker Caspari. Chicago: Regnery, 1957.

ANGELUS SILESIUS (i.e., Johannes Scheffler), 1624-1677.
The Cherubinic Wanderer [Der Cherubinische Wandersmann]; tr. Willard R. Trask. New York: Pantheon, 1953.

ARNIM, LUDWIG ACHIM VON, 1781-1831.
See Hermann Kesten, *The Blue Flower.*

BACHMANN, INGEBORG, 1926–
See Jerome Rothenberg, *New Young German Poets.*

BAMM, PETER (i.e., Kurt Emmrich), 1897–
The Invisible Flag [Die unsichtbare Flagge]; New York: Day, 1956.

The Invisible Flag [Die unsichtbare Flagge]; New York: New American Library, (1958?).

BARLACH, ERNST, 1870-1938.
Two Acts from The Flood [Die Sündflut]; *A Letter on Kandinsky; Eight Sculptures.* Northampton: Printed at the Gehenna Press for the Massachusetts Review, 1960.

BARTHEL, MAX, 1893-
See Herman Salinger, *Twentieth-Century German Verse.*

BAUMANN, HANS, 1914-
Angelina and the Birds [Kleine Schwester Schwalbe]; tr. Katharine Potts. New York: Watts, 1959.
The Barque of the Brothers: A Tale of the Days of Henry the Navigator [Die Barke der Brüder aus der Zeit Heinrichs des Seefahrers]; tr. Isabel and Florence McHugh. New York: Walch, 1958.
The Caves of the Great Hunters [Die Höhlen der grossen Jäger]; tr. Isabel and Florence McHugh. New York: Pantheon, 1954.
Jackie the Pit Pony [Hänschen in der Grube]. New York: Watts, 1958.
Son of Columbus [Der Sohn des Columbus]; tr. Isabel and Florence McHugh. New York: Oxford, 1957.
Sons of the Steppe [Steppensöhne]; tr. Isabel and Florence McHugh. New York: Oxford, 1957.
The World of the Pharaohs [Die Welt der Pharaonen]; tr. Richard and Clara Winston. New York: Pantheon, 1960.

BECHER, ULRICH, 1910-
See Herman Salinger, *Twentieth-Century German Verse.*

BEKESSY, EMERY, 1887-   and ANDREAS HEMBERGER
Barabbas; A Novel of the Time of Jesus; tr. Richard and Clara Winston. New York: Prentice-Hall, 1946*.
Barabbas; A Novel of the Time of Jesus; tr. Richard and Clara Winston. New York: Garden City, 1948*.

BENARY-ISBERT, MARGOT, 1889-

The Ark [Die Arche Noah]; tr. Richard and Clara Winston. New York: Harcourt, Brace, 1953.

Blue Mystery; Richard and Clara Winston. New York: Harcourt, Brace, 1957.

Castle on the Border [Schloss an der Grenze]; tr. Richard and Clara Winston. New York: Harcourt, Brace, 1956.

The Long Way Home; tr. Richard and Clara Winston. New York: Harcourt, Brace, 1959.

Rowan Farm [Der Ebereschenhof]; tr. Richard and Clara Winston. New York: Harcourt, Brace, 1954.

The Shooting Star; tr. Richard and Clara Winston. New York: Harcourt, Brace, 1954.

The Wicked Enchantment; tr. Richard and Clara Winston. New York: Harcourt, Brace, 1955.

BENN, GOTTFRIED, 1886-1956.

Primal Vision: Selected Writings; ed. E. B. Ashton (pseud.). Norfolk, Conn.: Laughlin, 1960.

See also Stephen Spender, *Great German Short Stories.*

BENTZ, HANS GEORG, 1902-

Dogs Are Company [Der Bund der Drei]; tr. Marjorie Deans. New York: Dutton, 1954.

BERGENGRÜN, WERNER, 1892-

The Last Captain of Horse, A Portrait of Chivalry [Der letzte Rittmeister]; tr. Eric Peters. New York: Vanguard, 1954*.

The Last Captain of Horse, A Portrait of Chivalry [Der letzte Rittmeister]; tr. Eric Peters. New York: Thames and Hudson, 1954.

A Matter of Conscience [Der Grosstyrann und das Gericht]; tr. Norman Cameron. New York: Thames and Hudson, 1952.

BERNARD, DENIS F., 1915-

The Suspended Man [Mensch ohne Gegenwart]; tr. Robert Molly. New York: Putnam, 1960.

BERSTL, JULIUS, 1883-
The Tentmaker; A Novel Based on the Life of St. Paul; tr. Clarissa Graves. Murray Hill, N.Y.: Reinhart, 1952.
The Cross and the Eagle: A Novel Based on the Life of St. Paul; tr. Clarissa Graves. Philadelphia: Muhlenberg, 1955.

BINDING, RUDOLF G., 1867-1938.
See Herman Salinger, *Twentieth-Century German Verse.*

BIRKENFELD, GÜNTHER, 1901-1966.
A Room in Berlin [Dritter Hof links]; tr. Eric Sutton. New York: Avon, 1955★.

BÖHME, JAKOB, 1575-1624.
Confessions; ed. W. Scott Palmer. New York: Harper, 1954.
Dialogues on the Supersensual Life [Vom übersinnlichen Leben]; tr. William Law and others. New York: Ungar, 1958.
Six Theosophic Points, and Other Writing; tr. John Rolleston Earle. Ann Arbor: University of Michigan, 1958.
Way to Christ, Discovered and Described by Jacob Behmen [Weg zu Christo]. Los Angeles: Wetzel, 1946★.
Way to Christ [Weg zu Christo]; tr. John Joseph Stoudt. New York: Harper, 1947★.

BÖLL, HEINRICH, 1917-
Acquainted with the Night [Und sagte kein einziges Wort]; tr. Richard Graves. New York: Holt, 1954.
Acquainted with the Night [Und sagte kein einziges Wort]; tr. Richard Graves. New York: Criterion, 1954★.
Adam, Where Art Thou? [Wo warst du, Adam?]; tr. Mervyn Savill. New York: Criterion, 1955.
Tomorrow and Yesterday [Haus ohne Hüter]; tr. Mervyn Savill. New York: Criterion, 1957.
The Train was on Time [Der Zug war pünktlich]; tr. Richard Graves. New York: Criterion, 1956.
See also Stephen Spender, *Great German Short Stories.*

BONSELS, WALDEMAR, 1881-1952.
The Adventures of Maya the Bee [Die Biene Maja]; tr. Adele Szold Seltzer. New York: Pellegrini and Cudahy, 1951.

BORCHERT, WOLFGANG, 1921-1947.
The Man Outside [Draussen vor der Tür]: *The Prose Works;* tr. David Porter. Norfolk, Conn., New Directions, 1952.

BRECHT, BERTOLT, 1898-1956.
Galileo [Leben des Galilei]. Typescript of acting version used by Charles Laughton (1947?).
The Good Woman of Setzuan [Der gute Mensch von Sezuan]; tr. Eric Bentley (Royal Court Theatre version). New York: 1956.
In the Jungle of the Cities [Im Dickicht der Städte]; tr. Gerhard Nellhaus. Microfilm of typescript, 1957.
A Man's a Man [Mann ist Mann]. Microfilm of typescript, 1957.
Mother Courage and Her Children [Mutter Courage und ihre Kinder]; tr. J. Kirkup. Microfilm of typescript, 1957.
On Agreement; tr. Lee Baxandall. Microfilm of typescript, 1959.
On 'Tao te Ching' [Zu Taoteking]. Lexington, Ky.: Anvil, 1959.
Parables for the Theatre; Two Plays: The Good Woman of Setzuan [Der gute Mensch von Sezuan] *and The Caucasian Chalk Circle* [Der kaukasische Kreidekreis]; tr. Eric and Maja Bentley. Minneapolis: University of Minnesota, 1948.
Puntila [Herr Puntila und sein Knecht Matti]; tr. Gerhard Nellhaus. Microfilm of typescript, 1959.
The Rise of Arturo Ui [Der aufhaltsame Aufstieg des Arturo Ui]; tr. H. R. Hays. Microfilm of typescript, 1957.
Schweyk [Schweik im zweiten Weltkrieg]; tr. Alfred Kreymborg. New York, 1957.
Two Plays: The Good Woman of Setzuan [Der gute Mensch von Sezuan]; *The Caucasian Chalk Circle* [Der kaukasische Kreidekreis]; tr. Eric Bentley and Maja Apelman. New York: Grove, 1957.
Selected Poems; tr. H. R. Hays. New York: Reynal and Hitchcock, 1947.
Selected Poems; tr. H. R. Hays. New York: Grove, 1959.

Threepenny Novel [Der Dreigroschenroman]; tr. Desmond I. Vesey. New York: Grove, 1956.
See also Eric Bentley, *From the Modern Repertoire*, and *The Modern Theatre*.

BREMER, KLAUS, 1924-
See Jerome Rothenberg, *New Young German Poets*.

BRENTANO, CLEMENS, 1778-1842.
See Angel Flores, *An Anthology of German Poetry;* Hermann Kesten, *The Blue Flower;* Victor Lange, *Great German Short Novels and Stories;* and Robert Pick, *German Stories and Tales*.

BROCH, HERMANN, 1886-1951.
Death of Virgil [Der Tod des Vergil]; tr. Jean Starr Untermeyer. New York: Pantheon, 1945.
The Sleepwalkers [Die Schlafwandler]; tr. Willa and Edwin Muir. New York: Pantheon, 1947.
See also Robert Pick, *German Stories and Tales*.

BROD, MAX, 1884-
The Master [Der Meister]; tr. Heinz Norden. New York: Philosophical Library, 1951.
Unambo [Unambo]; tr. Ludwig Lewisohn. New York: Farrar, Straus, 1952.

BRUCKNER, KARL, 1906-
The Golden Pharaoh [Der goldene Pharao]; tr. Frances Lobb. New York: Pantheon, 1959.

BUBER, MARTIN, 1878-1965.
For the Sake of Heaven [Gog u-Magog]; tr. Ludwig Lewisohn. Philadelphia: Jewish Publication Society, 1945*.
For the Sake of Heaven [Gog u-Magog]; tr. Ludwig Lewisohn. 2d ed. New York: Harper, 1953.

For the Sake of Heaven [Gog u-Magog]; tr. Ludwig Lewisohn. Cleveland and New York: World, and Philadelphia: Jewish Publication Society, 1958, 1959.

The Legend of Baal-Shem [Die Legende des Baalschem]; tr. Maurice Friedman. New York: Harper, 1955.

Tales of Angels, Spirits & Demons [Erzählungen von Engeln, Geistern und Dämonen]; tr. David Antin and Jerome Rothenberg. New York: Hawk's Well, 1958.

Tales of the Hasidim [Die chassidischen Bücher]; tr. Olga Marx. Volume I, The Early Masters; Volume II, The Later Masters. New York: Schocken, 1947-1948.

Ten Rungs: Hasidic Sayings; tr. Olga Marx. New York: Schocken, 1947.

BÜCHNER, GEORG, 1813-1837.

The Plays of Georg Büchner; tr. Geoffrey Dunlop. New York: Ravin, 1952.

See also Eric Bentley, *From the Modern Repertoire,* and *The Modern Theatre;* and Stephen Spender, *Great German Short Stories.*

CAROSSA, HANS, 1878-1956.

See Herman Salinger, *Twentieth-Century German Verse.*

CARWIN, SUSANNA (i.e., Herta Schubart-Karpeles), 1908-

Faith and Inquisitions; tr. Melville Sanders. New York: Hutchinson, 1950.

CELAN, PAUL, 1920-

See Jerome Rothenberg, *New Young German Poets.*

CHAMISSO, ADELBERT VON, 1781-1838.

The Wonderful History of Peter Schlemihl [Peter Schlemihls wundersame Geschichte]; tr. William Howitt. Emmaus, Pa.: Story Classics, 1954*.

CHONZ, SELINA (i.e., Selina Könz), 1911-
A Bell for Ursli. New York: Oxford, 1950, 1957.
Florina and the Wild Bird [Flurina und das Wildvöglein]; tr. Anne and Ian Serraillier. New York: Oxford, 1953.
The Snowstorm [Der grosse Schnee]. New York: Walch, 1958.

CLAUDIUS, HERMANN, 1878-
See Herman Salinger, *Twentieth-Century German Verse*.

CONTE, MANFRED
Jeopardy [Cassia und der Abenteuer]; tr. Cressida Ridley. New York: Sloane, 1956.

DEICH, FRIEDRICH (i.e., Friedrich August Weeren), 1907-
The Sanity Inspectors [Wundarzt und Apfelsinenpfarrer]; tr. Robert Kee. New York: Rinehart, 1957.

DENNEBORG, HEINRICH MARIA, 1909-
Grisella the Donkey [Das Eselchen Grisella]; tr. Emile Capouya. New York: McKay, 1957.
Jan and the Wild Horse [Jan und das Wildpferd]; tr. Emile Capouya. New York: McKay, 1958.

DIETMAR VON AIST, 12th cent.
See Hubert Creekmore, *Lyrics of the Middle Ages*.

DÖBLIN, ALFRED, 1878-1957.
Alexanderplatz Berlin [Berlin Alexanderplatz]; tr. Eugene Jolas. New York: Ungar, 1958.

DREYER, ERNST JÜRGEN, 1934-
See Jerome Rothenberg, *New Young German Poets*.

DROSTE-HÜLSHOFF, ANNETTE VON, 1797-1848.
See Angel Flores, *An Anthology of German Poetry;* and Victor Lange, *Great German Short Novels and Stories*.

DÜRRENMATT, FRIEDRICH, 1921-

The Judge and His Hangman [Der Richter und sein Henker]; tr. Therese Pol. New York: Harper, 1955.

The Judge and His Hangman [Der Richter und sein Henker]; tr. Therese Pol. New York: Berkley, 1958*.

The Pledge [Das Versprechen]; tr. Richard and Clara Winston. New York: Knopf, 1959.

The Pledge [Das Versprechen]; tr. Richard and Clara Winston. New York: New American Library, 1960.

Traps [Die Panne]; tr. Richard and Clara Winston. New York: Knopf, 1960.

The Visit [Der Besuch der alten Dame]; tr. Maurice Valency. New York: French, 1958.

The Visit [Der Besuch der alten Dame]; tr. Maurice Valency. New York: Random House, 1958.

EBNER-ESCHENBACH, MARIA VON, 1830-1916.

See Robert Pick, *German Stories and Tales*.

ECKHART, MEISTER, 1260?-1327.

Meister Eckhart: An Introduction to the Study of His Works, with an Anthology of His Sermons; tr. James M. Clark. New York: Nelson, 1957.

Meister Eckhart: A Modern Translation; tr. Raymond Bernard Blakney. New York: Harper, 1957.

Meister Eckehart [sic] *Speaks: A Collection of the Teachings of the Famous German Mystic* [Meister Eckehart spricht]; tr. Elizabeth Strakosch. New York: Philosophical Library, 1957.

Sermon on Beati pauperes spiritu; tr. Raymond Bernard Blakney. Pawlet, (Vt.?): Claude Fredericks, 1960.

Treatises and Sermons; tr. James M. Clark and John V. Skinner. New York: Harper, 1958.

Works; tr. C. de B. Evans. 2 vols., Naperville, Ill.: Alec R. Allenson, I, 1956; II, 1952*.

EICHENDORFF, JOSEPH FREIHERR VON, 1788-1857.
Memoirs of a Good-for-Nothing [Aus dem Leben eines Taugenichts]; tr. B. Q. Morgan. New York: Ungar, 1955, 1960.
See also Angel Flores, *An Anthology of German Poetry*.

EKERT-ROTHOLZ, ALICE MARIA, 1900-
A Net of Gold [Strafende Sonne - lockender Mond]; tr. Richard and Clara Winston. New York: Viking, 1960.
The Time of the Dragons [Wo Tränen verboten sind]; tr. Richard and Clara Winston. New York: Viking, 1958.
The Time of the Dragons [Wo Tränen verboten sind]; tr. Richard and Clara Winston. New York: New American Library, 1959.

EKKEHARDUS I, DEAN OF ST. GALL, d. 973.
Walter of Aquitaine: Materials for the Study of His Legend; tr. F. P. Magoun, Jr., and H. M. Smyser. New London: Connecticut College, 1950.

ELBOGEN, PAUL, 1894-
The Jealous Mistress; tr. Ruth Lachenbruch. New York: Random House, 1953.
The Jealous Mistress. New York: Pyramid, (1956?).

EMMERICH, ANNA KATHARINA, 1774-1824.
The Life of the Blessed Virgin Mary; From the Visions of Anne Catherine Emmerich; tr. Sir Michael Palairet. Springfield, Ill.: Templegate, 1954★.
The Life of Our Lord and Savior Jesus Christ, Combined with The Bitter Passion, and The Life of Mary; From the Revelations of Anna Catharina Emmerick as Recorded in the Journals of Clemens Brentano. Fresno, Calif.: Academy Library Guild, 1954★.

ENZENSBERGER, HANS MAGNUS, 1929-
See Jerome Rothenberg, *New Young German Poets*.

ESKA, KARL (i.e., Kurt Stein), 1905-
The Five Seasons [Fünf Jahreszeiten]; tr. Robert Kee. New York: Viking, 1954.

FALLADA, HANS (i.e., Rudolf Ditzen), 1893-1947.
The Drinker [Der Trinker]; tr. Charlotte and A. L. Lloyd. New York: Didier, 1952.
The Drinker [Der Trinker]; tr. Charlotte and A. L. Lloyd. New York: Dell, (1956?).
Little Man, What Now? [Kleiner Mann, was nun?]; tr. Eric Sutton. New York: Ungar, 1958.
That Rascal, Fridolin [Fridolin, der freche Dachs]; tr. Ruth Michaelis-Jena and Imre Hofbauer. New York: Pantheon, 1959.

FANGER, HORST, 1919-
A Life for a Life [Wir selber sind das Rad]; tr. Richard and Clara Winston. New York: Ballantine, 1954.

FEUCHTWANGER, LION, 1884-1958.
Jephta and His Daughter [Jefta und seinte Tochter]; tr. Eithne Wilkins and Ernst Kaiser. New York: Putnam, 1958.
Jephta and His Daughter [Jefta und seine Tochter]; tr. Eithne Wilkins and Ernst Kaiser. New York: New American Library, 1960.
Marianne in India, and Other Stories [Marianne in Indien und sieben andere Erzählungen]. New York: Avon, 1948.
Odysseus and the Swine, and Other Stories. New York: Hutchinson 1949.
Power [Jud Süss]; tr. Willa and Edwin Muir. New York: Viking, 1948.
Proud Destiny [Waffen für Amerika]; tr. Moray Firth. New York: Viking, 1947.
Proud Destiny [Waffen für Amerika]; tr. Moray Firth. New York: Garden City, 1949*.
Raquel, the Jewess of Toledo [Die Jüdin von Toledo]; tr. Ernst Kaiser and Eithne Wilkins. New York: Messner, 1956.
Raquel, the Jewess of Toledo [Die Jüdin von Toledo]; tr. Ernst Kaiser and Eithne Wilkins. New York: New American Library, 1957.

Simone; tr. G. A. Herman. New York: Garden City, 1946*.
Stories from Far and Near. New York: Viking, 1945.
This Is the Hour [Goya, oder Der arge Weg zur Erkenntnis]; tr. H. T. Lowe-Porter and Frances Fawcett. New York: Viking, 1951.
This Is the Hour [Goya, oder Der arge Weg zur Erkenntnis]; tr. H. T. Lowe-Porter and Frances Fawcett. New York: Heritage, 1956.
'Tis Folly to Be Wise, or Death and Transfiguration [Narrenweisheit oder Tod und Verklärung des Jean Jacques Rousseau]; tr. Frances Fawcett. New York: Messner, 1953.
The Ugly Duchess [Die hässliche Herzogin]; tr. Willa and Edwin Muir. New York: Avon, (1951?).
The Widow Capet [Die Witwe Capet]. Los Angeles: Pazifische Presse, 1956.

FLÜCKIGER, ALFRED, 1898-
Tuck, the Story of a Snow-Hare [Muck, Lebenstage eines Alpenhasen]; tr. Rose Fyleman. New York: Coward-McCann, (1951?)*.

FRANK, LEONHARD, 1882-1961.
Beloved Stranger; tr. Cyrus Brooks. New York: Fischer, 1946.
Desire Me [Karl und Anna]; tr. Cyrus Brooks. New York: Garden City, 1947*.
Desire Me [Karl und Anna] *and Other Stories;* tr. Cyrus Brooks. Baltimore: Penguin, 1948.
Desire Me [Karl und Anna]. New York: New American Library, (1957?).
Dream Mates [Die Traumgefährten]; tr. Maxim Newmark. New York: Philosophical Library, 1946.
Mathilde [Mathilde]; tr. Willard R. Trask. New York: Simon and Schuster, 1948.

FREY, ALEXANDER M., 1881-1957.
Birl, the Story of a Cat [Birl, die kühne Katze]; tr. Gwenda David and Eric Mosbacher. New York: British Book Centre, 1952.

The Stout-Hearted Cat; tr. Richard and Clara Winston. New York: Holt, 1947*.

FRIEBERGER, KURT, 1883-
Fisher of Men [Der Fischer Simon Petrus]; tr. A. L. Lloyd. New York: Appleton-Century-Crofts, 1954.

FRIEDRICH VON HAUSEN, 12th cent.
See Hubert Creekmore, *Lyrics of the Middle Ages*.

FRISCH, MAX, 1911-
Homo Faber; A Report [Homo Faber]; tr. Michael Bullock. New York: Abelard-Schuman, 1959.
I'm Not Stiller [Stiller]; tr. Michael Bullock. New York: Abelard-Schuman, 1958.

FUCHS, PETER, 1928-
The Land of Veiled Men [Im Land der verschleierten Männer]; tr. Bice Fawcett. New York: Citadel, 1956.

FÜLÖP-MILLER, RENÉ, 1891-
The Night of Time; tr. Richard and Clara Winston. Indianapolis: Bobbs-Merrill, 1955.
The Silver Bacchanal; tr. Richard and Clara Winston. New York: Atheneum, 1960.
Sing, Brat, Sing; tr. Richard Winston. New York: Holt, 1947*.
The Web: A Trilogy of Novellas; tr. Richard and Clara Winston. New York: Abelard-Schuman, 1950.

GAISER, GERD, 1908-
The Final Ball [Schlussball]; tr. Marguerite Waldman. New York: Pantheon, 1960.
The Last Squadron [Die sterbende Jagd]; tr. Paul Findlay. New York: Pantheon, 1956.
See also Stephen Spender, *Great German Short Stories*.

GEBHARDT, HERTHA VON, 1896-
The Girl from Nowhere [Das Mädchen von Irgendwoher]; tr. James Kirkup. New York: Criterion, 1959.

GEORGE, STEFAN ANTON, 1868-1933.
The Works of Stefan George; tr. Olga Marx and Ernst Morwitz. Chapel Hill: University of North Carolina, 1949.
See also Angel Flores, *An Anthology of German Poetry;* and Herman Salinger, *Twentieth-Century German Verse.*

GERLACH, HEINRICH, 1908-
The Forsaken Army [Die verratene Armee]; tr. Richard Graves. New York: Harper, 1959.

GERSTÄCKER, FRIEDRICH WILHELM CHRISTIAN, 1816-1872.
California Gold Mines. Oakland, Calif.: Biobooks, 1946*.
Germelshausen [Germelshausen]; tr. Alexander Gode-von Aesch. Great Neck, N.Y.: Barron, 1958.

GOES, ALBRECHT, 1908-
The Burnt Offering [Das Brandopfer]; tr. Michael Hamburger. New York: Pantheon, 1956.
Unquiet Night [Unruhige Nacht]; tr. Constantine Fitzgibbon. Boston: Houghton Mifflin, 1951.

GOETHE, JOHANN WOLFGANG VON, 1749-1832.
Botanical Writings; tr. Bertha Mueller. Honolulu: University of Hawaii, 1952.
Egmont; tr. Willard R. Trask. Great Neck, N.Y.: Barron, 1960.
Faust (I and II); tr. John Anster. New York: Oxford, 1946*.
Faust (I and II); tr. Max Diez. Bryn Mawr, Pa.: 1949.
Faust (I and II, abridged); tr. Louis MacNeice. New York: Oxford, 1952*, 1954, 1957, 1959 (5th Printing).
Faust (I and II); tr. Sir Theodore Martin. New York: Dutton, 1954.

Faust (I and II); tr. Philip Wayne. 2 vols., Baltimore: Penguin, I, 1958, 1960; II, 1959.
Faust (I and Act V of II); tr. B. Q. Morgan. New York: Liberal Arts, 1957.
Faust (I and selections of II); tr. J. F. L. Raschen. Ithaca, N.Y.: Thrift, 1949.
Faust (I); tr. Bayard Taylor, ed. B. Q. Morgan, New York: Crofts, 1946.
Faust (I); tr. Carlyle F. MacIntyre. New York: New Directions, 1947*, 1949*, 1957 (4th Printing).
Faust (I); tr. Bayard Taylor. New York: Hartsdale, 1947*.
Faust (I); tr. Bayard Taylor. New York: Modern Library, 1950.
Faust (I); tr. B. Q. Morgan. New York: Liberal Arts, 1954.
Faust (I); tr. Alice Raphael. New York: Rinehart, 1955, 1960 (4th Printing).
Faust (I); tr. George Madison Priest. Chicago: Encyclopaedia Britannica, 1955.
Faust (I); tr. Bertram Jessup. New York: Philosophical Library, 1958.
Faust (I); tr. John Shawcross. New York: Daub, 1959.
Faust (I); tr. Alice Raphael. New York: Heritage, 1959.
Goethe, the Lyrist; tr. Edwin H. Zeydel. Chapel Hill: University of North Carolina, 1955.
Goethe, the Lyrist; tr. Edwin H. Zeydel. 2d ed., rev. Chapel Hill: University of North Carolina, 1959.
Goethe, The Story of a Man, Being the Life of Johann Wolfgang Goethe as Told in His Own Words and the Words of His Contemporaries; tr. Ludwig Lewisohn. New York: Farrar, Straus, 1949.
Goethe's Autobiography: Poetry and Truth from My Own Life; tr. R. O. Moon. Washington, D.C.: Public Affairs, 1949.
Goethe's Botany: The Metamorphosis of Plants (1790) and Tobler's Ode to Nature (1782); tr. Agnes Arber. Waltham, Mass.: Chronica Botanica, 1946.
Goethe's World as Seen in His Letters and Memoirs. New York: New Directions, 1949.
Great Writings of Goethe; ed. Stephen Spender. New York: New American Library, 1958.

Iphigenia in Tauris [Iphigenie auf Tauris]; tr. Sidney E. Kaplan. Brooklyn: Barron, 1953.
Iphigenia in Tauris [Iphigenie auf Tauris]; tr. B. Q. Morgan. Stanford, Calif.: Academic Reprints, 1954.
Iphigenia in Tauris [Iphigenie auf Tauris]; tr. Roy Pascal. Microfilm of typescript, 1958.
Letters from Goethe; tr. M. von Herzfeld and C. Melvil Sym. New York: Nelson, 1957.
Most Famous Songs of Goethe; tr. Udo Rall. Arlington, Va.: Rall, 1949.
The Permanent Goethe; ed. Thomas Mann. New York: Dial, 1948.
Poems of Goethe: A Sequel to 'Goethe the Lyrist'; tr. Edwin H. Zeydel. Chapel Hill: University of North Carolina, 1957.
Sorrows of Young Werther [Die Leiden des jungen Werthers], *The New Melusina* [Die neue Melusine], *Novelle* [Die Novelle]; ed. Victor Lange. New York: Rinehart, 1949.
George Ticknor's The Sorrows of Young Werter [Die Leiden des jungen Werthers]; ed. Frank G. Ryder. Chapel Hill: University of North Carolina, 1952.
Stella; tr. B. Q. Morgan. Microfilm of typescript, 1958.
Story of Reynard the Fox [Reineke Fuchs]; tr. Thomas James Arnold. New York: Heritage, 1954.
The Story of Reynard the Fox [Reineke Fuchs]; tr. Thomas James Arnold. New York: Limited Editions Club, 1954.
The Sufferings of Young Werther [Die Leiden des Jungen Werthers]; tr. B. Q. Morgan. New York: Ungar, 1957.
Torquato Tasso; tr. Ben Kimpel and T. C. Duncan Eaves. Fayetteville: University of Arkansas, 1956.
Truth and Fantasy From My Own Life [Dichtung und Wahrheit]; tr. Eithne Wilkins and Ernst Kaiser. New York: Ravin, 1949*.
The Urfaust [Urfaust]; tr. Douglas M. Scott. Great Neck, N.Y.: Barron, 1958.
Wilhelm Meister's Apprenticeship [Wilhelm Meisters Lehrjahre]; tr. Thomas Carlyle. New York: Limited Editions Club, 1959.
Wisdom and Experience; tr. Hermann J. Weigand. New York: Pantheon, 1949.

Words of Goethe, Being the Conversations of Johann Wolfgang von Goethe, Recorded by His Friend Johann Peter Eckermann. New York: Tudor, 1949.
See also Eric Bentley, *The Classic Theatre;* and Victor Lange, *Great German Short Novels and Stories.*

GOTTFRIED VON STRASSBURG, 13th cent.
Tristan; tr. A. T. Hatto. Baltimore: Penguin, 1960.
Tristan; tr. A. T. Hatto. Gloucester, Mass.: Smith, 1960.
The 'Tristan and Isolde' of Gottfried von Strassburg; tr. E. H. Zeydel. Princeton: Princeton University, 1948.

GOTTHELF, JEREMIAS, 1797-1854.
See Angel Flores, *Nineteenth-Century German Tales.*

GRABBE, CHRISTIAN DIETRICH, 1801-1836.
See Eric Bentley, *From the Modern Repertoire.*

GRASS, GÜNTER, 1927-
See Jerome Rothenberg, *New Young German Poets.*

GREGOR, MANFRED, 1929-
The Bridge [Die Brücke]; tr. Robert S. Rosen. New York: Random House, 1960.

GRESSIEKER, HERMANN, 1903-
Royal Gambit; tr. George White. New York: French, 1959.

GRILLPARZER, FRANZ, 1791-1872.
A Dream is Life [Der Traum ein Leben]; tr. Henry H. Stevens. Yarmouthport, Mass.: Register, 1946.
Family Strife in Hapsburg [Ein Bruderzwist in Habsburg]; tr. Arthur Burkhard. Yarmouthport, Mass.: Register, 1949*.
Hero and Leander [Hero und Leander]; tr. B. Q. Morgan. Microfilm of typescript, 1958.

The Jewess of Toledo [Die Jüdin von Toledo]; and *Esther*; tr. Arthur Burkhard. Yarmouthport, Mass.: Register, 1953.
Medea; tr. Arthur Burkhard. Yarmouthport, Mass.: Register, 1956.
Sappho; tr. Arthur Burkhard. Yarmouthport, Mass.: Register, 1953.

GRIMM, JAKOB LUDWIG KARL, 1785-1863, and WILHELM, 1786-1859.
Fairy Tales; tr. Mrs. Edgar Lucas and others. New York: Grosset and Dunlap, 1945.
Fairy Tales; tr. Lucy Crane, Marian Edwardes, Mrs. Edgar Lucas, and others. Cleveland: World, 1947.
Fairy Tales. New York: Scribner, 1947.
Fairy Tales. New York: Chanticleer, 1950.
Fairy Tales. New York: Dutton, 1951.
Fairy Tales. New York: Garden City, 1954.
Grimms' Fairy Tales. New York: Dutton, 1949*.
Grimms' Fairy Tales. Garden City, N.Y.: Junior Editions, 1954*.
Grimms' Fairy Tales; retld. Rose Dobbs. New York: Random House, 1955.
Grimms' Fairy Tales: Snow White and Other Stories; retld. Shirley Goulden. New York: Grosset and Dunlap, 1957.
The Grimms' German Folk Tales; tr. Francis P. Magoun, Jr., and Alexander H. Krappe. Carbondale, Ill.: Southern Illinois University, 1960.
Grimms' Tales. New York: Oxford, 1954.
Favorite Fairy Tales Told in Germany, Retold from the Brothers Grimm; retld. Virginia Haviland. Boston: Little, Brown, 1959.
House in the Wood, and Other Old Fairy Stories. New York: Warne, 1947*, 1957.
Household Stories from the Collection of the Brothers Grimm; tr. Lucy Crane. New York: Macmillan, 1949, 1954.
More Tales from Grimm; tr. Wanda Gag. New York: Coward-McCann, 1947.
Snow White, and Other Stories from Grimm; retld. Jeanne Cappe (tr. from the French, Marie Ponsot). New York: Grosset and Dunlap, 1957.
Snow White, and Other Stories; retld. Shirley Goulden. New York: Grosset and Dunlap, 1957.

Tales from Grimm; retld. Sarah K. Wright. New York: Dutton, 1945.
Tales of Grimm and Andersen. New York: Modern Library, 1952.
Tales from Grimm and Andersen; retld. W. K. Holmes. New York: Oceana, 1958.
The Brave Little Tailor. New York: Simon and Schuster, 1953.
Cinderella; adpt. Harriet. New York: Maxton, 1947.
The Fisherman and His Wife. New York: Pantheon, 1957.
The Golden Goose. Boston: McLaughlin, 1945.
The Golden Goose. Boston: Houghton Mifflin, 1947.
The Golden Goose. New York: Simon and Schuster, 1954.
The Good-for-Nothing. New York: Harcourt, Brace, 1957.
The Story of Hansel and Gretel. New York: Lothrop, Lee and Shephard, 1945.
Hansel and Gretel. New York: Simon and Schuster, 1945, 1954.
Hansel and Gretel; adpt. Harriet. New York: Maxton, 1946.
Hansel and Gretel: A Play; adpt. Catherine Ellis Wilkinson. Chicago: Dramatic, 1946.
Hansel and Gretel; adpt. Lillian Decker Masters. New York: French, 1949★.
Hansel and Gretel. Chicago: Rand McNally, 1960.
The Story of What Happened to Hansel and Gretel; tr. P. H. Muir. New York: Limited Editions Club, 1952.
King Thrushbeard; adpt. Harriet. New York: Maxton, 1946.
The Musicians of Bremen. New York: Simon and Schuster, 1954.
Rumpelstiltskin; adpt. Patricia Jones. Chicago: Rand McNally, 1955.
The Shoes That Danced; adpt. Harriet. New York: Maxton, 1946.
The Shoemaker and the Elves; tr. Wayne Andrews. New York: Scribner, 1960.
The Sleeping Beauty; tr. Peter Collier. New York: Harcourt, Brace, 1959.
Snow White and Rose-Red; adpt. Harriet. New York: Maxton, 1946.
Snow White and the Seven Dwarfs. Chicago: Wilcox and Follett, 1946.
Snow White and the Seven Dwarfs. New York: Anthroposophic, 1946.
Snow White. New York: Garden City, 1946.
Snow White and the Seven Dwarfs. New York: Coward-McCann, 1960.

Walt Disney's Snow White and the Seven Dwarfs; adpt. Jane Werner. New York: Simon and Schuster, 1952*.
The Story of the Seven Ravens. New York: Lothrop, Lee and Shephard, 1946.
The Giant with Three Golden Hairs. New York: Simon and Schuster, 1955.
Three Gay Tales from Grimm. New York: Coward-McCann, 1960.
Traveling Musicians. Boston: McLaughlin, 1945.
The Travelling Musicians. New York: Harcourt, Brace, 1955.
The Twelve Dancing Princesses; retld. Sheilah Beckett. New York: Simon and Schuster, 1954.
The Wolf and the Seven Little Kids. New York: Harcourt, Brace, 1959.

GRZIMEK, BERNHARD, 1909-
Doctor Jimek, I Presume [Flug ins Schimpansenland]; tr. R. H. Stevens. New York: Norton, 1956.
No Room for Wild Animals [Kein Platz für wilde Tiere]; tr. R. H. Stevens. New York: Norton, 1957.

HABE, HANS (i.e., Jean Bekessy), 1911-
Aftermath; tr. Richard F. Hanser. New York: Viking, 1947*.
Black Earth [Die schwarze Erde]; tr. Basil Creighton. New York: Putnam, 1952.
The Devil's Agent [Im Namen des Teufels]; tr. Ewald Osers. New York: Fell, 1958.
The Devil's Agent [Im Namen des Teufels]. New York: Fawcett, (1959?).
Off. Limits; tr. Ewald Osers. New York: Fell, 1957.
Off Limits. New York: Fawcett, (1958?), (1960?).
Our Love Affair with Germany [Unsere Liebesaffaire mit Deutschland]. New York: Putnam, 1953.
Walk in Darkness [Der Weg ins Dunkel]; tr. Richard Hanser. New York Putnam, 1948.

HARDERS, GUSTAV
Yaalahn [Jaalahn, die Geschichte einer Indianerliebe]; tr. H. C. Nitz. Milwaukee: Northwestern, 1954.

HARTMANN VON AUE, 12th cent.
Gregorius; tr. Edwin H. Zeydel and B. Q. Morgan. Chapel Hill: University of North Carolina, 1955.
'Gregorius, the Good Sinner'; tr. Sheema Buehne. Unpubl. diss., Pennsylvania State University, 1960.
See also Hubert Creekmore, *Lyrics of the Middle Ages.*

HAUFF, WILHELM, 1802-1827.
Dwarf Long-Nose [Der Zwerg Nase]; tr. Doris Orgel. New York: Random House, 1960.

HAUPTMANN, GERHART, 1862-1946.
The Beaver Coat [Der Biberpelz]; tr. B. Q. Morgan. Microfilm of typescript, 1958.
The Heretic of Soana [Der Ketzer von Soana]; tr. B. Q. Morgan. New York: Ungar, 1958.
The Weavers [Die Weber]; tr. B. Q. Morgan. Microfilm of typescript, 1958.
The Weavers [Die Weber]; *Hannele* [Hanneles Himmelfahrt], *The Beaver Coat* [Der Biberpelz]; tr. Horst Frenz and Miles Waggoner. New York: Rinehart, 1951, 1959 (3d Printing).
See also Victor Lange, *Great German Short Novels and Stories.*

HAUSHOFER, ALBRECHT, 1903-1945.
See Herman Salinger, *Twentieth-Century German Verse.*

HEBBEL, FRIEDRICH, 1813-1863.
Agnes Bernauer; tr. B. Q. Morgan. Microfilm of typescript, 1958.
Herod and Mariamne [Herodes und Mariamne]; tr. Paul H. Curts. Chapel Hill: University of North Carolina, 1950.

The Nibelungs [Die Nibelungen]; tr. B. Q. Morgan. Microfilm of typescript, 1958.

HEBEL, JOHANN PETER, 1760-1826.
Francisca, and Other Stories; tr. Clavia Goodman and B. Q. Morgan. Lexington, Ky.: Anvil, 1957.
See also Robert Pick, *German Stories and Tales.*

HEIMANN, MORITZ, 1868-1925.
See Robert Pick, *German Stories and Tales.*

HEINE, HEINRICH, 1797-1856.
Bittersweet Poems; tr. Joseph Auslander. Mount Vernon, N.Y.: Peter Pauper, 1956.
Doctor Faust: A Dance Poem [Der Doktor Faust, ein Tanzpoem]; tr. Basil Ashmore. New York: British Book Centre, 1952*.
Heinrich Heine: A Biographical Anthology; tr. Moses Hadas. Philadelphia Jewish Publication Society of America, 1956.
The North Sea [Die Nordsee]; tr. Vernon Watkins. New York: New Directions, 1951.
Poems; tr. Louis Untermeyer. New York: Limited Editions Club, 1957.
Poems; tr. Louis Untermeyer. New York: Heritage, 1957.
Poems and Ballads; tr. Emma Lazarus. New York: Hartsdale, 1948.
Poems and Ballads; tr. Emma Lazarus. New York: Garden City, 1950.
The Poetry and Prose of Heinrich Heine; poetry tr. Louis Untermeyer and others, prose tr. Frederic Ewen, ed. Frederic Ewen. New York: Citadel, 1948, 1959.
The Rabbi of Bacherach; tr. E. B. Ashton (pseud.). New York: Schocken, 1947.
Religion and Philosophy in Germany: A Fragment [Zur Geschichte der Religion und Philosophie in Deutschland]; tr. John Snodgrass. Boston: Beacon, 1959.
The Sea and the Hills: The Harz Journey [Die Harzreise] *and The North Sea* [Die Nordsee]; tr. Frederic T. Wood. Boston: Chapman and Grimes, 1946.

Selections from the Poetry of Heinrich Heine; tr. K. S. Weimar. Providence?, 1951.
The Sword and the Flame: Selections from Heinrich Heine's Prose; tr. Charles Godfrey Leland. New York: Yoseloff, 1960.
See also Marjorie Fischer, *Strange to Tell;* Angel Flores, *An Anthology of German Poetry;* Hermann Kesten, *The Blue Flower;* and Victor Lange, *Great German Short Novels and Stories.*

HEINE, THOMAS THEODOR, 1867-1948.
I Wait for Miracles [Ich warte auf Wunder]; tr. Clara G. Stillman. New York: Greenberg, 1947.

HEINRICH VON MORUNGEN, 12th cent.
See Hubert Creekmore, *Lyrics of the Middle Ages.*

HEINRICH, WILLI, 1920-
Crack of Doom; tr. Oliver Coburn. New York: Farrar, Straus, 1958.
Crack of Doom; tr. Oliver Coburn. New York: Bantam, 1959.
The Cross of Iron [Das geduldige Fleisch]; tr. Richard and Clara Winston. Indianapolis: Bobbs-Merrill, 1956.
The Cross of Iron [Das geduldige Fleisch]; tr. Richard and Clara Winston. New York: Bantam, 1957.
Mark of Shame [Die Gezeichneten]; tr. Sigrid Rock. New York: Farrar, Straus, 1959.
Mark of Shame [Die Gezeichneten]; tr. Sigrid Rock. New York: Bantam, 1960.

HEISSENBÜTTEL, HELMUT, 1921-
See Jerome Rothenberg. *New Young German Poets.*

HESSE, HERMANN, 1877-1962.
Demian, the Story of a Youth [Demian, die Geschichte einer Jugend]; tr. N. H. Friday. New York: Holt, 1948.
Gertrude; tr. Hilda Rosner. Hollywood-by-the-Sea, Fla.: Transatlantic Arts, 1956.

Goldmund [Narziss und Goldmund]; tr. Geoffrey Dunlap. Chester Springs, Pa.: Dufour, 1959.
The Journey to the East [Die Morgenlandfahrt]; tr. Hilda Rosner. New York: Noonday, 1957.
Magister Ludi: The Nobel Prize Novel Das Glasperlenspiel; tr. Mervyn Savill. New York: Holt, 1949.
Magister Ludi [Das Glasperlenspiel]; tr. Mervyn Savill. New York: Ungar, 1957.
Siddhartha; tr. Hilda Rosner. New York: New Directions, 1951, 1957.
Steppenwolf [Der Steppenwolf]; tr. Basil Creighton. New York: Holt, 1947*.
Steppenwolf [Der Steppenwolf]; tr. Basil Creighton. New York: Ungar, 1957, 1960.
See also Robert Pick, *German Stories and Tales;* and Herman Salinger, *Twentieth-Century German Verse.*

HEYM, GEORG, 1887-1912.
See Stephen Spender, *Great German Short Stories.*

HILDESHEIMER, WOLFGANG, 1916-
See Stephen Spender, *Great German Short Stories.*

HOCHWÄLDER, FRITZ, 1911-
The Strong Are Lonely [Das heilige Experiment]; adpt. Eva La Gallienne (from the French version by J. Mercure and R. Thieberger). New York: French, 1954.

HÖLDERLIN, FRIEDRICH, 1770-1843.
Hölderlin: His Poems; tr. Michael Hamburger. New York: Pantheon, 1952.
Selected Poems; tr. J. B. Leishman. Hollywood-by-the-Sea, Fla.: Transatlantic Arts, 1945*.
Selected Poems; tr. J. B. Leishman. New York: Grove, 1956.
See also Angel Flores, *An Anthology of German Poetry.*

HÖLLERER, WALTER, 1922-
See Jerome Rothenberg, *New Young German Poets.*

HOFFMANN, ERNST THEODOR AMADEUS, 1776-1822.
Story of a Nutcracker; adpt. Desmond MacCarthy and Bryan Guiness. New York: Heinman, 1953*.
Tales from Hoffmann; ed. J. M. Cohen. New York: Coward-McCann, 1951.
Tales of Hoffmann; ed. Christopher Lazare. New York: Wyn, 1946.
Tales of Hoffmann. New York: Heritage, 1951*.
Tales of Hoffmann; ed. Christopher Lazare. New York: Grove, 1959.
See also Angel Flores, *Nineteenth-Century German Tales;* Hermann Kesten, *The Blue Flower;* and Victor Lange, *Great German Short Novels and Stories.*

HOFMANNSTHAL, HUGO VON, 1874-1929.
Arabella (Libretto for opera by Richard Strauss); tr. J. Gutmann. New York: Boosey and Hawkes, 1955.
Death and the Fool [Der Tor und der Tod]; tr. B. Q. Morgan. Microfilm of typescript, 1958.
Selected Prose; tr. Mary Hottinger and Tania and James Stern. New York: Pantheon, 1952.
See also Angel Flores, *An Anthology of German Poetry;* Robert Pick, *German Stories and Tales;* Herman Salinger, *Twentieth-Century German Verse;* and Stephen Spender, *Great German Short Stories.*

HOLTHUSEN, HANS EGON, 1913-
See Herman Salinger, *Twentieth-Century German Verse.*

HOMEYER, HEINZ VON, 1895-
The Radiant Mountain [Der leuchtende Berg]; tr. Elinor Castendyk Briefs. Chicago: Regnery, 1957.

HORBACH, MICHAEL, 1924-
The Betrayed [Die verratenen Söhne]; tr. Robert Kee. New York: Coward-McCann, 1959.

HUBER, HEINZ, 1922-
See Stephen Spender, *Great German Short Stories*.

HUCH, RICARDA, 1864-1947.
See Herman Salinger, *Twentieth-Century German Verse*.

HÜNERMANN, WILHELM
Miracle at Fatima [Der Himmel ist stärker als wir]; tr. Isabel and Florence McHugh. New York: Kenedy, 1959.

HUTTERER, FRANZ, 1925-
Trouble for Tomas [Treue findet ihren Lohn]; tr. Joyce Emerson. New York: Harcourt, Brace, 1959.

JARAY, HANS, 1906-
One Page Missing [Es fehlt eine Seite]; tr. Elizabeth Reynolds Hapgood. New York: Holt, 1948.

JENS, WALTER, 1923-
The Blind Man [Der Blinde]; tr. Michael Bullock. New York: Macmillan, 1954.

JOHANNES VON SAAZ (Johannes von Tepl), ca. 1350-1414.
Death and the Plowman, or The Bohemian Plowman [Der Ackermann aus Böhmen]; tr. Ernest N. Kirrmann. Chapel Hill: University of North Carolina, 1958.

JÜNGER, ERNST, 1895-
The Glass Bees [Gläserne Bienen]; tr. Louise Bogan and Elizabeth Mayer. New York: Noonday, 1960.
On the Marble Cliffs [Auf den Marmor-Klippen]; tr. Stuart O. Hood. Norfolk, Conn.: New Directions, 1947.
The Peace [Der Friede]; tr. Stuart O. Hood. Hinsdale, Ill.: Regnery, 1948.

KADES, HANS (i.e., Hans Werlberger), 1906-
The Doctor's Secret; tr. E. B. Ashton (pseud.). New York: Dell, 1959.
Without Sanction; tr. E. B. Ashton (pseud.). New York: Criterion, 1955.

KÄSTNER, ERICH, 1899-
The Animals' Conference [Konferenz der Tiere]; tr. Zita de Schauensee. New York: McKay, 1949, 1953*.
Baron Munchhausen: His Wonderful Travels and Adventures [Münchhausen]; tr. Richard and Clara Winston. New York: Messner, 1957.
Don Quixote [Don Quichotte]; tr. Richard and Clara Winston. New York: Messner, 1957.
Lisa and Lottie [Das doppelte Lottchen]; tr. Cyrus Brooks. Boston: Little, Brown, 1951.
Puss in Boots [Der gestiefelte Kater]; tr. Richard and Clara Winston. New York: Messner, 1957.
A Salzburg Comedy [Der kleine Grenzverkehr]; tr. Cyrus Brooks. New York: Ungar, 1957.
The Simpletons [Die Schildbürger]; tr. Richard and Clara Winston. New York: Messner, 1957.
Till Eulenspiegel, the Clown; tr. Richard and Clara Winston. New York: Messner, 1957.

KAFKA, FRANZ, 1883-1924.
Amerika; tr. Edwin Muir. New York: New Directions, 1946*.
Amerika; tr. Edwin Muir. Garden City, N.Y.: Doubleday, 1955.
The Castle [Das Schloss]; tr. Willa and Edwin Muir. New York: Knopf, 1954, 1956.
Dearest Father: Stories and Other Writings; tr. Ernst Kaiser and Eithne Wilkins. New York: Schocken, 1954.
Description of a Struggle; tr. Tania and James Stern. New York: Schocken, 1958.
The Diaries of Franz Kafka; tr. Joseph Kresch, Martin Greenberg, and Hannah Arendt. 2 vols. New York: Schocken, 1948-1949.
A Franz Kafka Miscellany: Pre-fascist Exile; tr. Sophie Prombaum. New York: Twice-a-Year Press, 1946.

The Great Wall of China [Beim Bau der chinesischen Mauer]: *Stories and Reflections;* tr. Willa and Edwin Muir. New York: Schocken, 1946 (2 Printings), 1948, 1960.
The Great Wall of China [Beim Bau der chinesischen Mauer] *and Other Pieces;* tr. Willa and Edwin Muir. Rev. ed. New York: Schocken, 1957.
Letters to Milena; tr. Tania and James Stern. New York: Schocken, 1953.
Metamorphosis [Die Verwandlung]; tr. A. L. Lloyd. New York: Vanguard, 1946.
Parables; tr. Willa and Edwin Muir and Clement Greenberg. New York: Schocken, 1947.
The Penal Colony [In der Strafkolonie]: *Stories and Short Pieces;* tr. Willa and Edwin Muir. New York: Schocken, 1948.
Selected Short Stories of Franz Kafka; tr. Willa and Edwin Muir. New York: Modern Library, 1952.
The Trial [Der Prozess]; tr. Willa and Edwin Muir. New York: Knopf, 1945*, 1957.
See also Marjorie Fischer, *Strange to Tell;* Victor Lange, *Great German Short Novels and Stories;* Robert Pick, *German Stories and Tales;* and Stephen Spender, *Great German Short Stories.*

KAISER, GEORG, 1878-1945.
Gas I; tr. Herman Scheffauer. New York: Ungar, 1957.

KATZ, LEO, 1892-
Seedtime; tr. Joel Ames (pseud.). New York: Knopf, 1947*.

KATZ, RICHARD, 1888-
Solitary Life [Einsames Leben]; tr. Hetty Kohn. New York: Reynal, 1959.

KAUFMANN, RICHARD, 1914-
Heaven Pays No Dividends [Der Himmel zahlt keine Zinsen]; tr. Eric Mosbacher. New York: Viking, 1952.

KELLER, GOTTFRIED, 1819-1890.
Green Henry [Der grüne Heinrich]; tr. A. M. Holt. New York: Grove, 1960.
Legends and People. Emmaus, Pa.: Story Classics, 1953.
A Village Romeo and Juliet [Romeo und Julia auf dem Dorfe]; tr. Paul Bernard Thomas and B. Q. Morgan. New York: Ungar, 1955, 1960.
See also Marjorie Fischer, *Strange to Tell;* Angel Flores, *Nineteenth-Century German Tales;* Hermann Kesten, *The Blue Flower;* Victor Lange, *Great German Short Novels and Stories;* Robert Pick, *German Stories and Tales;* and Stephen Spender, *Great German Short Stories.*

KESTEN, HERMANN, 1900–
Casanova; tr. James Stern and Robert Pick. New York: Harper, 1955.
Copernicus and His World [Copernicus und seine Welt]; tr. E. B. Ashton (pseud.) and Norbert Guterman. New York: Roy, 1945.
Ferdinand and Isabella. New York: Wyn, 1946*.
Happy Man [Glückliche Menschen]; tr. Edward Crankshaw. New York: Wyn, 1947*.
The Twins of Nuremberg [Die Zwillinge von Nürnberg]; tr. Andrew St. James and E. B. Ashton (pseud.). New York: Fischer, 1946.
See also Robert Pick, *German Stories and Tales.*

KEUN, IRMGARD, 1910–
The Bad Example; tr. Leila Berg and Ruth Baer. New York: Harcourt, Brace, 1955.

KIND, FRIEDRICH, 1768-1843.
The Devil's Bullet [Der Freischütz]. Libretto. New York: Oxford, 1948.
The Devil's Marksman [Der Freischütz]. New York: Boosey and Hawkes, 1951*.

KIRST, HANS HELLMUT, 1914–
Forward, Gunner Asch!; tr. Robert Kee. Boston: Little, Brown, 1956.

The Lieutenant Must Be Mad [Wir nannten ihn Galgenstrick]; tr. Richard and Clara Winston. New York: Harcourt, Brace, 1951.
The Return of Gunner Asch; tr. Robert Kee. Boston: Little, Brown, 1957.
The Revolt of Gunner Asch [In der Kaserne]; tr. Robert Kee. Boston: Little, Brown, 1955, 1956.
The Seventh Day [Keiner kommt davon]; tr. Richard Graves. Garden City, N.Y.: Doubleday, 1959.
The Seventh Day [Keiner kommt davon]; New York: Ace, (1960?).

KLEIST, HEINRICH VON, 1777-1811.
The Broken Pitcher [Der zerbrochene Krug]; tr. B. Q. Morgan. Microfilm of typescript, 1958.
Katie of Heilbronn, 1808; or Trial by Fire [Das Käthchen von Heilbronn]; tr. Arthur H. Hughes. Hartford: Trinity College, 1960.
The Marquise of O— [Die Marquise von O—] *and Other Stories;* tr. Martin Greenberg. New York: Criterion, 1960.
The Prince of Homburg [Der Prinz von Homburg]; tr. Charles E. Passage. New York: Liberal Arts, 1956.
See also Eric Bentley, *The Classic Theatre;* Angel Flores, *Nineteenth-Century German Tales;* Hermann Kesten, *The Blue Flower;* Victor Lange, *Great German Short Novels and Stories;* and Stephen Spender, *Great German Short Stories.*

THE KNIGHT OF KÜRENBERG, 12th cent.
See Hubert Creekmore, *Lyrics of the Middle Ages.*

KRAMER, GERHARD, 1904-
We Shall March Again [Wit werden weitermarschieren]; tr. Anthony G. Powell. New York: Putnam, 1955.

KROLOW, KARL, 1915-
See Jerome Rothenberg, *New Young German Poets.*

KUBY, ERICH, 1905-
Rosemarie [Rosemarie, des deutschen Wunders liebstes Kind]; tr. R. C. J. Muller. New York: Knopf, 1960.

Rosemarie [Rosemarie, des deutschen Wunders liebstes Kind]. New York: Dell, (1960?).

KURZ, ISOLDE, 1853-1944.
See Herman Salinger, *Twentieth-Century German Verse*.

LANGGÄSSER, ELISABETH, 1899-1950.
The Quest [Märkische Argonautenfahrt]; tr. Jane Bannard Greene. New York: Knopf, 1953.

LANIA, LEO (i.e. Lazar Herrmann), 1886-1961.
The Foreign Minister; tr. James Stern. Boston: Houghton Mifflin, 1956.

LEDIG, GERT, 1921-
The Tortured Earth [Die Stalinorgel]; tr. Mervyn Savill. Chicago: Regnery, 1956.

LE FORT, GERTRUD VON, 1876-
Eternal Woman [Die ewige Frau], *The Woman in Time* [Die Frau in der Zeit], *Timeless Woman* [Die zeitlose Frau]; tr. M. C. Buehrle. Milwaukee: Bruce, 1954*.
The Fearless Heart (Based on the novel *The Song from the Scaffold* [Die letzte am Schafott]); tr. (from the Frech) Michael Legat. Westminster, Md.: Newman, 1952*.
The Song at the Scaffold [Die Letzte am Schafott]; drm. Emmet Lavery. New York: French, 1949.
The Song at the Scaffold [Die Letzte am Schafott]; tr. Olga Marx. New York: Sheed and Ward, 1951.
The Song at the Scaffold [Die Letzte am Schafott]. Kirkwood, Mo.: Catholic Authors Press, (1960?).
The Wife of Pilate [Die Frau des Pilatus]; tr. Marie C. Buehrle. Milwaukee: Bruce, 1957.

LEHMANN, ARTHUR HEINZ, 1909-1956.
The Noble Stallion [Liebesgeschichte zweier Menschen und eines edlen Pferdes]; tr. James and Morika Cleugh. New York: Holt, 1955.

LENAU, NIKOLAUS, 1802-1850.
See Angel Flores, *An Anthology of German Poetry*.

LERNET-HOLENIA, ALEXANDER, 1897-
Count Luna, Two Tales of the Real and the Unreal: Baron Bagge [Der Baron Bagge] *and Count Luna* [Der Graf Luna]; tr. Richard and Clara Winston and Jane B. Greene. New York: Criterion, 1956.
See also Robert Pick, *German Stories and Tales*.

LERSCH, HEINRICH, 1889-1936.
See Herman Salinger, *Twentieth-Century German Verse*.

LESSING, GOTTHOLD EPHRAIM, 1729-1781.
Emilia Galotti; tr. Anna Johanna Gode-von Aesch. Great Neck, N.Y.: Barron, 1959.
Laocoön; tr. Ellen Frothingham. New York: Noonday, 1957.
Laocoön, Nathan the Wise [Nathan der Weise], *Minna von Barnhelm;* tr. William A. Steel and Anthony Dent. New York: Dutton, 1959.
Nathan the Wise [Nathan der Weise]; tr. Guenther Reinhardt. Brooklyn: Barron, 1950.
Nathan the Wise [Nathan der Weise]; tr. B. Q. Morgan. New York: Ungar, 1955.
Theological Writings; tr. Henry Chadwick. Stanford, Calif.: Stanford University, 1957.
Three Rings; retld. (from Nathan der Weise, Act III) Margaret K. Soifer. Brooklyn: Furrow, 1947*.

LICHTENBERG, GEORG CHRISTOPH, 1742-1799.
The Lichtenberg Reader; tr. Franz H. Mautner and Henry Hatfield. Boston: Beacon, 1959.
Lichtenberg: A Doctrine of Scattered Occasions, Reconstructed from His Aphorisms and Reflections; ed. Joseph Peter Stern. Bloomington: Indiana University, 1959.

LOBE, MIRA, 1913-

The Zoo Breaks Out [Der Tiergarten reisst aus]; tr. Norman Dale. New York: Barnes, 1960.

LOEWENSTEIN, PRINCE HUBERTUS, 1906-

The Child and the Emperor [Kind und Kaiser]. New York: Macmillan, 1945*.
The Eagle and the Cross [Der Adler und das Kreuz]. New York: Macmillan, 1947*.
Lance of Longinus [Die Lanze des Longinus]. New York: Macmillan, 1946*.

LOTHAR, ERNST, 1890-

The Door Opens [Die Tür geht auf]; tr. Marion A. Werner. New York: Doubleday, 1945*.
The Prisoner; tr. James A. Galston. New York: Doubleday, 1945*.
Return to Vienna [Die Rückkehr]. Garden City, N.Y.: Doubleday, 1949*

LUDWIG, EMIL, 1881-1948.

Abraham Lincoln, the Full Life Story of Our Martyred President; tr. Eden and Cedar Paul. New York: Liveright, 1949*.
Abraham Lincoln, and the Times that Tried His Soul; tr. Eden and Cedar Paul. New York: Fawcett, 1956.
Cleopatra; tr. Bernard Miall. New York: Bantam, 1959.
The Mediterranean, Saga of the Sea; tr. Barrows Mussey. New York: McGraw, 1952*.
Napoleon. New York: Pocket Books, 1954.
The Nile, the Life-Story of a River [Der Nil, Lebenslauf eines Stromes]; tr. Mary Lindsay. Garden City, N.Y.: Garden City, 1947*.
Of Life and Love. New York: Philosophical Library, 1945.
Of Life and Love. Garden City, N.Y.: Blue Ribbon Books, 1946.
Othello; tr. Franz von Hildebrand. New York: Putman, 1947.
Son of Man, the Story of Jesus [Der Menschensohn, Geschichte eines Propheten]; tr. Eden and Cedar Paul. New York: Liveright, 1945*.
The Son of Man. Greenwich, Conn.: Fawcett, 1957.

LÜTGEN, KURT, 1911-
Two Against the Arctic [Kein Winter für Wölfe]; tr. Isabel and Florence McHugh. New York: Pantheon, 1957.

MAASS, EDGAR, 1896-1964.
Imperial Venus [Kaiserliche Venus]. Indianapolis: Bobbs-Merrill, 1946.
A Lady at Bay; tr. Richard and Clara Winston. New York: Scribner, 1953.
The Magnificent Enemies. New York: Scribner, 1955*.
The Queen's Physician [Der Arzt der Königin]. New York: Scribner, 1948.
The Queen's Physician [Der Arzt der Königin]. Garden City, N.Y.: Sun Dial, 1950*.
World and Paradise. New York: Scribner, 1950*.

MAASS, JOACHIM, 1901-
The Gouffé Case [Der Fall Gouffé]; tr. Michael Bullock. New York: Harper, 1960.
The Weeping and the Laughter [Ein Testament]; tr. Erika Meyer. New York: Wyn, 1947.

MAHNER-MONS, HANS
The Sword of Satan [Der Kavalier von Paris]; tr. Richard Hanser. New York: McKay, 1952.

MANN, HEINRICH, 1871-1950.
Blue Angel [Professor Unrat]. New York: New American Library, (1959?).
Little Superman [Der Untertan]; tr. Ernest Boyd. New York: Creative Age, 1945.
See also Victor Lange, *Great German Short Novels and Stories.*

MANN, KLAUS, 1906-1949.
Pathetic Symphony [Symphonie Pathétique]. New York: Allen, Towne and Heath, 1948.

MANN, THOMAS, 1875-1955.

Buddenbrooks; tr. H. T. Lowe-Porter. New York: Pocket Books, 1952.

Buddenbrooks; tr. H. T. Lowe-Porter. New York: Vintage, (1960?).

The Beloved Returns [Lotte in Weimar]; tr. H. T. Lowe-Porter. New York: Knopf, 1957.

The Black Swan [Die Betrogene]; tr. Willard R. Trask. New York: Knopf, 1954.

Confessions of Felix Krull, Confidence Man [Bekenntnisse des Hochstaplers Felix Krull]; tr. Denver Lindley. New York: Knopf, 1955.

Confessions of Felix Krull, Confidence Man [Bekenntnisse des Hochstaplers Felix Krull]; tr. Denver Lindley. New York: New American Library, 1957.

Death in Venice [Der Tod in Venedig] *and Seven Other Stories;* tr. H. T. Lowe-Porter. New York: Vintage, 1954, 1959.

Doctor Faustus [Doktor Faustus]; tr. H. T. Lowe-Porter. New York: Knopf, 1948.

Essays; tr. H. T. Lowe-Porter. New York: Vintage, 1957, 1958.

Essays of Three Decades; tr. H. T. Lowe-Porter. New York: Knopf, 1947.

Germany and the Germans [Deutschland und die Deutschen]. Washington: Library of Congress, 1945.

Goethe and Democracy [Goethe und die Demokratie]. Washington: Library of Congress, 1950.

The Holy Sinner [Der Erwählte]; tr. H. T. Lowe-Porter. New York: Knopf, 1951.

Joseph and His Brothers [Joseph und seine Brüder]; tr. H. T. Lowe-Porter. New York: Knopf, 1948*, 1956, 1958.

Last Essays; tr. Richard and Clara Winston, Tania and James Stern, H. T. Lowe-Porter. New York: Knopf, 1959.

Letters to Paul Amann, 1915-1952 [Briefe an Paul Amann, 1915-1952]; tr. Richard and Clara Winston. Middletown, Conn.: Wesleyan University, 1960.

The Magic Mountain [Der Zauberberg]; tr. H. T. Lowe-Porter. New York: Knopf, 1946*, 1953*.

Nietzsche's Philosophy in Light of Contemporary Events. Washington: Library of Congress, 1947★.

A Sketch of My Life [Lebensabriss]; tr. H. T. Lowe-Porter. New York: Knopf, 1960.

Tables of the Law [Das Gesetz]; tr. H. T. Lowe-Porter. New York: Knopf, 1945.

The Thomas Mann Reader; ed. Joseph Warner Angell. New York: Knopf, 1950.

The Thomas Mann Reader; ed. Joseph Warner Angell. New York: Grosset and Dunlap, 1950★, 1957.

The Transposed Heads [Die vertauschten Köpfe]; tr. H. T. Lowe-Porter. New York: Vintage, 1959.

See also Marjorie Fischer, *Strange to Tell;* Victor Lange, *Great German Short Novels and Stories;* Robert Pick, *German Stories and Tales;* and Stephen Spender, *Great German Short Stories.*

MARNAU, ALFRED, 1918–

Free Among the Dead [Der steinerne Gang]; tr. Eithne Wilkins. New York: Pellegrini and Cudahy, (1952?)★.

MAY, KARL FRIEDRICH, 1842–1912.

In the Desert [Durch die Wüste]; tr. F. Billerbeck-Gentz. Bamberg, N.Y.: Ustad-Verlag, 1955★.

MEHRING, WALTER, 1896–

The Lost Library [Die verlorene Bibliothek]; tr. Richard and Clara Winston. Indianapolis: Bobbs-Merrill, 1951★.

MEICHSNER, DIETER, 1928–

The Answer in the Sky [Weisst du, warum?]; tr. Charlotte and Albert Lloyd. New York: Funk and Wagnalls, 1953.

MEYER, CONRAD FERDINAND, 1825–1898.

See Victor Lange, *Great German Short Novels and Stories.*

MIEGEL, AGNES, 1879-1964.
See Herman Salinger, *Twentieth-Century German Verse*.

MÖRIKE, EDUARD FRIEDRICH, 1804-1875.
Mozart on the Way to Prague [Mozart auf der Reise nach Prag]; tr. Walter and Catherine Alison Phillips. New York: Pantheon, 1947.
Mozart's Journey to Prague [Mozart auf der Reise nach Prag]; tr. Leopold von Loewenstein-Wertheim. New York: British Book Centre, 1958.
See also Angel Flores, *An Anthology of German Poetry*, and *Nineteenth-Century German Tales*.

MOOSDORF, JOHANNA, 1911-
Flight to Africa [Flucht nach Afrika]; tr. Richard and Clara Winston. New York: Harcourt, Brace, 1954.

MORGENSTERN, CHRISTIAN, 1871-1914.
See Angel Flores, *An Anthology of German Poetry;* and Herman Salinger, *Twentieth-Century German Verse*.

MORGENSTERN, SOMA, 1896-
In my Father's Pastures; tr. Ludwig Lewisohn. Philadelphia: Jewish Publication Society, 1947.
The Son of the Lost Son [Der Sohn des verlorenen Sohnes]; tr. Joseph Leftwich and Peter Gross. New York: Rinehart, 1946*.
The Son of the Lost Son; tr. Joseph Leftwich and Peter Gross. Philadelphia: Jewish Publication Society, 1946.
The Testament of the Lost Son; tr. Jacob Sloan and Maurice Samuel. Philadelphia: Jewish Publication Society, 1950.
The Third Pillar; tr. Ludwig Lewisohn. New York: Farrar, Straus, 1955.

MÜHLENWEG, FRITZ, 1898-1961.
Big Tiger and Christian [In geheimer Mission durch die Wüste Gobi]; tr. Isabel and Florence McHugh. New York: Pantheon, 1952.

MÜLLER, MARGARETHE, 1862-   and CARLA WENCKEBACH.
Good Luck! [Glück auf]; tr. Helen Stoddard Reed. N.p., 195-?.

MÜLLER-GUGGENBÜHL, FRITZ, 1922-
Swiss-Alpine Folk-Tales; tr. Katherine Potts. New York: Walck, 1958.

MUSIL, ROBERT, 1880-1942.
The Man Without Qualities [Der Mann ohne Eigenschaften]; tr. Eithne Wilkins and Ernst Kaiser. 2 vols. New York: Coward-McCann, 1953-1954.
Young Törless [Die Verwirrungen des Zöglings Törless]; tr. Eithne Wilkins and Ernst Kaiser. New York: Pantheon, 1955.
Young Törless [Die Verwirrungen des Zöglings Törless]; tr. Eithne Wilkins and Ernst Kaiser. New York: Noonday, 1958.

NEIDHART VON REUENTHAL, 13th cent.
See Hubert Creekmore, *Lyrics of the Middle Ages.*

NEUMANN, ALFRED, 1895-1952.
Six of Them [Es waren ihrer sechs]; tr. Anatol Murad. New York: Macmillan, 1945.
Six of Them [Es waren ihrer sechs]; tr. Anatol Murad. New York: Hutchinson, 1945*.
Strange Conquest [Der Pakt]; tr. Ransom T. Taylor. New York: Ballantine, 1954.

NIBELUNGENLIED
The Nibelungenlied; tr. Margaret Armour. New York: Limited Editions Club, 1960.

NOSSACK, HANS ERICH, 1901-
See Stephen Spender, *Great German Short Stories.*

NOVALIS (i.e., Friedrich von Hardenberg), 1772-1801.
Hymns to the Night [Hymnen an die Nacht]; tr. Mabel Cotterell. Hollywood-by-the-Sea, Fla.: Transatlantic Arts, 1949*.

Hymns to the Night [Hymnen an die Nacht] *and Other Selected Writings;* tr. Charles E. Passage. New York: Liberal Arts, 1960.
The Novices of Sais [Die Lehrlinge zu Sais]; tr. Ralph Manheim. New York: C. Valentin, 1949.
See also Angel Flores, *An Anthology of German Poetry.*

OLIVIER, STEFAN (i.e., Reinhart Stalman), 1917-
I Swear and Vow; tr. Helen Sebba. Garden City, N.Y.: Doubleday, 1960.

OPITZ, KARLLUDWIG, 1914-
The General [Mein General]; tr. Constantine Fitzgibbon. New York: Day, 1957.
The General [Mein General]; tr. Constantine Fitzgibbon. New York: Ace, 1957.

OTT, WOLFGANG, 1923-
Sharks and Little Fish [Haie und kleine Fische]; tr. Ralph Manheim. New York: Pantheon, 1957, 1958.
Sharks and Little Fish [Haie und kleine Fisch]; tr. Ralph Manheim. New York: Dell, 1959.

PARACELSUS VON HOHENHEIM, 1493-1541.
Selected Writings [Lebendiges Erbe]; tr. Norbert Guterman. New York: Pantheon, 1951, 1958.
Volumen Medicinae Paramirum; tr. Kurt F. Leidecker. Baltimore: Johns Hopkins, 1949*.

PAUL, JEAN (i.e., Johann Paul Friedrich Richter), 1763-1825.
See Angel Flores, *Nineteenth-Century German Tales.*

PICARD, JACOB, 1883-
The Marked One [Der Gezeichnete] *and Twelve Other Stories;* tr. Ludwig Lewisohn. Philadelphia: Jewish Publishing Society, 1956.

PIDOLL, CARL FREIHERR VON, 1888-1965.
Eroica [Verklungenes Spiel]; tr. Anthony Powell. New York: Vanguard, 1957.

PIONTEK, HEINZ, 1925-
See Jerome Rothenberg, *New Young German Poets.*

PLATEN, AUGUST GRAF VON, 1796-1835.
See Angel Flores, *An Anthology of German Poetry.*

PLIEVIER, THEODOR, 1892-1955.
Berlin; tr. Louis Hagen and Vivian Milroy. New York: Ace, 1956.
Berlin; tr. Louis Hagen and Vivian Milroy. Garden City, N.Y.: Doubleday, 1957.
Moscow; tr. Stuart Hood. New York: Doubleday, 1954.
Moscow; tr. Stuart Hood. New York: Ace, (1957?).
Stalingrad; tr. Richard and Clara Winston. New York: Appleton-Century-Crofts, 1948.
Stalingrad; tr. Richart and Clara Winston. New York: Royal Books, (1952?).
Stalingrad; tr. Richard and Clara Winston. New York: Berkley Books, 1958.
The World's Last Corner [Im letzten Winkel der Erde]; tr. Robert Pick. New York: Appleton-Century-Crofts, 1951.

PUMP, HANS WILHELM, 1915-1957.
Before the Great Snow [Vor dem grossen Schnee]; tr. Robert Kee. New York: Harcourt, Brace, 1958.

PÜCKLER-MUSKAU, HERMANN LUDWIG HEINRICH VON, 1785-1871.
A Regency Visitor; the English Tour of Prince Pückler-Muskau Described in His Letters, 1826-1828 [Briefe eines Verstorbenen]; tr. Sarah Austin. New York: Dutton, 1958.

RAIMUND, FERDINAND, 1790-1836.
The Spendthrift [Der Verschwender]; tr. Erwin Tramer. New York: Ungar. 1949.

RASP-NURI, GRACE, 1899-
Yusuf, Boy of Cyprus [Jusauf, der Türkenjunge]; tr. J. Maxwell Brownjohn. New York: Criterion, 1958.

REINMAR VON HAGENAU, 12th cent.
See Hubert Creekmore, *Lyrics of the Middle Ages.*

REINMAR VON SWETER, 13th cent.
See Hubert Creekmore, *Lyrics of the Middle Ages.*

REMARQUE, ERICH MARIA, 1898-
All Quiet on the Western Front [Im Westen nichts Neues]; New York: Fawcett, (1958?), (1959?).
Arch of Triumph [Arc de Triomphe]; tr. Walter Sorell and Denver Lindley. New York: Appleton-Century, 1945.
Arch of Triumph [Arc de Triomphe]; tr. Walter Sorell and Denver Lindley. New York: Grosset and Dunlap, 1947★.
Arch of Triumph [Arc de Triomphe]; tr. Walter Sorell and Denver Lindley. New York: New American Library, 1950, (1959?).
The Black Obelisk [Der schwarze Obelisk]; tr. Denver Lindley. New York: Harcourt, Brace, 1957.
The Black Obelisk [Der schwarze Obelisk]; tr. Denver Lindley. New York: Fawcett, (1958?).
The Road Back [Der Weg zurück]. New York: Avon, (1960?).
Spark of Life [Der Funke Leben]; tr. James Stern. New York: Appleton-Century-Crofts, 1952.
Spark of Life [Der Funke Leben]; tr. James Stern. New York: New American Library, 1953.
Three Comrades [Drei Kameraden]; tr. A. W. Wheen. Boston: Little, Brown, 1946★.
Three Comrades [Drei Kameraden]; tr. A. W. Wheen. New York: Popular Library, 1953, (1958?).
A Time to Love and a Time to Die [Zeit zu leben und Zeit zu sterben]; tr. Denver Lindley. New York: Harcourt, Brace, 1954.

A Time to Love and a Time to Die [Zeit zu leben und Zeit zu sterben]; tr. Denver Lindley. New York: Popular Library, 1955, (1959?), (1960?).

RENCK, ALEX T., pseud.
The Wrong Way Home; tr. E. M. Valk. Philadelphia: Lippincott, 1954.

REZZORI, GREGOR VON, 1914-
First Meeting with the Hussar [Ein Hermelin in Tschernopol]; tr. Catherine Hutter. New York: Harcourt, Brace, 1959.
The Hussar [Ein Hermelin in Tschernopol]; tr. Catherine Hutter. New York: Harcourt, Brace, 1960.

RICHTER, HANS WERNER, 1908-
Beyond Defeat [Die Geschlagenen]; tr. Robert Kee. New York: Putnam, 1950.
Beyond Defeat [Die Geschlagenen]; tr. Robert Kee. New York: Fawcett, (1957?).
They Fell from God's Hands [Sie fielen aus Gottes Hand]; tr. Geoffrey Sainsbury. New York: Dutton, 1956.

RILKE, RAINER MARIA, 1875-1926.
The Duino Elegies [Die Duineser Elegien]; tr. Harry Behn. Mt. Vernon, N.Y.: Peter Pauper, 1957.
Ewald Tragy; tr. Lola Gruenthal. New York: Twayne, 1958.
Five Prose Pieces; tr. Carl Niemeyer. Cummington, Mass.: Cummington, 1947.
From the Remains of Count C. W.: A Poem Cycle; tr. J. B. Leishman. New York: British Book Centre, 1953*.
The Lay of Love and Death of Cornet Christopher Rilke [Die Weise von Liebe und Tod des Cornets Christoph Rilke]; tr. Leslie Phillips and Stefan Schimanski. Forest Hills, N.Y.: Transatlantic Arts, 1949*.
The Lay of the Love and Death of Cornet Christopher Rilke [Die Weise von Liebe und Tod des Cornets Christoph Rilke]; tr. M. D. Herter Norton. Rev. ed. New York: Norton, 1959.

Letters of Rainer Maria Rilke; tr. Jane Bannard Greene and M. D. Herter Norton. Volume I, 1892-1910; Volume 2, 1910-1926. New York: Norton, 1945-1948.

The Letters of Rainer Maria Rilke and Princess Marie von Thurn und Taxis [Briefwechsel: Rainer Maria Rilke und Maria von Thurn und Taxis]; tr. Nora Wydenbruck. Norfolk, Conn.: New Directions, 1958.

Letters to Benvenuta [So lass ich mich zu Träumen gehen]; tr. Heinz Norden. New York: Philosophical Library, 1951.

Letters to a Young Poet; tr. M. D. Herter Norton. Rev. ed. New York: Norton, 1954.

The Life of the Virgin Mary [Das Marien-Leben]; tr. C. F. MacIntyre. Berkeley: University of California, 1947.

The Life of the Virgin Mary [Das Marien-Leben]; tr. Stephen Spender. New York: Philosophical Library, 1951.

The Notebooks of Malte Laurids Brigge [Die Aufzeichnungen des Malte Laurids Brigge]; tr. M. D. Herter Norton. New York: Norton, 1949.

The Notebooks of Malte Laurids Brigge [Die Aufzeichnungen des Malte Laurids Brigge]; tr. M. D. Herter Norton. New York: Capricorn, 1958.

Poems: 1906 to 1926; tr. J. B. Leishman. Norfolk, Conn.: Laughlin, 1957.

Rainer Maria Rilke: His Last Friendship; tr. (from the French) William H. Kennedy. New York: Philosophical Library, 1952.

Rodin; tr. Jessie Lemont and Hans Trausil. New York: Fine Editions, 1945.

Selected Letters; ed. Harry T. Moore. Garden City, N.Y.: Doubleday, 1960.

Selected Poems; tr. C. F. MacIntyre. 2d ed. Berkeley: University of California, 1947*, 1956, 1958, 1960 ('Second Edition, Sixth Printing [First Paper-bound Edition, Fourth Printing]').

Selected Works. Volume I, Prose; tr. G. Craig Houston. Volume 2, Poetry; tr. J. B. Leishman. New York: New Directions, 1960.

The Song of the Life and Death of the Cornet Christoph Rilke [Die Wise von

Liebe und Tod des Cornets Christoph Rilke]; tr. Howard Steven Strouth. N.p., 1950.
Sonnets to Orpheus [Die Sonette an Orpheus], *Duino Elegies* [Die Duineser Elegien]; tr. Jessie Lemont. New York: Fine Editions, 1945.
Sonnets to Orpheus [Die Sonette an Orpheus]; tr. C. F. MacIntyre. Berkeley: University of California, 1960.
Thirty-One Poems by Rainer Maria Rilke; tr. Ludwig Lewisohn. New York: Ackerman, 1946.
See also Marjorie Fischer, *Strange to Tell;* Angel Flores, *An Anthology of German Poetry;* Victor Lange, *Great German Short Novels and Stories;* Herman Salinger, *Twentieth-Century German Verse;* and Stephen Spender, *Great German Short Stories.*

RINSER, LUISE, 1911-
Nina [Mitte des Lebens]; tr. Richard and Clara Winston. Chicago: Regnery, 1956.
Rings of Glass [Die gläsernen Ringe]; tr. Richard and Clara Winston. Chicago: Regnery, 1958.

RISSE, HEINZ, 1898-
The Earthquake [Wenn die Erde bebt]; tr. Rita Eldon. New York: Farrar, Straus, 1953.

ROEHLER, KLAUS, 1929-
The Dignity of Night [Die Würde der Nacht]; Philadelphia: Lippincott, (1960?).

ROTHGIESSER, RUBEN, 1895-
The Well of Gerar; tr. Harry Schneiderman. Philadelphia: Jewish Publication Society, 1953.

RÜBER, JOHANNES, 1928-
Bach and the Heavenly Choir [Die Heiligsprechung des Johann Sebastian Bach]; tr. Maurice Michael. Cleveland: World, 1956.

RUODLIEB
Ruodlieb: The Earliest Courtly Novel; tr. Edwin H. Zeydel. Chapel Hill: University of North Carolina, 1959.

RUTENBORN, GUENTER, 1912-
The Sign of Jonah [Das Zeichen des Jonas]; tr. B. Ohse and G. Elston. Chicago: Lutheran Student Association, 1954.
The Sign of Jonah [Das Zeichen des Jonas]; tr. George White. New York: Nelson, 1960.
The Word Was God [Biblische Fremdenführung]; tr. Elmer E. Foelber. New York: Nelson, 1959.

RUTHERFORD, DOROTHEA, 1890-
The Threshold [Vor Tag]; tr. Moura Budberg and Tania Alexander. Boston: Little, Brown, 1955.

SACHER-MASOCH, LEOPOLD RITTER VON, 1836-1895.
Venus in Furs [Venus im Pelz]; New York: Printed privately for the Sylvan Press, 1947*.

SALOMON, ERNST VON, 1902-
The Questionnaire [Der Fragebogen]; tr. Constantine Fitzgibbon. Garden City, N.Y.: Doubleday, 1955.

SALTEN, FELIX, 1869-1945.
Bambi. Garden City, N.Y.: Junior Deluxe Editions, 1956.
Bambi's Children. New York: Grosset and Dunlap, 1948.
Bambi's Children; adpt. Allen Chaffee. New York: Random House, 1950.
Bambi's Children. New York: Wonder Books, 1951.
Fairy Tales from Far and Near; tr. Clara Stillman. New York: Philosophical Library, 1945.
Felix Salten's Favorite Animal Stories. New York: Messner, 1948*.
Fifteen Rabbits [Fünfzehn Hasen]; tr. Whittaker Chambers. New York: Grosset and Dunlap, 1951*.

Jibby the Cat [Djibi, das Kätzchen]. New York: Messner, 1948.
Perri: From the Walt Disney Motion Picture. New York: Simon and Schuster, 1958.
Walt Disney's Bambi. New York: Simon and Schuster, 1948*, 1949.
Walt Disney's Perri and Her Friends [Die Jugend des Eichhörnchens Perri]. New York: Simon and Schuster, 1956.

SANDEN, WALTER VON, 1888-
Ingo: The Story of My Otter [Ingo der Fischotter]; tr. Desmond I. Vesey. New York: Longmans, 1959.

SCHAPER, EDZARD HELLMUTH, 1908-
The Dancing Bear [Das Tier]; tr. Norman Denny. New York: Day, 1960.
Star Over the Frontier [Stern über der Grenze]; tr. Isabel and Florence McHugh. Baltimore: Helicon, 1960.

SCHIEKER, SOFIE, 1892-
The House at the City Wall [Das Haus an der Stadtmauer]; tr. Eva Hearst. Chicago: Follett, 1955.

SCHILLER, JOHANN CHRISTOPH FRIEDRICH VON, 1759-1805.
Don Carlos, Infante of Spain; tr. Charles E. Passage. New York: Ungar, 1959.
Friedrich Schiller: An Anthology for Our Time; tr. Jane Bannard Greene, Charles E. Passage, Alexander Gode-von Aesch. New York: Ungar, 1959.
Intrigue and Love [Kabale und Liebe]; tr. Guenther Reinhardt. Brooklyn: Barron, 1953.
The Maiden of Orleans [Die Jungfrau von Orleans]; tr. John T. Krumpelmann. Chapel Hill: University of North Carolina, 1959.
Mary Stuart [Maria Stuart]; tr. Guenther Reinhardt. Brooklyn: Barron, 1950, 1958.
Mary Stuart [Maria Stuart]; adpt. Jean Stock Goldstone and John Reich. New York: Dramatists Play Service, 1958.

Mary Stuart [Maria Stuart]; tr. Sophie Wilkins. Great Neck, N.Y.: Barron, 1959.
On the Aesthetic Education of Man, in a Series of Letters [Über die ästhetische Erziehung des Menschen]; tr. Reginald Snell. New Haven: Yale University, 1954.
Song of the Bell [Das Lied von der Glocke]; tr. Amilie Knoke. N.p., 1947*.
Wallenstein; tr. Charles E. Passage. New York: Ungar, 1958, 1960.
William Tell [Wilhelm Tell]; tr. Theodore Martin. New York: Heritage, 1952.
William Tell [Wilhelm Tell]; tr. Sydney E. Kaplan. Brooklyn: Barron, 1954.
See also Eric Bentley, *The Classic Theatre;* Hermann Kesten, *The Blue Flower;* and Victor Lange, *Great German Short Novels and Stories.*

SCHILLIGER, JOSEF, 1918-
The Saint of the Atom Bomb [Der Heilige der Atombombe]; tr. David Heimann. Westminster, Md.: Newman, 1955.

SCHILLING, WILFRID, 1919-
The Fear Makers [Die Angstmacher]; tr. Oliver Coburn. Garden City, N.Y.: Doubleday, 1960.

SCHMELTZER, KURT, 1888-
Axe of Bronze. New York: Sterling, 1958.
The Long Arctic Night [Die Hütte im ewigen Eis]; tr. Elizabeth Brommer. New York: Watts, 1952.

SCHNABEL, ERNST, 1913-
Anne Frank, a Portrait in Courage [Anne Frank, Spur eines Kindes]; tr. Richard and Clara Winston. New York: Harcourt, Brace, 1958.
The Footsteps of Anne Frank [Anne Frank, Spur eines Kindes]; tr. Richard and Clara Winston. New York: Longmans, 1959.
The Voyage Home; tr. Denver Lindley. New York: Harcourt, Brace, 1958.

SCHNEIDER, REINHOLD, 1903-1958.
The Hour of Saint Francis of Assisi; tr. James Meyer. Chicago: Franciscan Herald, 1953.
Imperial Mission [Las Casas vor Karl V]; tr. Walter Oden. New York: Gresham, 1948.

SCHNITZLER, ARTHUR, 1862-1931.
Casanova's Homecoming [Casanovas Heimfahrt]. New York: Privately printed for the Sylvan Press, 1947.
Casanova's Homecoming [Casanovas Heimfahrt]. New York: Avon, 1948.
Casanova's Homecoming [Casanovas Heimfahrt]. New York: Citadel, 1949*.
Merry-Go-Round [Reigen]; tr. Frank and Jacqueline Marcus. New York: British Book Centre, 1954.
See also Eric Bentley, *From the Modern Repertoire,* and *The Modern Theatre;* Victor Lange, *Great German Short Novels and Stories;* Robert Pick, *German Stories and Tales;* and Herman Salinger, *Twentieth-Century German Verse.*

SCHOLZ, HANS, 1911-
Through the Night [Am grünen Strand der Spree]; tr. Elisabeth Abbott. New York: Crowell, 1959.

SEGHERS, ANNA (i.e., Netty Radvanyi), 1900-
The Dead Stay Young [Die Toten bleiben jung]. Boston: Little, Brown, 1950.

SEIDEL, INA, 1885-
See Herman Salinger, *Twentieth-Century German Verse.*

SELINKO, ANNEMARIE, 1914-
Désirée; tr. Arnold Bender and E. W. Dickes. New York: Morrow, 1953.
Désirée. New York: Pocket Books, 1954*.

SENTJURC, IGOR, 1927-
Prayer for an Assassin [Gebet für den Mörder]; tr. Cornelia Schaeffer. Garden City, N.Y.: Doubleday, 1959.

SOMMER, FEDOR, 1864-1930.
The Iron Collar [Die Schwenkfelder]; tr. Andrew S. Berky. Pennsburg, Pa.: Schwenkfelder Library, 1956.

SPERBER, MANES, 1905-
The Abyss; tr. Constantine Fitzgibbon. Garden City, N.Y.: Doubleday, 1952.
The Achilles Heel; tr. Constantine Fitzgibbon. Garden City, N.Y.: Doubleday, 1960.
The Burned Bramble [Der verbrannte Dornbusch]; tr. Constantine Fitzgibbon. Garden City, N.Y.: Doubleday, 1951.
Journey Without End [La baie perdue]; tr. Constantine Fitzgibbon. Garden City, N.Y.: Doubleday, 1954.
To Dusty Death; tr. Constantine Fitzgibbon. New York: Wingate, 1952.

SPYRI, JOHANNA, 1827-1901.
All Alone in the World: The Story of Rico and Wiseli's Way; tr. M. E. Calthrop. New York: Dutton, 1959.
The Children's Christmas Carol; adpt. Darlene Geis. Englewood Cliffs. N. J.: Prentice-Hall, 1957.
Heidi; adpt. Marie Agnes Foley. Evanston, Ill.: Row, 1945.
Heidi; tr. Helen B. Dole. New York: Grosset and Dunlap, 1945, 1948*.
Heidi. Cleveland and New York: World, 1946.
Heidi; adpt. Florence Hayes. New York: Random, 1946.
Heidi. Philadelphia: Lippincott, 1948.
Heidi. New York: Chanticleer, 1950*.
Heidi, Child of the Mountains. New York: Wonder Books, 1950, 1954.
Heidi. New York: Dutton, 1951*, 1952.
Heidi. Philadelphia: Winston, 1952, 1957.
Heidi; tr. Louise Brooks. Garden City, N.Y.: Doubleday, 1954.
Heidi. New York: Simon and Schuster, 1954, 1956.

Heidi. Racine, Wis.: Whitman, 1955.
Heidi. New York: Pocket Books (1955?).
Heidi. New York: Scribner, 1958.
Heidi. New York: Teen Age Book Club, (1958?).
Heidi; tr. Louise Brooks. New York: Random House, 1959.
Heidi; tr. Joy Law. New York: Watts, 1959.
The Pet Lamb and Other Swiss Stories; tr. M. E. Calthrop and E. M. Popper. New York: Dutton, 1956.

STEFFEN, ALBERT, 1884-1963.
Christ or Barrabas? [Barrabas]; tr. Arnold D. Wadler and Paul M. Allen. New York: American Press for Art and Science, 1950.
From a Notebook [Merkbuch]; tr. Arvia MacKaye. New York: Adonis, 1945.

STEINER, ALEXIS (i.e., Alois Rottensteiner), 1911-
Kriki and the Fox [Kriki und ihre Kinder]; tr. Renata Symonds. New York: Watts, 1960.
Kriki, the Wild Duck [Kriki, das tapfere Entlein]; tr. E. Hurd. New York: Watts, 1960.

STEINMANN-BRUNNER, ELSA, 1901-
Liz and the Red Carnations [Liz und die roten Nelken]; tr. Richard and Clara Winston. New York: Pantheon, 1960.
The Son of the Gondolier; tr. Richard and Clara Winston. New York: Pantheon, 1958.

STERN, SELMA, 1890-
The Court Jew; tr. Ralph Weimar. Philadelphia: Jewish Publication Society, 1950.
The Spirit Returneth; tr. Ludwig Lewisohn. Philadelphia: Jewish Publication Society, 1946.

STERNHEIM, CARL, 1878-1942.
See Eric Bentley, *From the Modern Repertoire*, and *The Modern Theatre*.

STIFTER, ADALBERT, 1805-1868.
Brigitta; tr. Edward Fitzgerald. Emmaus, Pa.: Rodale, 1957.
Rock Crystal, A Christmas Tale [Der Bergkristall]; tr. Elisabeth Mayer and Marianne Moore. New York: Pantheon, 1945.
The Village on the Heath [Das Heidedorf]; tr. Helen Stoddard Reed. N.p., 195–?*
See also Angel Flores, *Nineteenth-Century German Tales;* Robert Pick, *German Stories and Tales;* and Stephen Spender, *Great German Short Stories.*

STORM, THEODOR, 1817-1888.
Immensee; tr. Guenther Reinhardt. Brooklyn: Barron, 1950.
Viola Tricolor; tr. B. Q. Morgan, [and] *Curator Carsten;* tr. Frieda M. Voigt. New York: Ungar, 1956.
See also Victor Lange, *Great German Short Novels and Stories.*

TAULER, JOHANNES, ca. 1300-1361.
The Book of the Poor in Spirit, by a Friend of God [Nachfolgung des armen Lebens]; tr. C. F. Kelley. New York: Harper, 1954.
Signposts to Perfection: A Selection from the Sermons of Johann Tauler; tr. Elisabeth Strakosch. St. Louis: Herder, 1958.

TESSIN, BRIGITTE VON, 1917-
The Bastard [Der Bastard]; tr. Mervyn Savill. New York: McKay, 1959.
The Long-Haired Elephant Child [Die Geschichte vom haarigen Elefantenkind]. New York: Pantheon, 1958.

THIEL, RUDOLF, 1899-
And There Was Light [Und es ward Licht]; tr. Richard and Clara Winston. New York: Knopf, 1957.
And There Was Light [Und es ward Licht]; tr. Richard and Clara Winston. New York: New American Library, 1960.
Luther; tr. Gustav K. Wiencke. Philadelphia: Muhlenberg, 1955.

THUN, RODERICH
The Magic Jewel [Das indische Zauberkästchen]. New York: Viking, 1960.

TIECK, JOHANN LUDWIG, 1773-1853.
See Hermann Kesten, *The Blue Flower.*

TOMAN, WALTER, 1920-
A Kindly Contagion; tr. Harry Zohn. Indianapolis: Bobbs-Merrill, 1959.

TRAKL, GEORG, 1887-1914.
See Angel Flores, *An Anthology of German Poetry;* and Herman Salinger, *Twentieth-Century German Verse.*

TUCHOLSKY, KURT, 1890-1935.
The World is a Comedy: A Tucholsky Anthology; tr. Harry Zohn. Cambridge, Mass.: Sci-Art, 1957.

ULRICH VON ZATZIKHOVEN, ca. 1200.
Lanzelet; tr. Kenneth G. T. Webster and Roger Sherman Loomis. New York: Columbia University, 1951.

UNRUH, FRITZ VON, 1885-
The End is Not Yet: A Novel of Hate and Love [Der nie verlor]. New York: Storm, 1947.
The Saint [Die Heilige]; tr. Willard R. Trask. New York: Random House, 1950.

VOEGELI, MAX (i.e., Michael West,) 1921-
Wonderful Lamp [Die wunderbare Lampe]; tr. E. M. Prince. New York: Oxford, 1955.

VOLLMOELLER, KARL GUSTAV, 1878-1948.
The Last Miracle; tr. Louise Salm. New York: Duell, Sloan and Pearce, 1949.

WALEWSKA, MATHILDE, 1930-1958.
My Lovely Mama [Meine schöne Mama]; tr. Constantine Fitzgibbon. Indianapolis: Bobbs-Merrill, 1956.

WALSER, ROBERT, 1878-1956.
See Stephen Spender, *Great German Short Stories*.

WALTHER VON DER VOGELWEIDE, 12th cent.
Poems; tr. Edwin H. Zeydel and B. Q. Morgan. Ithaca, N.Y.: Thrift, 1952.
See also Hubert Creekmore, *Lyrics of the Middle Ages*.

WASSERMANN, JAKOB, 1873-1934.
Alexander in Babylon [Alexander in Babylon]. Chicago: Ziff-Davis, 1949.
The Maurizius Case [Der Fall Maurizius]; tr. Caroline Newton. New York: Liveright, 1959.
See also Robert Pick, *German Stories and Tales*.

WEDEKIND, FRANK, 1864-1918.
Five Tragedies of Sex; tr. Frances Fawcett and Stephen Spender. New York: Theatre Arts, 1952.
The Tenor [Der Kammersänger]. Opera by Hugo Weisgall; libretto by Karl Shapiro and Ernst Lert. Bryn Mawr, Pa.: Merion Music, 1957.
The Solar Spectrum (*Those Who Buy the Gods of Love*); tr. Dietrich Faehl and Eric Vaughn. N.p. (1958?).
See also Eric Bentley, *From the Modern Repertoire*, and *The Modern Theatre;* and Victor Lange, *Great German Short Novels and Stories*.

WEINHEBER, JOSEF, 1892-1945.
See Herman Salinger, *Twentieth-Century German Verse*.

WEIRAUCH, ANNA ELISABET, 1887-
The Outcast; tr. Guy Endore. New York: Willey, 1948.
Of Love Forbidden (*The Scorpion*) [Skorpion]. New York: Fawcett, (1958?).
The Scorpion [Skorpion]; tr. Whittaker Chambers. New York: Willey, 1948.

WEISKOPF, FRANZ CARL, 1900-
Children of Their Time; tr. Heinz Norden and Ilona Ralf Sues. New York: Knopf, 1948.
Twilight on the Danube; tr. Olga Marx. New York: Knopf, 1946.

WEISS, ERNST, 1884-1940.
See Robert Pick, *German Stories and Tales.*

WEISS-SONNENBURG, HEDWIG, 1889-
Plum Blossom and Kai Lin [Pflaumenblüte und Kai Lin]; tr. Joyce Emerson. New York: Watts, 1960.

WEISSBERG, ALEXANDER, 1901-
The Accused; tr. Edward Fitzgerald. New York: Simon and Schuster, 1951.

WERFEL, ALMA MAHLER, 1879?-1964.
And the Bridge is Love. New York: Harcourt, Brace, 1958.
Gustav Mahler: Memories and Letters; tr. Basil Creighton. New York, Viking, 1946.

WERFEL, FRANZ V., 1890-1945.
Between Heaven and Earth [Zwischen oben und unten]; tr. Maxim Newmark. New York: Hutchinson, 1947.
Embezzled Heaven [Der veruntreute Himmel]; adpt. L. Bush-Fekete and Mary Helen Fay. New York: Viking, 1945.
Embezzled Heaven [Der veruntreute Himmel]; tr. Moray Firth. New York: Dell, 1959.
The Forty Days of Musa Dagh [Die vierzig Tage des Musa Dagh]; tr. Geoffrey Dunlop. New York: Modern Library, 195-?*
Poems; tr. Edith Abercrombie Snow. Princeton, N. J.: Princeton University, 1945.
The Song of Bernadette [Das Lied von Bernadette]; tr. Ludwig Lewisohn. New York: Viking, 1946 (12th Printing)*, 1956.

The Song of Bernadette [Das Lied von Bernadette]; tr. Ludwig Lewisohn. New York: Pocket Books, 1947*, 1953.

Star of the Unborn [Stern der Ungeborenen]; tr. Gustave O. Arlt. New York: Viking, 1946.

Verdi; tr. Helen Jessiman. New York: Allen, Towne and Heath, 1947.

See also Herman Salinger, *Twentieth-Century German Verse.*

WERNER, BRUNO ERICH, 1896-1964.

The Slave Ship [Die Galeere]; tr. Eithne Wilkins and Ernst Kaiser. New York: Pantheon, 1951.

WIECHERT, ERNST, 1887-1950.

The Earth is Our Heritage [Die Jeromin-Kinder]; tr. Robert Maxwell. New York: Nevil, 1950.

The Earth is Our Heritage [Die Jeromin-Kinder]; tr. Robert Maxwell. Westport, Conn.: Associated Books, 1955.

Forest of the Dead [Der Totenwald]; tr. Ursula Stechow. New York: Greenberg, 1947.

Girl and the Ferryman [Die Magd des Jürgen Doskocil]; tr. Eithne Wilkins and Ernst Kaiser. New York: Pilot, 1947.

Missa Sine Nomine; tr. Marie Heynemann and Margery B. Ledward. New York: British Book Centre, 1954.

The Poet and His Time: Three Addresses [Der Dichter und die Zeit]; tr. Irene Taeuber. Hinsdale, Ill.: Regnery, 1948.

Tidings [Missa sine nomine]; tr. Marie Heynemann and Margery B. Ledward. New York: Macmillan, 1959.

See also Herman Salinger, *Twentieth-Century German Verse.*

WINTERFELD, HENRY, 1901-

Castaways in Lilliput [Telegramm aus Liliput]; tr. Kyrill Schabert. New York: Harcourt, Brace, 1960.

Detective in Togas [Caius ist ein Dummkopf]; tr. Richard and Clara Winston. New York: Harcourt, Brace, 1956.

Star Girl [Kommt ein Mädchen geflogen]; tr. Kyrill Schabert. New York: Harcourt, Brace, 1957.

WITTENWILER, HEINRICH, 15th cent.
Wittenwiler's Ring and the Anonymous Scots Poem, 'Colkebie Sow': Two Comic-Didactic Works from the Fifteenth Century; tr. George Fenwick Jones. Chapel Hill: University of North Carolina, 1956.

WOLFRAM VON ESCHENBACH, 12th cent.
Parzival; tr. Edwin H. Zeydel and B. Q. Morgan. Chapel Hill: University of North Carolina, 1951.
See also Hubert Creekmore, *Lyrics of the Middle Ages.*

WOLFSKEHL, KARL, 1869-1948.
1933, A Poem Sequence [Die Stimme spricht]; tr. Carol North Valhope (pseud.) and Ernst Morwitz. New York: Schocken, 1947.

WOLLER, OLGA
Sex Alarm; tr. James A. Galston. New York: Richard R. Smith, 1946*.
Strange Conflict; tr. James A. Galston. New York: Pageant, 1955*.

WYSS, JOHANN DAVID, 1743-1818.
Swiss Family Robinson [Der schweizerische Robinson]. Cleveland: World, 1947.
Swiss Family Robinson [Der schweizerische Robinson]. New York: Macmillan, 1948*.
Swiss Family Robinson [Der schweizerische Robinson]. New York: Grosset and Dunlap, 1949.
Swiss Family Robinson [Der schweizerische Robinson]. New York: Chanticleer, 1950*.
Swiss Family Robinson [Der schweizerische Robinson]. New York: Dutton, 1951*, 1958.
Swiss Family Robinson [Der schweizerische Robinson]. Garden City, N. Y.: Junior Deluxe Editions, 1954.
Swiss Family Robinson [Der schweizerische Robinson]. New York: Garden City, 1956.
Swiss Family Robinson [Der schweizerische Robinson]. New York: Pocket Books, (1959?).

Swiss Family Robinson [Der schweizerische Robinson]; adpt. Felix Sutton. New York: Grosset and Dunlap, 1960.
Swiss Family Robinson [Der schweizerische Robinson]. New York: Dell, (1960?).

ZIESER, BENNO, 1922-
The Road to Stalingrad; tr. Alex Brown. New York: Ballentine, 1956.

ZIMNIK, REINER, 1930-
Jonah the Fisherman [Jonas der Angler]; tr. Richard and Clara Winston. New York: Pantheon, 1956.
Proud Circus Horse [Der stolze Schimmel]. New York: Pantheon, 1957.

ZWEIG, ARNOLD, 1887-
Axe of Wandsbek [Das Beil von Wandsbek]; tr. Eric Sutton. New York: Viking, 1947.
See also Marjorie Fischer, *Strange to Tell*.

ZWEIG, STEFAN, 1881-1942.
Balzac; tr. William and Dorothy Rose. New York: Viking, 1946.
Balzac; tr. William and Dorothy Rose. New York: Garden City, 1948.
Erasmus of Rotterdam; tr. Eden and Cedar Paul. New York: Viking, 1956.
Marie Antoinette. New York: Pocket Books, (1956?).
Stefan and Friderike Zweig: Their Correspondence, 1912-1942; tr. Henry G. Alsberg and Erna MacArthur. New York: Hastings, 1954.

ANTHOLOGIES

Collections Devoted Exclusively to Translations from the German

BENTLEY, ERIC, 1916-   ed.
The Classic Theatre. Volume II. *Five German Plays.* Garden City: N.Y., Doubleday, 1959.

Goethe, Johann Wolfgang von: Egmont; tr. Michael Hamburger.
Kleist, Heinrich von: Penthesilea; tr. Humphrey Trevelyan.
Kleist, Heinrich von: The Prince of Homburg; tr. James Kirkup.
Schiller, Friedrich von: Don Carlos; tr. James Kirkup.
Schiller, Friedrich von: Mary Stuart; tr. Joseph Mellish and Eric Bentley.

FLORES, ANGEL, 1900-   ed.
An Anthology of German Poetry from Hölderlin to Rilke in English Translation. Garden City, N.Y.: Doubleday, 1960.

    Brentano, Clemens, (10)
    Droste-Hülshoff, Annette von (8)
    Eichendorff, Joseph Freiherr von (17)
    George, Stefan Anton (23)
    Heine, Heinrich (29)
    Hölderlin, Friedrich (15)
    Hofmannsthal, Hugo von (10)
    Lenau, Nikolaus (9)
    Mörike, Eduard Friedrich (20)
    Morgenstern, Christian (24)
    Novalis (11)
    Platen, August Graf von (16)
    Rilke, Rainer Maria (29)
    Trakl, Georg (21)

FLORES, ANGEL, 1900-   ed.
Nineteenth-Century German Tales. Garden City, N.Y.: Doubleday, 1959.

Gotthelf, Jeremias: The Black Spider; tr. Mary Hottinger.
Hoffmann, E. T. A.: The Mines at Falun; tr. Peggy Sard.
Keller, Gottfried: Meret; tr. Mary Hottinger.
Kleist, Heinrich von: Michael Kohlhaas; tr. Charles E. Passage.
Mörike, Eduard Friedrich: Mozart on His Way to Prague; tr. Mary Hottinger.

Richter, Johann Paul Friedrich: Life of the Cheerful Schoolmaster Maria Wuz; tr. John D. Grayson.
Stifter, Adalbert: Brigitta; tr. Herman Salinger.

LANGE, VICTOR, 1908-   ed.
Great German Short Novels and Stories. New York: Modern Library, 1952.

Brentano, Clemens: The Story of Just Caspar and Fair Annie; tr. Carl Schreiber.
Droste-Hülshoff, Annette von: The Jew's Beech Tree; tr. E. N. Bennett.
Goethe, Johann Wolfgang von: The Sorrows of Young Werther; tr. William Rose.
Hauptmann, Gerhart: Flagman Thiel; tr. Adele S. Seltzer.
Heine, Heinrich: Gods in Exile; tr. M. Fleishman.
Hoffmann, E. T. A.: The Cremona Violin; tr. J. T. Bealby.
Kafka, Franz: A Country Doctor; tr. Willa and Edwin Muir.
Keller, Gottfried: The Naughty Saint Vitalis; tr. Martin Wyness.
Kleist, Heinrich von: The Earthquake in Chile; tr. Victor Lange.
Mann, Heinrich: Three Minute Novel; tr. Victor Lange.
Mann, Thomas: Death in Venice; tr. Kenneth Burke.
Meyer, Conrad Ferdinand: Plautus in the Convent; tr. William Guild Howard.
Rilke, Rainer Maria: How Old Timofei Died Singing; tr. M. D. Herter Norton and Nora Purtscher-Wydenbruck.
Schiller, Friedrich von: The Sport of Destiny; tr. Marian Klopfer.
Schnitzler, Arthur: A Farewell; tr. Beatrice Marshall.
Storm, Theodor: Immensee; tr. C. W. Bell.
Wedekind, Frank: The Burning of Egliswyl; tr. F. Eisemann.

PICK, ROBERT, 1898-   ed.
German Stories and Tales. New York: Knopf, 1954.

Brentano, Clemens: The Picnic of Mores the Cat; tr. Jane B. Greene.
Broch, Hermann: Zerline, the Old Servant Girl; tr. Jane B. Greene.

Ebner-Eschenbach, Maria von: Krambambuli; tr. Paul Pratt.
Hebel, Johann Peter: The Hussar; tr. Paul Pratt.
Hebel, Johann Peter: Kannitverstan; tr. Paul Pratt.
Hebel, Johann Peter: Unexpected Reunion; tr. Paul Pratt.
Heimann, Moritz: The Message That Failed; tr. E. B. Ashton (pseud.).
Hesse, Hermann: Youth, Beautiful Youth; tr. Richard and Clara Winston.
Hofmannsthal, Hugo von: Episode in the Life of the Marshal de Bassompierre; tr. Mary Hottinger.
Kafka, Franz: The Metamorphosis; tr. Willa and Edwin Muir.
Keller, Gottfried: A Little Legend of the Dance; tr. M. D. Hottinger.
Kesten, Hermann: The Friend in the Closet; tr. Richard and Clara Winston.
Lernet-Holenia, Alexander: Mona Lisa; tr. Jane B. Greene.
Mann, Thomas: Death in Venice; tr. H. T. Lowe-Porter.
Schnitzler, Arthur: The Bachelor's Death; tr. Richard and Clara Winston.
Stifter, Adalbert: Rock Crystal: tr. Elizabeth Mayer and Marianne Moore.
Wassermann, Jakob: Lukardis; tr. Lewis Galantière.
Weiss, Ernst: Cardiac Suture; tr. E. B. Ashton (pseud.).

ROTHENBERG, JEROME, 1931-   ed.
New Young German Poets. San Franscisco [sic]: City Light Books, 1959.

Bachmann, Ingeborg (3)
Bremer, Klaus (2)
Celan, Paul (8)
Dreyer, Ernst Jürgen (3)
Enzensberger, Hans Magnus (6)
Grass, Günter (4)
Heissenbüttel, Helmut (5)
Höllerer, Walter (2)
Krolow, Karl (5)
Piontek, Heinz (3)

SALINGER, HERMAN, 1905-   ed.
Twentieth-Century German Verse. Princeton: Princeton University Press, 1952.

    Barthel, Max (1)
    Becher, Ulrich (1)
    Binding, Rudolf G. (1)
    Carossa, Hans (1)
    Claudius, Hermann (3)
    George, Stefan Anton (2)
    Haushofer, Albrecht (2)
    Hesse, Hermann (8)
    Hofmannsthal, Hugo von (1)
    Holthusen, Hans Egon (2)
    Huch, Ricarda (1)
    Kurz, Isolde (1)
    Lersch, Heinrich (1)
    Miegel, Agnes (1)
    Morgenstern, Christian (3)
    Rilke, Rainer Maria (8)
    Seidel, Ina (1)
    Trakl, Georg (1)
    Weinheber, Josef (1)
    Werfel, Franz (1)
    Wiechert, Ernst (1)

SPENDER, STEPHEN, 1909-   ed.
Great German Short Stories. New York: Dell, 1960.

    Aichinger, Ilse: The Bound Man; tr. Eric Mosbacher.
    Benn, Gottfried: The Conquest; tr. Christopher Middleton.
    Böll, Heinrich: The Man With the Knives; tr. Richard Graves.
    Büchner, Georg: Lenz; tr. Goronwy Rees.
    Gaiser, Gerd: The Game of Murder; tr. H. M. Waidson.
    Heym, Georg: The Autopsy; tr. Michael Hamburger.
    Hildesheimer, Wolfgang: A World's End; tr. Christopher Holme.

Hofmannsthal, Hugo von: A Tale of Cavalry; tr. James Stern.
Huber, Heinz: The New Apartment; tr. Christopher Holme.
Kafka, Franz: In the Penal Colony: tr. Edwin and Willa Muir.
Keller, Gottfried: A Little Legend of the Dance; tr. M. D. Hottinger.
Kleist, Heinrich von: The Earthquake in Chile; tr. Michael Hamburger.
Mann, Thomas: Gladius Dei; tr. H. T. Lowe-Porter.
Nossack, Hans Erich: The Meeting in the Hallway; tr. Christopher Middleton.
Rilke, Rainer Maria: Gym Period; tr. Carl Niemeyer.
Stifter, Adalbert: Brigitta; tr. Ilsa Barea.
Walser, Robert: A Village Tale; tr. Christopher Middleton.

Collections of Literature from Various Countries,
Containing Numerous Translations from the German

BENTLEY, ERIC, 1916-   ed.
From the Modern Repertoire. Series One. Denver: University of Denver Press, 1949.

    Brecht, Bertolt: The Threepenny Opera; tr. Desmond Vesey and Eric Bentley.
    Büchner, Georg: Danton's Death; tr. Stephen Spender and Goronwy Rees.
    Schnitzler, Arthur: Round Dance; tr. Keene Wallis.
    Sternheim, Carl: The Snob; tr. Eric Bentley.

From the Modern Repertoire. Series Two. Denver: University of Denver Press, 1952.

    Brecht, Bertolt: Galileo; tr. Charles Laughton.
    Grabbe, Christian: Jest, Satire, Irony; tr. Maurice Edwards.
    Wedekind, Frank: The Marquis of Keith; tr. Beatrice Gottlieb.

From the Modern Repertoire. Series Three. Bloomington: Indiana University Press, 1956.

Brecht, Bertolt: Saint Joan of the Stockyards; tr. Frank Jones.
Büchner, Georg: Leonce and Lena; tr. Eric Bentley,
Schnitzler, Arthur: Anatol; tr. H. Granville-Barker.

The Modern Theatre. Volume I. Garden City, N.Y.: Doubleday, 1955.

Brecht, Bertolt: The Threepenny Opera; tr. Eric Bentley and Desmond Vesey.
Büchner, Georg: Woyzeck; tr. Theodore Hoffman.

The Modern Theatre. Volume II. Garden City, N.Y.: Doubleday, 1955.

Brecht, Bertolt: Mother Courage; tr. Eric Bentley.
Schnitzler, Arthur: La Ronde; tr. Eric Bentley.

The Modern Theatre. Volume V. Garden City, N.Y.: Doubleday, 1957.

Büchner, Georg: Danton's Death; tr. John Holmstrom.

The Modern Theatre. Volume VI. Garden City, N.Y.: Doubleday, 1960.

Brecht, Bertolt: The Measure Taken; tr. Eric Bentley.
Sternheim, Carl: The Underpants; tr. Eric Bentley.
Wedekind, Frank: Spring's Awakening; tr. Eric Bentley.

CREEKMORE, HUBERT, ed.
Lyrics of the Middle Ages. New York: Grove, 1959.

Anonymous (2)
Dietmar von Aist (2)
Friedrich von Hausen (1)
Hartmann von Aue (1)
Heinrich von Morungen (3)
The Knight of Kürenberg (2)
Neidhart von Reuenthal (1)
Reinmar von Hagenau (2)
Reinmar von Sweter (1)

Walther von der Vogelweide (4)
Wolfram von Eschenbach (1)

FISCHER, MARJORIE, and ROLFE HUMPHRIES, ed.
Strange to Tell: Stories of the Marvelous and Mysterious. New York: Julian Messner, 1946.

    Feuchtwanger, Lion: Faithful Peter; tr. Renate Oppenheimer.
    Goethe, Johann Wolfgang von: The New Melusina; tr. Jean Starr Untermeyer.
    Goethe, Johann Wolfgang von: The Waterman; tr. T. Aytoun.
    Grimm Brothers: The Devil Turned Pleader; tr. Thomas Roscoe.
    Grimm Brothers: Gambling Hansel; tr. Margaret Hunt.
    Hauff, Wilhelm: The Story of the Haunted Ship; tr. S. Mendel.
    Heine, Heinrich: The Waterwitch Lurley; tr. Alexander Macmillan.
    Kafka, Franz: The City Coat of Arms; tr. Willa and Edwin Muir.
    Kafka, Franz: The Hunter Gracchus; tr. Willa and Edwin Muir.
    Keller, Gottfried: The Virgin as Nun; tr. Ellie Schleussner.
    Mann, Thomas: The Wardrobe; tr. H. T. Lowe-Porter.
    Munch: Hindenburg's March into London; tr. E. Redmond-Howard.
    Rilke, Rainer Maria: The Unicorn; tr. Rolfe Humphries.
    Zweig, Arnold: The Apparition; tr. Emma D. Ashton.

KESTEN, HERMANN, 1900-   ed.
The Blue Flower. New York: Roy, 1946.

    Arnim, Ludwig Achim von: The Mad Veteran of the Fort Ratonneau; tr. William Metcalfe.
    Brentano, Clemens: Loreley and Marmot; tr. E. B. Ashton (pseud.).
    Goethe, Johann Wolfgang von: The New Melusina; tr. Thomas Carlyle.
    Grillparzer, Franz: The Poor Fiddler; tr. E. B. Ashton (pseud.).
    Grimm, Jakob and Wilhelm: The Story of the Youth Who Went Forth to Learn What Fear Was; tr. Margaret Hunt.
    Heine, Heinrich: Florentine Nights-Second Night; (tr. not given).

Hoffmann, E. T. A.: The Cremona Violin; tr. J. T. Bealby.
Keller, Gottfried: Spiegel, the Kitten; tr. E. B. Ashton (pseud.).
Kleist, Heinrich von: The Earthquake in Chile; tr. Roman Brown.
Schiller, Friedrich von: The Sport of Destiny; tr. Thomas Roscoe.
Tieck, Johann Ludwig: Auburn Egbert; tr. Thomas Roscoe.

A SELECTIVE BIBLIOGRAPHY

BIBLIOGRAPHICAL SOURCES

Books in Print: An Author-Title-Series Index to the Publishers' Trade List Annual.
A Catalog of Books Represented by Library of Congress Cards (title varies).
Cumulative Book Index: World List of Books in the English Language.
Index Translationum: International Bibliography of Translations.
Paperbound Books in Print.
The Publishers' Trade List Annual.

Baldensperger, Fernand, and Werner P. Friederich. *Bibliography of Comparative Literature.* Chapel Hill, 1950; reprinted by Russell & Russell. New York, 1960. Continued in *Yearbook of Comparative and General Literature.*
Mönnig, Richard. *Amerika und England im deutschen, österreichischen und schweizerischen Schriftum der Jahre 1945-1949: Eine Bibliographie.* Stuttgart, 1951.
Mönnig, Richard. *Bibliography of Paperbound Books Translated from the German and of Works on Germany.* 2d ed. Bonn, 1965.
Mönnig, Richard. *Deutschland und die Deutschen im englisch-sprachigen Schriftum, 1948-1955: Eine Bibliographie.* Göttingen, 1957.
Morgan, B. Q. *A Critical Bibliography of German Literature in English Translation, 1481-1927; Supplement Embracing the Years 1928-1955.* 2 vols. New York and London, 1965.
Mummendey, Richard. *Belle [sic] Lettres of the United States of America in German Translations: A Bibliography.* Charlottesville, 1961.
Mummendey, Richard. *Die schöne Literatur der Vereinigten Staaten von Amerika in deutschen Übersetzungen: Eine Bibliographie.* Bonn, 1961.
Pochmann, Henry A., and Arthur R. Schultz. *Bibliography of German Culture in America to 1940.* Madison, 1953.
Sternfeld, Wilhelm, and Eva Tiedemann. *Deutsche Exil-Literatur: Eine Bio-Bibliographie.* Heidelberg, 1962.

RELATED STUDIES

BOOKS

Faust, Albert Bernhardt. *The German Element in the United States, With Special Reference to Its Political, Moral, Social, and Educational Influence.* New York, 1927.

Frese, Hans. *Das deutsche Buch in Amerika: Übersetzungen der Jahre 1918-1935.* Zeulenroda (Thür.), 1937.

Goodnight, Scott Holland. *German Literature in American Magazines Prior to 1846.* Madison, 1909.

Haertel, Martin Henry. *German Literature in American Magazines: 1846-1880.* Madison, 1908.

Hathaway, Lillie V. *German Literature of the Mid-Nineteenth Century in England and America as Reflected in the Journals, 1840-1914.* Boston, 1935.

Hawgood, John A. *The Tragedy of German America: The Germans in the United States of America during the Nineteenth Century – and After.* New York, 1940.

Herford, Charles H. *Studies in the Literary Relations of England and Germany in the Sixteenth Century.* Cambridge, Eng., 1886.

Hewett-Thayer, Harvey W. *American Literature as Viewed in Germany: 1818-1861.* Chapel Hill, 1958.

Huebener, Theodore. *The Germans in America.* Philadelphia, 1962.

Long, Orie W. *Literary Pioneers: Early American Explorers of European Culture.* Cambridge, Mass., 1935.

Möhl, Gertrud. *Die Aufnahme amerikanischer Literatur in der deutschsprachigen Schweiz während der Jahre 1945-1950.* Zurich, 1961.

Morgan, B. Q., and A. R. Hohlfeld, ed. *German Literature in British Magazines: 1750-1860.* Madison, 1949.

Pochmann, Henry A. *German Culture in America: Philosophical and Literary Influences, 1600-1900.* Madison, 1957.

Price, Lawrence Marsden. *Die Aufnahme englischer Literatur in Deutschland: 1500-1960.* Bern, 1961.

Price, Lawrence Marsden. *English-German Literary Influences: Bibliography and Survey.* Berkeley, 1919-20.

Price, Lawrence Marsden. *English Literature in Germany.* Berkeley, 1953.

Price, Lawrence Marsden. *The Reception of English Literature in Germany.* Berkeley, 1932.

Price, Mary Bell, and Lawrence Marsden Price. *The Publication of English Humaniora in Germany in the Eighteenth Century.* Berkeley, 1955.

Price, Mary Bell, and Lawrence Marsden Price. *The Publication of English Literature in Germany in the Eighteenth Century.* Berkeley, 1934.

Schirmer, Walter F. *Der Einfluss der deutschen Dichtung auf die englische im neunzehnten Jahrhundert.* Halle/Saale, 1947.

Schlösser, Anselm. *Englische Literatur in Deutschland von 1895-1934 mit einer vollständigen Bibliographie der deutschen Übersetzungen und der im deutschen Sprachgebiet erschienenen englischen Ausgaben.* Jena, 1937.

Shelley, Philip Allison, Arthur O. Lewis, Jr., (and, vol. 1 only, William W. Betts, Jr.). *Anglo-German and American-German Crosscurrents.* 2 vols. Chapel Hill, Volume One, 1957; Volume Two, 1962.

Springer, Anne M. *The American Novel in Germany: A Study of the Critical Reception of Eight American Novelists Between the Two World Wars.* Hamburg, 1960.
Stockley, Violet. *German Literature as Known in England: 1750-1830.* London, 1929.
Stokoe, F. W. *German Influence in the English Romantic Period, 1788-1818, With Special References to Scott, Coleridge, Shelley and Byron.* Cambridge, Eng., 1926.
Thomas, J. Wesley. *Amerikanische Dichter und die deutsche Literatur.* Goslar, 1950.
Timpe, Eugene F. *American Literature in Germany, 1861-1872.* Chapel Hill, 1964.
Vogel, Stanley M. *German Literary Influences on the American Transcendentalists.* New Haven, 1955.
Walz, John A. *German Influence in American Education and Culture.* Philadelphia, 1936.
Waterhouse, Gilbert. *The Literary Relations of England and Germany in the Seventeenth Century.* Cambridge, Eng., 1914.
Wellek, René. *Confrontations: Studies in the Intellectual and Literary Relations between Germany, England, and the United States during the Nineteenth Century.* Princeton, 1965.
Wiem, Irene. *Das englische Schrifttum in Deutschland von 1518-1600.* Leipzig, 1940.

ARTICLES AND DISSERTATIONS

Ballenger, Sara E. 'The Reception of the American Novel in German Periodicals, 1945-1957.' Unpubl. diss., Indiana Univ., 1959.
Blume, Bernhard. 'Amerika und die deutsche Literatur,' *Deutsche Akademie für Sprache und Dichtung, Darmstadt, Jahrbuch 1959* (Darmstadt, 1960), pp. 137-148.
Crispin, Robert L. 'The Currency and Reception of German Short Prose Fiction in England and America as Reflected in the Periodicals, 1790-1840.' Unpubl. diss., Pennsylvania State Univ., 1955.
Dietel, Günther. 'Studien zur Aufnahme und Beurteilung der deutschen Literatur in Amerika, 1919-1939.' Unpubl. diss., Jena, 1952.
Feller, Max F. 'Die Aufnahme amerikanischer Literatur in der deutschsprachigen Schweiz.' Unpubl. diss., Humboldt-Univ., Berlin, 1949.
Hatfield, Henry C., and Joan Merrick. 'Studies of German Literature in the United States, 1939-46,' *MLR*, XLIII (1948), 353-392.
Jantz, Harold S. 'German Thought and Literature in New England, 1620-1820,' *JEGP*, XLI (1942), 1-45.
Jantz, Harold S. 'Amerika im deutschen Dichten und Denken,' *Deutsche Philologie im Aufriss*, ed. Wolfgang Stammler, III (Berlin, 1957), 145-204.
Kant, Hermann. 'Darmstädter Dilemma [Zu einem Vortrag von Bernhard Blume über "Amerika und die deutsche Literatur"],' *Neue Deutsche Literatur*, VIII (1960), 161-163.
Leitel, Erich. 'Die Aufnahme der amerikanischen Literatur in Deutschland: Übersetzungen der Jahre 1914-1944; Mit einer Bibliographie.' Unpubl. diss., Jena, 1958.
Rie, Robert. 'Amerika und die österreichische Literatur,' *Wort in der Zeit*, VII (1961), 42-45.
Rose, Ernst. 'Die Leistungen der amerikanischen Germanistik während des letzten Jahrzehnts (1939-1951),' *Wirkendes Wort*, III (1952), 34-46.
Rosenberg, Ralph P. 'American Doctoral Studies in Germanic Cultures. A Study in German-American Relations, 1873-1949,' *Yearbook of Comparative and General Literature*, IV (1955), 30-44.

Townsend, Stanley R. 'Die moderne deutsche Literatur in Amerika,' *Die Sammlung: Zeitschrift für Kultur und Erziehung*, IX (1954), 237-243.
Waidson, H. M. 'Zeitgenössische deutsche Literatur in englischer Übersetzung,' *Deutschunterricht für Ausländer*, VIII (1958), 65-71.
Weisstein, Ulrich. 'The Reception of Twentieth Century German Literature in the United States,' *Comparative Literature: Proceedings of the Second Congress of the International Comparative Literature Association*, II (Chapel Hill, 1959), 548-557.

GOETHE

BOOKS

Adams, Henry. *A Catalogue of the Books of John Quincy Adams Deposited in the Boston Athenaeum, With Notes on Books, Adams Seals and Book Plates*. Boston, 1938.
Atkins, Stuart Pratt. *The Testament of Werther in Poetry and Drama*. Cambridge, Mass., 1949.
Baumann, Lina. *Die englischen Übersetzungen von Goethes Faust*. Halle, 1907.
Bergstraesser, Arnold, ed. *Goethe and the Modern Age: The International Convocation at Aspen, Colorado, 1949*. Chicago, 1950.
Brown, Herbert Ross. *The Sentimental Novel in America, 1789-1860*. Durham, N.C., 1940.
Catalogue of Books in the Boston Athaneum [sic]; *to which are added the By-Laws of the Institution and a list of its proprietors and subscribers*. Boston, 1827.
Frantz, Adolf Ingram. *Half a Hundred Thralls to Faust: A Study Based on the British and the American Translators of Goethe's Faust, 1823-1949*. Chapel Hill, 1949.
Hinz, Stella M. *Goethe's Lyric Poems in English Translation after 1860*. Madison, 1928.
Oswald, Eugene. *Goethe in England and America*. 2d ed., London, 1909.
Schreiber, Carl F., ed. *Goethe's Works with the Exception of Faust: A Catalogue Compiled by the Members of the Yale University Library Staff*. New Haven, 1940.
Simmons, Lucretia Van Tuyl. *Goethe's Lyric Poems in English Translation Prior to 1860*. Madison, 1919.

ARTICLES AND DISSERTATIONS

Betts, William W., Jr. 'The Fortunes of Faust in American Literature.' Unpubl. diss., Pennsylvania State Univ., 1954.
Charles, Robert Alan. 'French Intermediaries in the Transmission of German Literature and Culture to England, 1750-1815.' Unpubl. diss., Pennsylvania State Univ., 1952.
Charles, Robert Alan. 'French Mediation and Intermediaries, 1750-1815,' *Anglo-German and American-German Crosscurrents*, ed. Philip Allison Shelley, Arthur O. Lewis, Jr., and William W. Betts, Jr., I (1957), 1-38.
Hammer, Carl J., Jr. 'Longfellow's Lyrics "From the German,"' *Studies in Comparative Literature*, ed. Waldo McNeir (Baton Rouge, 1962), pp. 155-172.
Hill, C. J. 'The First English Translation of *Werther*,' *MLN*, XLVII (1932), 8-12.
Jantz, Harold S. 'Samuel Miller's Survey of German Literature, 1803,' *GR*, XVI (1942), 267-277.
Kornbluth, Martin L. 'The Reception of *Wilhelm Meister* in America,' *Symposium*, XIII (1959), 128-134.
Lieder, Frederick W. C. 'Goethe in England and America,' *JEGP*, X (1911), 535-556.

Long, Orie W. 'English Translations of Goethe's Werther,' *JEGP*, XIV (1915), 169-203.
Long, Orie W. 'Werther in America,' *Studies in Honor of John Albrecht Walz*, ed. Fred O. Nolte, Harry W. Pfund, and George J. Metcalfe (Lancaster, Pa., 1941). pp. 86-116.
Morris, Walter John. 'John Quincy Adams: Germanophile.' Unpubl. diss., Pennsylvania State Univ., 1963.
Perry, Bliss. 'The Road to Weimar,' *American Scholar*, I (1932), 272-291.
Ryder, Frank G. 'George Ticknor's *Sorrows of Young Werter*,' *Comparative Literature*, I (1949), 360-372.
Shelley, Philip Allison. 'A German Art of Life in America: The American Reception of the Goethean Doctrine of Self-Culture,' *Anglo-German and American-German Crosscurrents*, ed. Philip Allison Shelley, Arthur O. Lewis, Jr., and William W. Betts, Jr., I (1957), 241-292.

SCHILLER

BOOKS

Ewen, Frederic. *The Prestige of Schiller in England, 1788-1859*. New York, 1932.
Parry, Ellwood Comly. *Friedrich Schiller in America: A Contribution to the Literature of the Poet's Centenary, 1905*. Philadelphia, 1905.
Pick, Robert, ed. *Schiller in England, 1787-1960: A Bibliography*. London, 1961.
Rea, Thomas. *Schiller's Dramas and Poems in England*. London, 1906.

ARTICLES

Barnstorff, Hermann. 'German and American Interest in Schiller During the Inter-Bellum Period 1918-1939,' *GQ*, XIII (1940), 92-100.
Burkhard, Arthur. 'Charles Timothy Brooks's *Mary Stuart*,' *Studies in German Literature*, ed. Carl Hammer, Jr. (Baton Rouge, 1963), pp. 3-17.
Dummer, H. Heyse. 'Schiller in English,' *MDU*, XXXV (1943), 334-337.
Frey, John R. 'American Schiller Literature: A Bibliography,' *Schiller 1759/1959: Commemorative American Studies*, ed. John R. Frey (Urbana, 1959), pp. 203-213.
Frey, John R. 'Maria Stuart "Off Broadway," 1957,' *A-GR*, XXIV (August-September, 1958), 6-8, 27.
Frey, John R. 'Schiller in Amerika, insbesonders in der amerikanischen Forschung,' *Jahrbuch der deutschen Schillergesellschaft*, ed. Herbert Stubenrauch and Bernhard Zeller, III (1959), 338-367.
Guthke, Karl S. 'Schiller auf der Bühne der Vereinigten Staaten,' *Maske und Kothurn*, V (1960), 227-242.
Knepler, Henry W. 'Schiller's *Maria Stuart* on the Stage in England and America,' *Anglo-German and American-German Crosscurrents*, ed. Philip Allison Shelley and Arthur O. Lewis, Jr., II (1962), 5-31.
Willoughby, L. A. 'Schiller's "Kabale und Liebe" in English Translation,' *Publications of the English Goethe Society*, N.S. I (London, 1924), 44-66.
Witte, W. 'Schiller: Reflections on a Bicentenary,' *Schiller Bicentenary Lectures*, ed. Frederick Norman (London, 1960), pp. 145-168.

BOOKS

Arnold, Armin. *Heine in England and America: A Bibliographical Check-List.* London, 1959.
Burkhard, Arthur. *Franz Grillparzer in England and America.* Vienna, 1961.
Henel, Heinrich. *The Poetry of Conrad Ferdinand Meyer.* Madison, 1954.
Hiebel, Friedrich. *Novalis: German Poet, European Thinker, Christian Mystic.* Chapel Hill, 1954.
Liptzin, Sol. *The English legend of Heinrich Heine.* New York, 1954.
Matenko, Percy. *Ludwig Tieck and America.* Chapel Hill, 1954.
Peacock, Ronald. *The Poet in the Theatre.* New York, 1946.
Pollak, Gustav. *Franz Grillparzer and the Austrian Drama.* New York, 1907.
Sachs, H. B. *Heine in America.* Philadelphia, 1916.
Williams, W. D. *The Stories of Conrad Ferdinand Meyer.* Oxford, 1962.
Wormley, S. G. *Heine in England.* Chapel Hill, 1943.

ARTICLES AND DISSERTATIONS

Barnstorff, Hermann. 'German Literature in Translation Published by Poet Lore, 1891-1939,' *MLJ*, XXV (1941), 711-715.
Blankenagel, John C. 'Early Reception of Hauptmann's *Die Weber* in the United States,' *MLN*, LXVIII (1953), 334-340.
Cappel, Edith. 'The Reception of Gerhart Hauptmann in the United States.' Unpubl. diss., Columbia Univ., 1952.
Cobb, Palmer. 'The Influence of E. T. A. Hoffmann on the Tales of Edgar Allan Poe,' *Studies in Philology*, III. Philadelphia, 1908.
Crane, T. F. 'The External History of the *Kinder- und Hausmärchen* of the Brothers Grimm,' *Modern Philology*, XIV (1917), 577-610; XV (1917), 65-77, and 355-383.
Dummer, E. H. 'Gerhart Hauptmann and the Chicago Stage,' *A-GR*, VI (December, 1939), 17-19.
Eisenmeier, Eduard. 'Nachtrag zu Stifters Werk in Amerika und England: Eine Bibliographie,' *Vierteljahrsschrift der Adalbert-Stifter-Institut des Landes Oberösterreich*, IX (1960), 129-132.
Fife, Robert H., Jr. 'The Real E. A. Hoffman,' *Nation*, LXXXV (November 28, 1907), 491.
Foltinek, Herbert. 'Arthur Schnitzler in Amerika,' *Österreich und die angelsächsische Welt*, ed. Otto Hietsch (Vienna, 1961), pp. 207-214.
Friebert, Stuart Alyn. 'A Chronicle of Conrad Ferdinand Meyer's Life with a Collection of His Comments on His Own Works.' Unpubl. diss., Univ. of Wisconsin, 1958.
Funke, Lewis. 'Theatre: Wedekind's "The Awakening of Spring,"' New York *Times* (May 14, 1964), p. 40.
Gohdes, Clarence. 'Heine in America: A Cursory Survey,' *Georgia Review*, XI (1959), 44-49.
Guthke, Karl S. 'Georg Büchner und William Mudford?,' *Archiv für das Studium der neueren Sprachen und Literaturen*, CLXVIII (1961-62), 170-171.
Hand, Wayland D. 'Die Märchen der Brüder Grimm in den Vereinigten Staaten,' *Brüder Grimm Gedenken 1963: Gedenkschrift zur hundertsten Wiederkehr des Todestages von*

Jacob Grimm, ed. Ludwig Denecke and Ina-Maria Greverus (Marburg, 1963), pp. 525-544.

Krumpelmann, John T. 'Gerstäcker's *Germelshausen* and Lerner's *Brigadoon*,' *MDU*, XL (1948), 396-400.

Landa, Bjarne Emil. 'The American Scene in Friedrich Gerstäcker's Works of Fiction.' Unpubl. diss., Univ. of Minnesota, 1952.

Majut, Rudolf. 'Georg Büchner and Some English Thinkers,' *MLR*, XLVIII (1953), 310-322.

Majut, Rudolf. 'Some Literary Affiliations of Georg Büchner with England,' *MLR*, L (1955), 30-43.

Mann, Klaus. 'Dream-America,' *Accent*, VIII (1947-48), 173-184.

O'Donnell, George H. R. 'Gerstäcker in America, 1837-1843,' *PMLA*, XLII (1927), 1036-43.

Plath, Otto. 'Washington Irvings Einfluss auf Wilhelm Hauff: Eine Quellenstudie,' *Euphorion*, XX (1913), 459-471.

Prahl, A. J. 'America in the Works of Gerstäcker,' *MLQ*, IV (1943), 213-224.

Read, Helen Appleton. 'Karl May: Germany's James Fenimore Cooper,' *A-GR*, II (June, 1936), 4-6.

Reichart, Walter A. 'Fifty Years of Hauptmann Study in America (1894-1944): A Bibliography,' *MDU*, XXXVII (1945), 1-31.

Reichart, Walter A. 'Gerhart Hauptmann's Dramas on the American Stage,' *Maske und Kothurn*, VIII (1962), 223-232.

Reichart, Walter A. 'Gerhart Hauptmann: His Work in America,' *A-GR*, XXIX (April-May, 1963), 11-12.

Reichart, Walter A. 'Hauptmann Study in America: A Continuation Bibliography,' *MDU*, LIV (1962), 297-310.

Reichart, Walter A. 'Hebbel in Amerika und England: Eine Bibliographie,' *Hebbel Jahrbuch 1961* (Heide in Holstein, 1961), pp. 118-135.

Reichart, Walter A., and Werner H. Grilk. 'Stifters Werk in Amerika und England: Eine Bibliographie,' *Vierteljahrsschrift des Adalbert-Stifter-Instituts des Landes Oberösterreich*, IX (1960), 39-42.

Reinhold, Ernest. 'The Reception of Franz Grillparzer's Works in England during the Nineteenth Century.' Unpubl. diss., Univ. of Michigan, 1956.

Rosenberg, Ralph P. 'Georg Büchner's Early Reception in America,' *JEGP*, XLIV (1945), 270-273.

Schrumpf, Beatrice M. 'The Reception of Arthur Schnitzler in the United States.' Unpubl. M.A. thesis, Columbia Univ., 1931.

Seidlin, Oskar. 'Frank Wedekind's German-American Parents,' *A-GR*, XII (August, 1946), 24-26.

Straubinger, O. Paul. 'Grillparzer-Bibliographie: 1937-1952,' *Jahrbuch der Grillparzer-Gesellschaft, Dritte Folge/Erster Band* (Vienna, 1953), pp. 34-80.

Straubinger, O. Paul. 'Grillparzer's Reception in England,' *Moderne Sprachen*, IV (November-December, 1959), 20-25.

Straubinger, O. Paul. 'The Reception of Raimund and Nestroy in England and America,' *Österreich und die angelsächsische Welt*, ed. Otto Hietsch (Vienna, 1961), pp. 481-494.

Weisert, John J. 'Critical Reception of Gerhart Hauptmann's "The Sunken Bell" on the American Stage,' *MDU*, XLIII (1951), 221-234.

Zylstra, Henry. 'E. T. A. Hoffmann in England and America.' Unpubl. diss., Harvard Univ., 1940.

BOOKS

THE TWENTIETH CENTURY

Bareiss, Otto. *Hermann Hesse: Eine Bibliographie der Werke über Hermann Hesse*, I. Basel, 1962; *Zeitschriften- und Zeitungsaufsätze*, II. Basel, 1964.
Brennan, Joseph Gerard. *Thomas Mann's World*. New York, 1962.
Bürgin, Hans. *Das Werk Thomas Manns*. Frankfurt am Main, 1959.
Esslin, Martin. *Brecht, The Man and His Work*. New York, 1961.
Euler, Walter, and Hans-Rolf Ropertz. *Karl Wolfskehl*. Darmstadt, n.d.
Flores, Angel. *Franz Kafka: A Chronology and Bibliography*. Houlton, Maine, 1944.
Flores, Angel, and Homer Swander, ed. *Franz Kafka Today*. Madison, 1958.
Flores, Angel, ed. *The Kafka Problem*. New York, 1963.
Foltin, Lore B., ed. *Franz Werfel, 1890-1945*. Pittsburgh, 1961.
Hemmerle, Rudolf. *Franz Kafka: Eine Bibliographie*. Munich, 1958.
Järv, Harry. *Die Kafka-Literatur*. Malmö-Lund, 1961.
Jonas, Klaus W. *Fifty Years of Thomas Mann Studies: A Bibliography of Criticism*. Minneapolis, 1955.
Landsmann, Georg Peter. *Stefan George und sein Kreis: Eine Bibliographie*. Hamburg, 1960.
Lohner, Edgar. *Gottfried Benn Bibliographie, 1912-1956*. Wiesbaden, 1958.
Mason, Eudo C. *Rilke, Europe, and the English-Speaking World*. Cambridge, Eng., 1961.
Mileck, Joseph. *Hermann Hesse and His Critics; The Criticism and Bibliography of Half a Century*. Chapel Hill, 1958.
Obermiller, Paul, and Herbert Steiner, with Ernst Zinn. *Katalog der Rilke-Sammlung Richard von Mises*. Frankfurt am Main, 1966.
Ritzer, Walter. *Rainer Maria Rilke Bibliographie*. Vienna, 1951.
Willett, John. *The Theatre of Bertolt Brecht: A Study from Eight Aspects*. New York, 1960.

ARTICLES AND DISSERTATIONS

Benson, Ann. 'The American Criticism of Franz Kafka, 1930-1948.' Unpubl. diss., Univ. of Tennessee, 1958.
Boyle, Kay. 'A Voice from the Future,' *Holiday*, XXXVI (October, 1964), 20-22.
Frey, John R. 'America and Franz Werfel,' *GQ*, XIX (1946), 121-128.
Heller, Peter. 'Die deutsche Literatur aus amerikanischer Sicht,' *Welt und Wort*, XI (1956), 105-107.
Hodge, Francis. 'German Drama and the American Stage,' *The German Theatre Today: A Symposium*, ed. Leroy R. Shaw (Austin, 1963), pp. 69-88.
Jonas, Klaus W. 'Additions to the Bibliography of Hermann Hesse,' *Papers of the Bibliographical Society of America*, XLIX (1955), 358-360.
Jonas, Klaus W. 'Franz Kafka: An American Bibliography,' *Bulletin of Bibliography*, XX (1952), 212-216, and 231-233.
Jonas, Klaus W. 'Hermann Hesse in America,' *MDU*, XLIV (1952), 95-99.
Jonas, Klaus W. 'Rainer Maria Rilke in Amerika,' *Börsenblatt für den deutschen Buchhandel*, Frankfurt edition, LXXII (October 11, 1963), 1864-65.
Jonas, Klaus W. 'Rilke and America,' *Etudes Germaniques*, IX (1954), 55-59.
Jonas, Klaus W. 'Rilke and America,' *GLL*, VIII (1954), 45-49.

Leppmann, Wolfgang. 'Vermisst wird das deutsche Kulturwunder: Warum der deutsche Einfluss in den Vereinigten Staaten nach wie vor weit hinter dem Frankreichs zurücksteht,' *Die Zeit* (May 31, 1963), p. 21.
Loram, Ian C. ' "Der Besuch der alten Dame" and "The Visit," ' *MDU*, LIII (1961), 15-21.
Mann, Klaus. 'Dream-America,' *Accent*, VIII (1948), 173-184.
Metelmann, Ernst. 'Hermann Hesse,' *Die schöne Literatur*, XXVIII (1927), 299-312.
Mileck, Joseph. 'Hesse Bibliographies,' *MDU*, XLIX (1957), 201-205.
Ramras, Herman. 'Main Currents in American Criticism of Thomas Mann.' Unpubl. diss., Univ. of Wisconsin, 1949.
Reichart, Walter A. 'Thomas Mann: An American Bibliography,' *MDU*, XXXVII (1945), 389-408.
Roswell, May MacGinnis. 'Bertolt Brecht's Plays in America.' Unpubl. diss., Univ. of Maryland, 1961.
Ruland, Richard. 'The American Plays of Bertolt Brecht,' *American Quarterly*, XV (1963), 371-389.
Schroeder, Adolf E. 'Rainer Maria Rilke in America: A Bibliography, 1926-1951,' *MDU*, XLIV (1952), 27-38.
Steiner, George. 'The Hollow Miracle: Notes on the German Language,' *Reporter*, XXII (February 18, 1960), 36-41.
Waidson, H. M. 'Zeitgenössische deutsche Literatur in englischer Übersetzung,' *Deutschunterricht für Ausländer*, VIII (1958), 65-71.
Weisstein, Ulrich. 'Brecht in America: A Preliminary Survey,' *MLN*, LXXVIII (1963), 373-396.
Wirl, Julius. 'Englische Übertragungen von Rilkes erster Duineser Elegie,' *Österreich und die angelsächsische Welt*, ed. Otto Hietsch (Vienna, 1961), pp. 432-453.

REPRINTS

WITH THE UNIVERSITY OF NORTH CAROLINA PRESS

2. Werner P. Friederich. DANTE'S FAME ABROAD, 1350-1850. The Influence of Dante Alighieri on the Poets and Scholars of Spain, France, England, Germany, Switzerland and the United States. Rome, 1950, 1966. Pp. 584. Paper, $10.00.
10. Charles E. Passage. DOSTOEVSKI THE ADAPTER. A Study in Dostoevski's Use of the Tales of Hoffmann. 1954. Reprinted 1963. Pp. x, 205. Paper, $3.50. Cloth, $4.50.
11. Werner P. Friederich and David H. Malone. OUTLINE OF COMPARATIVE LITERATURE. From Dante Alighieri to Eugene O'Neill. 1954. Fourth Printing, 1967. Pp. 460. Paper, $6.00.

WITH RUSSELL & RUSSELL, INC. 156 FIFTH AVENUE, NEW YORK

1. Fernand Baldensperger and Werner P. Friedrich. BIBLIOGRAPHY of Comparative Literature, 1950. Pp. XXVI and 705. Cloth $15.00.
6, 7, 9, 14, 16, 18, 21, 25 and 27 YEARBOOKS OF COMPARATIVE AND GENERAL LITERATURE, Vols I-IX, 1952-60. Cloth $6.50 each.

WITH THE JOHNSON REPRINT CORPORATION, III FIFTH AVENUE, NEW YORK

4. Frank G. Ryder. GEORGE TICKNOR'S THE SORROWS OF YOUNG WERTER, edited with Introduction and Critical Analysis. 1952. Pp. XXXIII and 108. Cloth $8.00.
5. Helmut A. Hatzfeld. A CRITICAL BIBLIOGRAPHY OF THE NEW STYLISTICS APPLIED TO THE ROMANCE LITERATURES, 1900-1952. 1953. Pp. XXII and 302. Cloth $12.00.
19. Philip A. Shelley, Arthur O. Lewis, Jr., and William W. Betts, Jr., Editors. ANGLO-GERMAN AND AMERICAN-GERMAN CROSSCURRENTS. Vol. I. 1957. Pp. XVI, 304. Cloth $15.00.
26. J. Chesley Mathews. DANTE'S VITA NUOVA, TRANSLATED BY RALPH WALDO EMERSON. Edited and annotated. 1960. Pp. XIII and 145. Cloth $8.00.
28. Haskell M. Block. THE TEACHING OF WORLD LITERATURE. A University of Wisconsin Symposium. 1960. Pp. 96. Cloth $6.00.
30. Oskar Seidlin. ESSAYS IN GERMAN AND COMPARATIVE LITERATURE. 1961. Pp. 254. $10.00.